ROUTLEDGE LIBRARY EDITIONS:
AGRIBUSINESS AND LAND USE

Volume 11

TRENDS OF AGRICULTURE AND POPULATION IN THE GANGES VALLEY

TRENDS OF AGRICULTURE AND POPULATION IN THE GANGES VALLEY

A Study in Agricultural Economics

BIRENDRANATH
GANGULI, M.A., PH.D.

Routledge
Taylor & Francis Group

LONDON AND NEW YORK

First published in 1938 by Methuen & Co. Ltd

This edition first published in 2024
by Routledge
4 Park Square, Milton Park, Abingdon, Oxon OX14 4RN

and by Routledge
605 Third Avenue, New York, NY 10158

Routledge is an imprint of the Taylor & Francis Group, an informa business

British Library Cataloguing in Publication Data
A catalogue record for this book is available from the British Library

ISBN: 978-1-032-48321-4 (Set)
ISBN: 978-1-032-49873-7 (Volume 11) (hbk)
ISBN: 978-1-032-49892-8 (Volume 11) (pbk)
ISBN: 978-1-003-39592-8 (Volume 11) (ebk)

DOI: 10.4324/9781003395928

Publisher's Note
The publisher has gone to great lengths to ensure the quality of this reprint but points out that some imperfections in the original copies may be apparent.

Disclaimer
The publisher has made every effort to trace copyright holders and would welcome correspondence from those they have been unable to trace.

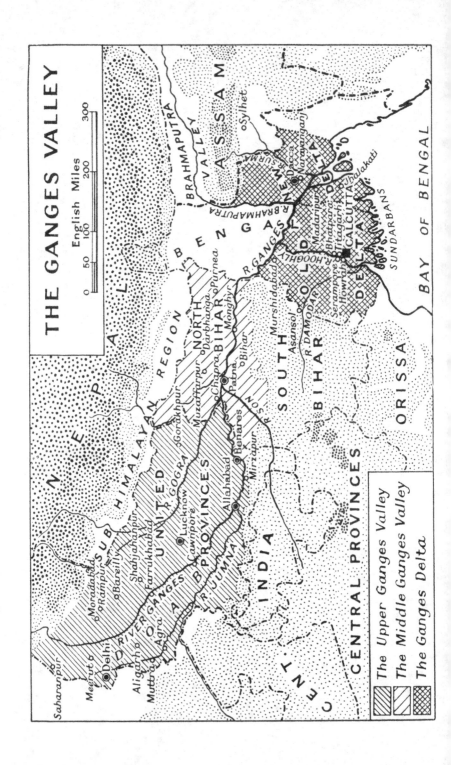

TRENDS OF AGRICULTURE
AND POPULATION IN THE
GANGES VALLEY

A Study in Agricultural Economics

by

BIRENDRANATH GANGULI, M.A., Ph.D.

PROFESSOR OF ECONOMICS, HINDU COLLEGE, DELHI, AND READER IN
ECONOMICS, UNIVERSITY OF DELHI

With a Map

METHUEN & CO. LTD. LONDON
36 Essex Street, Strand, W.C.2

DEDICATED

TO MY COUNTRYMEN

First published in 1938

PRINTED IN GREAT BRITAIN

PREFACE

In the present volume, which has grown out of a thesis approved for the degree of Doctor of Philosophy of the University of Calcutta, I have studied the problem of the adjustment of the population to the agricultural-economic environment in a geographical and economic setting. The region surveyed is the Ganges Valley, one of the most ancient and predominantly agricultural regions of the world which has witnessed the vicissitudes of civilizations.

Under modern conditions of economic life the pressure of the population on economic resources generates stresses and strains, which act and react not only on the process of economic equilibrium but also on social and cultural values, biological efficiency, political ideology, and public policy. Thus a study of the modern problem of population is really one of human adjustment in its wider sense to the whole of the environment which is an ensemble of various interdependent factors. In this work I have tried to visualize one segment of this integrated pattern, viz. the adjustment of the population to the agricultural-economic environment.

The study naturally has been based on a classification of agricultural regions in the entire Ganges Valley which shows some of the world's highest records of rural density and agricultural productivity under exceedingly favourable conditions of soil and rainfall, irrigation and floods. Rural density in the crowded monsoon zone supplies an invaluable index of economic exploitation, on the one hand, and the ensemble of natural agricultural advantages on the other. It is seen to vary with such distinct measurable factors as extension of cultivation and intensive subsistence farming, which again have definite correlation with geographical and ecological factors, viz., fertility and the amount and distribution of agricultural water-supply. A meticulous survey of the different agricultural regions reveals certain limiting as well as optimal factors of agricultural productivity and density. The operation of the limiting agents is of course due to an indefinite multiplication of population and an inevitable process of close regional adjustment of crops, crop rotations, and agricultural practices to feed the enormous population. Absence of industrialization and of migration account for the limiting factors being operative more quickly and on a larger scale than in other agricultural communities. Such a study of the variability, limits, and optimal conditions of agriculture and human density accordingly may contribute to change agricultural economics, which is so far mostly an assemblage of merely geographical and agricultural data, into a science, though it has still to struggle hard for recognition. It is also an indispensable prelude to rational agricultural planning, which will be seen to vary according to the economic limits and possibilities of different regions. My labour will be amply rewarded if this survey helps towards the development of exact methods in the treatment of agricultural-economic data and of a sound agricultural policy for the amelioration of the economic condition of the teeming millions of this historic region under the new regime of Provincial Autonomy.

In conclusion my grateful thanks are due to my uncle, Dr. Radha Kamal Mukherji, Professor of Economics and Sociology, University of Lucknow, whose personality has been a source of inspiration to me and whose valuable work on population problems has helped me immensely in my investigations.

B. N. GANGULI

HINDU COLLEGE,
    UNIVERSITY OF DELHI
    July 20, 1938

CONTENTS

Map of the Ganges Valley   *Frontispiece*
(*Drawing by L. J. Newell*)

PART I

TRENDS OF AGRICULTURE AND POPULATION IN THE UPPER GANGES VALLEY

PART II

TRENDS OF AGRICULTURE AND POPULATION IN THE MIDDLE GANGES VALLEY

PART III

TRENDS OF AGRICULTURE AND POPULATION IN THE GANGES DELTA

vii

INTRODUCTION

As an economic concept 'density of population' signifies the economic relation subsisting between population and the area over which it is concentrated. In higher stages of economic life, this relation is complicated by the mutual inter-dependence of the different types of economic exploitation. Workers whether they are engaged in agriculture, in extractive and elaborative industries, in occupations ancillary to these, or in the professions, are no doubt, with few exceptions, associated with a definite area. But, as Professor Bowley says, in the case of industrial countries, 'permanence of residence and areal dependence are not co-extensive.' Both population and area represent two heterogeneous totals, and consequently the density which is worked out by dividing the one by the other has little or no economic significance. In such a case the density of population can only be interpreted from the point of view of 'sufficiency of space for health'. Thus the problem of the density of population resolves itself into one of overcrowding and mal-distribution of population. It is not a problem of the 'suitability of the land for direct or indirect production of the means of subsistence', or, in other words, the problem of the adjustment of population to economic resources and possibilities.

The relation of persons to areas can, however, be examined from the economic point of view in the case of a predominantly agricultural country. As Professor Bowley remarks, while the density figures in the case of an industrial country 'convey little or no meaning that has any practical bearing', a comparison of densities becomes significant in the case of a predominantly agricultural country, for we can properly consider the 'number of people supported by consumption or sale of pastoral or agricultural products'. Population and area do not, in this case, represent 'heterogeneous totals', and 'permanence of residence and areal dependence' are co-extensive for all practical purposes.

But even in the case of a predominantly agricultural country like India, if we want to visualize the problem of what Professor Bowley calls 'adequacy of cultivation' at a given stage of economic enterprise and agricultural technique, the growth and distribution of population have to be viewed in a geographical and regional setting. If this method of approach is not followed, and if the area to which the population is correlated represents a heterogeneous total, we obviously confuse the variability of the natural environment governing agriculture and economic enterprise with the 'adequacy of cultivation' and the population capacity of a particular region. In fact, the merit of such a method of approach is that it reveals the limiting factors of population growth so far as they are traceable to man's agricultural-economic environment. It is obvious that, whenever the limits set by nature are ignored, and there is unwise and violent interference with man's agricultural-economic environment, nature reasserts herself with destructive energy. Such a phenomenon is witnessed in some of the agricultural regions of India surveyed in this work. As the writer has demonstrated, in certain tracts the increasing pressure of the population upon the soil has led to denudation of forest, soil erosion, and agricultural decadence. In other tracts, owing to artificial derangement of drainage levels there is widespread water-logging of land, and the conditions of health and subsistence have become so unfavourable that there is rural depopulation on a large scale. Elsewhere, owing to the construction of canals, the land has sometimes suffered from saline efflorescence, and the sub-soil water has become brackish, while the fall of the sub-soil water-level due to the constantly flowing high-level canals has increased the difficulty and insecurity of agriculture by rendering well irrigation more difficult than ever. It is clear that a study of the limits within which man may control and modify his agricultural-economic environment is particularly fruitful when we wish to understand the process of the adjustment of population to economic resources and possibilities in the particular regions which are the subject of our study.

The writer would hasten to mention at this stage that he is fully conscious of the limits of his present inquiry. From a comprehensive point of view the density of population is a reflex of various factors constituting the whole of the environment, factors which are biological, social, and political, no less than agricultural-economic, in character. These factors, acting and reacting on one another, form an integral pattern the intricate ramifications of which compose the complex web of life; they may be properly envisaged as a *complex* or *ensemble* constituting a given dynamic situation in the growth and movement of population, such a situation persisting as a balance or equilibrium which marks a particular stage of adaptation and adjustment of human life to the whole of its environment. Obviously the scope of the present work has been deliberately restricted to a study of the salient factors of the agricultural-economic environment which operate as the determining as well as the limiting factors of population growth. Thus an attempt has been made to visualize only an important facet of the whole picture, viz., the interesting process of the adjustment of population to the agricultural-economic environment.

The vital factors of the agricultural-economic environment which have been studied in relation to the density of population are: (1) Extension of cultivation, (2) Double-cropping, (3) Agricultural water-supply, and (4) Choice and combination of crops. It is necessary to examine as briefly as possible the bearing of each of these factors on the density of population.

I. EXTENSION OF CULTIVATION

In India agricultural development which accompanies the growth of population does not imply exploitation of the possibilities of intensive commercial cropping. As Mr. P. C. Tallents, I.C.S., observed in his report on census operations in Bihar and Orissa in 1911, 'experience generally shows that it is extension and not increased efficiency of cultivation that leads to an increase of the agricultural population, in so far as increased efficiency involves the use of labour-saving devices and the economy of man-power'. Such a process of agricultural development is characteristic of oriental countries in general, and, as Professor Siroshi Nasu rightly observes,

'the over-population in those countries is due to the restricted
area of the land which has been occupied from time immemorial and is not due to the changes in the means of production
or to economic cycles'. Hence a convenient method of
approach to the problem of the density of population in any
agricultural region in India is to observe the process and stages
of agricultural development as determined by the extension
of cultivation. In fact, the extent to which cultivation has
expanded or contracted, or has a tendency to expand or contract, is a clear indication of the agricultural possibilities of a
particular tract and of its population capacity. Thus a
statistical concept like the percentage of cropped land reflects
all the vital factors of the agricultural-economic environment.
Whenever these factors are favourable to agricultural development cultivation has a tendency to extend to its final limit,
and there is progressive increase in the density of population.
But such a process of agricultural development has its limit.
As the writer has shown, in some of the agricultural tracts
the situation is so alarming that an acre of land has to support
more than one person, and there is extension of cultivation
into lands which scarcely repay tillage, while there is encroachment even on the reserve necessary for fodder crops
and pasture. Again, wherever the factors of the agricultural-
economic environment are adverse to agricultural enterprise,
there is shrinkage of the cultivated area, general agricultural
decadence, and rural depopulation. But the percentage of
cultivated area, as a statistical concept, cannot be really
significant unless we properly interpret the statistics of cultivation as a whole. Possibilities of agricultural development
through extension of cultivation depend not only on the *scope*
for agricultural enterprise, but also on the *extent* of such
enterprise. The percentage of cultivated area to total area
is an index of both. But if we want to ascertain the scope
for agricultural development we must fix our attention on the
percentage of cultivable to total area. At the same time, if
we wish to realize the extent of agricultural enterprise we must
examine the percentage of cultivated to cultivable area.

II. DOUBLE-CROPPING

Double-cropping is one of those factors of agricultural economy which counteract the serious maladjustment between the increase of population and the extension of cultivation. When the population multiplies at an alarming rate and there is extreme scarcity of good arable land which can be brought under the plough, one of the alternatives before the farmer is to supplement his income by more extensive double-cropping. Thus extensive double-cropping in the densely populated regions surveyed in this work signifies the widespread tendency to resort to more intensive subsistence farming which has been forced upon the cultivators by the growth of population. The system of double-cropping modifies the ordinary standard rotation of *Rabi* and *Kharif* alternately, by which the *Rabi* harvest is followed by nearly three months' rest, and the *Kharif* harvest by nine or ten months' rest. In regions of dense population, where the average size of the holding is very small and the cultivator does not deliberately leave land fallow for successive seasons, these lengthy periods of rest give time for fresh supplies of mineral plant-food to become available and for bacteria in the soil to develop. Hence it is apparent that double-cropping involves a wasteful utilization of land. Sometimes, no doubt, double-cropping is practised on highly manured land near the village sites and is guided by intelligent methods of agriculture. Again, in the deltaic portion of the Ganges Plain in which the soil is fertile, and its fertility is renewed by the fertilizing deposit of silt due to the seasonal rise of the deltaic rivers, double-cropping does not mean predatory cultivation. But usually throughout the Ganges Plain extensive double-cropping is a sign of intensive subsistence farming and improvident husbandry. The cheaper varieties of *Kharif* and *Rabi* food-grains which are essential for the subsistence of the cultivator and his family are commonly raised by means of double-cropping. Although there is a limit to the development of subsistence farming which is based on over-cropping and wasteful cultivation of land, yet we notice a statistical correspondence between the high density of population and the *extent* of the double-cropped area in this region. But it must also be recognized that the contribution of double-cropping to agricultural productivity and agricultural security depends also on the *value* of the second crops raised on the same land in the same season. When we apply this test we find interesting regional contrasts which explain the variations in the distribution of rural density.

III. AGRICULTURAL WATER-SUPPLY

Environment, as understood in relation to agriculture, is a complex or ensemble of many factors of which relief, climate and soil are the most important. Relief or elevation of land profoundly influences climate and agricultural practice. The two other uncontrollable factors of the agricultural-economic environment, climate and soil, act and react on each other in a subtle manner. This question is discussed in detail in Chapter III, Part I. It has been shown that the efficiency of rainfall is profoundly influenced by the structure or texture of the soil, just as the efficiency of the soil, in respect of its physical and chemical conditions and in the matter of the supply of sufficient plant-food, depends upon rainfall and temperature. Thus there seems to be no sharp line of distinction between the physical and chemical conditions of the soil and the climatic conditions, although the distinction is clearly marked. But, on the whole, in a monsoon region like the Ganges Plain the importance of soil as a factor of agricultural productivity is overshadowed by the importance of climate. It is the variation in the amount and distribution of rainfall rather than the variation in the character of the soil which has far-reaching effects on agriculture, on the trend and rhythm of economic life in general and on the distribution of population. The natural regions of India are essentially Rainfall Tracts, and the order of these regions in regard to rainfall is the same as their order in regard to the density of population. The explanation of such a correlation may be very briefly discussed here. Where the rainfall is heavy heavy-yielding food crops as well as valuable commercial crops are raised with the help of monsoon rainfall and spill irrigation. Land also is so fertile that it yields bumper crops

even without judicious rotation and manuring, and after the
summer harvest is reaped so much moisture is still left in the
soil that another winter crop can often be taken off the same
land in the same season without manuring and irrigation.
But it should be remembered that artificial irrigation is also
an important factor of rural economy in considerable portions
of the Ganges Plain. Here the density of population may not
be entirely a function of artificial irrigation as in the Punjab
and the Sind Plains or in the coastal plain of South India.
But it has a productive as well as a protective function, at
any rate, in the upper portions of the Ganges Plain. Hence
both rainfall and irrigation, which may be characterized as
agricultural water-supply, are the determining factors of
agricultural productivity and the density of population.
There is another important aspect of the problem of the
density of population which should not be ignored. The
density of population, which depends so much on the stability
of agricultural economy, is profoundly influenced by agricultural security. Experience shows that population has a
tendency to decrease in those agricultural tracts which normally receive a scanty rainfall and are liable to drought, and
in which, at the same time, farmers cannot offer increasing
resistance to it by means of protective irrigation works. In
such ill-fated regions famine causes mortality either directly
by starvation or indirectly by beating down resistance to
disease, and also perhaps lowers fertility. Moreover, recurring
scarcity induces migration of people to localities where the
productivity as well as the security of agriculture is greater,
owing to greater facilities of natural or artificial irrigation.
A study of the geography of crop failure and famine reveals a
correlation between the amount and distribution of rainfall
and agricultural security in regions where agriculture depends
precariously on rainfall. In regions of very heavy rainfall
agriculture is secure, as there is little danger of deficiency of
rainfall, and even a substantial shortage sometimes becomes
a matter of indifference. In certain portions of the Ganges
Plain, however, while the normal rainfall is heavy, its bad
distribution leads to crop failure and famine, because the
timing of agricultural operations and the growth and maturity

of crops are so delicately adjusted to favourable meteorological conditions that a failure of rainfall at the critical
time ruins the winter rice crop which is the only important
food crop. Here artificial irrigation has been a difficult
process, and agriculture has become a gamble in rainfall. In
other dry regions of India, where rainfall hardly exceeds ten
inches, the density of population is no doubt low, but failure of
rainfall does not count for much, as the farmers do not depend
on rainfall at all. Again, in the Punjab Plains the rainfall is
moderate and is subject to sharp deviation from the normal, but
there the farmers depend upon artificial irrigation from the great
snow-fed rivers rather than on precarious rainfall, and have
evolved a stable agricultural economy based on farming of an
extremely remunerative type which may be more strenuous, but
is certainly more secure, than the farming of those agricultural
regions which depend too precariously on the bounty of nature.
Consequently in such regions the increase of population has kept
pace with the development of the sources of artificial irrigation.

IV. CHOICE AND COMBINATION OF CROPS

The choice as well as the combination of crops in any
region, which determines its agricultural productivity and
population capacity, is conditioned by the climatic factors
which determine the range of environment of crops and their
varying importance. But the importance of a particular
crop depends not only upon its own range of environment,
but also upon the range of environment of other valuable
crops which may be grown in preference to it. Hence it is
necessary to fix our attention not only upon the variety of
crops grown in any region, but also upon the choice of more
or less valuable staples and their varying economic importance.
In this connexion we discover how the pressure of the population on the soil and the choice and combination of crops
act and react on each other. In every country the increasing
pressure of the population on the soil has led to the substitution of heavy-yielding for light-yielding crops. In the
Ganges Plain we find a similar change in the choice of crops
which has been brought about by the increasing pressure of

the population upon land. The prevailing type of farming that has evolved there may be characterized as intensive subsistence farming based on the production of heavy-yielding crops as far as possible within the limits of the natural environment and the economic resources of the agriculturists. In fact, when the cultivators grow valuable commercial crops from which they raise money for cash payments, they have naturally to depend for their subsistence on the cultivation of heavy-yielding food crops. But there are regions in which the exclusive dependence on a single heavy-yielding crop of winter rice has increased economic insecurity, because the maturity of this crop depends too precariously on a short spell of rainfall at a critical time.

The region surveyed in this work forms part of the Region of the Plains situated in northern India. According to Vidal de la Blache the distribution of the ancient centres of dense population 'seems to be confined approximately to a zone bounded by the Tropic of Cancer and the fortieth parallel of latitude'. The Region of the Plains in northern India, which maintains some of the world's highest densities of population, is one of those ancient centres of dense population which eventually also became centres of civilization at a comparatively early time. Generally speaking, it is a monsoon region characterized by the comparatively dry winters and wet summers. But the succession and combination of crops, the system of farming, and the productivity and security of agriculture vary from one part of this vast region to another according to the variations in the amount and distribution of rainfall. Thus we may distinguish between a number of rainfall tracts or natural regions included in the vast Region of the Plains of Northern India. One part of the Bay of Bengal branch of the summer monsoon as it moves upward is diverted by the Himalayas and strikes them sideways and moves up the valley of the Ganges. As the monsoon current has to pass through a broad plain which rises very gradually from the sea to the mountains, it distributes itself more or less evenly over the vast stretches of the Region of the Plains. But as it moves westward it gives more rain in the northern sub-montane tract of the Ganges Valley than in the southern tracts and grows weaker and weaker as it moves up from east to west. Hence, generally speaking, the monsoon rainfall in the Plains of Northern India decreases from east to west and from north to south. Thus the natural regions arranged in order of diminishing rainfall are the Valley of the Brahmaputra and the Surma, the Valley of the Ganges and its distributaries (the Ganges Delta, the Middle Ganges Valley and the Upper Ganges Valley) and the Valley of the Indus and its tributaries (the Punjab Plain and the Sind Plain). The region surveyed in this work is the Valley of the Ganges, which includes three distinct rainfall tracts, and which, considered *in order of increasing rainfall* (the order conveniently followed in this work) are the Upper Ganges Valley, the Middle Ganges Valley and the Ganges Delta. Although the natural boundaries of these rainfall tracts seem to shade off into one another by imperceptible degrees, yet these regions, as classified on the basis of the variability of the agricultural-economic environment, have, broadly speaking, distinctive characteristics. It may be contended, as Wells does in one of his scientific essays, that every individual as well as every phenomenon is unique, and that 'It is only from the point of view of numerical law and what might be termed statistical equilibrium that an atom resembles an atom or a mammal a mammal', so that scientific classification merely serves the purpose of convenience of expression.[1] From this point of view any classification of agricultural regions will appear rather artificial. But for convenience of economic analysis and interpretation the broad divisions proposed here are sufficiently significant. Moreover, the writer has not shirked a meticulous survey as far as practicable. He has compared and contrasted the different sub-regions which may exhibit striking differences in the character of the agricultural-economic environment, in spite of the fact that they fall within one or other of the three regions. In fact, sometimes even the agricultural tracts within the same sub-region are compared and contrasted for the purpose of giving, as far as possible, an accurate perspective.

[1] André Maurois, *Poets and Prophets* (Cassell, 1936), p. 45.

PART I

TRENDS OF AGRICULTURE AND POPULATION IN THE UPPER GANGES VALLEY

EXTENSION OF CULTIVATION AND DENSITY

DENSITY is the relation of persons to areas. But this relation must not be regarded as merely a mathematical relation. Density is fundamentally a geographical expression by which we can envisage the relation between the earth and man through all its intricate ramifications which compose the complex web of life. A study of this relation reveals, among other things, the romantic episodes of the story of man's 'plant and animal conquest' and his conquest of the soil. Nature in her struggle against man's exploitation has jealously guarded the secrets of her life-cycles by which plant life responds to the needs of man. These secrets have been discovered by gradual stages, very often through accidents and adventures. Economic advantages of a particular location or environment have not been apparent to him during the early stages of his life on this earth. It is true, no doubt, that even in these early stages a benign climate and an abundant natural food-supply have favoured the increase of density.[1] But such a fact does not adequately explain the early distribution of population over the earth. Some of the early centres of dense population were found in forest retreats and mountainous tracts, because they afforded natural protection to people who were driven out of the fertile zone of the steppes which was more exposed to devastations caused by invasions and warfare. This was not, however, the normal course of events. The early centres of population were very often those in which land was not necessarily the most fertile, but was most easily cultivable. Once such favoured tracts were occupied density began to increase as a result of concentration of activities within a limited area surrounded by natural

[1] But it must also be remembered that the superabundance of vegetable and insect life, as in a tropical region, has stifled human effort and checked the increase of population.

I

barriers. 'Men built up their institutions and concentrated their efforts, while the surrounding country was neglected or uninhabited altogether.'[1] It is remarkable that primitive populations could reach a very high degree of density within these narrow limits imposed by nature. But gradually the isolation was broken. These centres of population gradually became the centres of ever-widening circles held together by a mutual interdependence of different types of exploitation. Such a stage presupposes an organized social life. It was at this stage that man realized more fully than ever the potentialities of different environments, and found scope for expansion of activities which results from a surer control over his environment. It was at this stage that density became a real expression of the natural agricultural factors which favour human agglomerations in certain regions rather than in others.

One of the signs of man's increasing control over natural environment is his conquest of the soil, which is the cause, and, in comparatively primitive times, also the effect, of a high density of population. This conquest has been possible by modifying the vegetational covering of the earth. As Vidal De La Blache says: 'Vegetation has been attacked in the most sensitive spot, so to speak.'[2] At a few degrees' distance from the equator the forest driven from the plateaux and hillsides has taken refuge in valleys and ravines. Various types of underbrush in regions which are now treeless and of aerial lianas which have become half subterranean in order to adapt themselves to new conditions of life, seem to indicate that a part of the immense area now occupied by savannas was formerly forested.[3] The great river valleys in the tropics have attracted men by the abundant animal and vegetable life which they offer. Here a high density of population has been possible by regulating and utilizing the available sources of irrigation and by clearing the tropical forests. But the conquest of the soil in these regions has always required a co-operative effort on the part of a sufficiently numerous and organized population

[1] P. Vidal De La Blache, *Principles of Human Geography*, p. 66.
[2] Ibid., p. 47.　　　　　　　　　　　　　　[3] Ibid., p. 47.

in the extent of cultivated area, the cultivable area being smaller in the eastern than in the central and the western portions of the Upper Ganges Valley.

Regions of the Upper Ganges Valley	Rural Density	Percentage of cultivable area still available for cultivation		
		1931	1921	1911
Indo-Gangetic Plain, East .	686	5·9	10·1	11·2
Sub-Himalaya, East . .	624	5·5	4·0	7·9
Indo-Gangetic Plain, Central .	504	8·6	8·9	9·5
Indo-Gangetic Plain, West .	459	8·5	10·1	9·8

INDO-GANGETIC PLAIN, EAST

A descriptive survey of the growth of population in relation to the extension of cultivation in the Upper Gangetic Plain should properly start with the Indo-Gangetic Plain, East, in which the density of population is the highest to be found in any of its natural divisions, both including and excluding the urban areas. The extreme pressure of the population on the soil in this region is evidenced by the steady emigration of people which has continued during successive decades in the past. In 1931 the emigrants outnumbered the immigrants in this region by more than two to one, and the density of population was only 1·6 per cent higher than what it had been fifty years ago.[1]

BENARES

Benares, one of the representative districts of this natural division, had a very high average density of 930 persons to the square mile in 1931. This unusually high density is, however, due to the population of the town. If its area and population be excluded, the average rural density drops to 742 persons to the square mile, which is exceeded by many other districts of this region. So far as the rural density is

[1] Speaking of this region as well as Sub-Himalaya, East, Mr. Turner says that 'a large volume of emigration takes place from these divisions owing to the pressure on the soil'. (*Census Report*, U.P., 1931, p. 106.)

concerned it has increased from 691 in 1911 to 742 in 1931.

The cultivated area in this district has increased from 73·7 per cent of the total area in 1901 to 74·7 per cent of the total area in 1931. The extension of cultivation has been mostly on land available for cultivation as a result of alluvial formations. The district area has increased by 54,470 acres most of which has been possibly brought under cultivation. The rest of the increase in the cultivated area has been at the expense of culturable waste proper. The clay tracts in the uplands east of the Ganges are by far the best tracts in the district, and the extension of cultivation has been greatest in these tracts. In Majhwar, for example, the cultivated area is more than 80 per cent of the total area, and in Narwan, a typical clay tract, it is more than 86 per cent; whereas in other parganas it is always less than 61 per cent. In the clay tracts cultivation is also more intensive, because 30 per cent of the cultivated area bears two crops in a season as compared with a little above 14 per cent in other parganas.

The culturable area including current fallow shows an increase of only 6,938 acres between 1909 and 1926–7. The real increase is much more, as there has been an increase of 54,470 acres in the district area owing to alluvial formations in the same period; whereas, there has been an increase in the area recorded as barren waste by only 1,397 acres, so that most of the increase in the district area means a corresponding increase in the culturable area.

Moreover, cultivation has not extended as in the Sub-Himalaya, East, by resumed cultivation of old fallow land or by reclamation of *usar* lands. The area not available for cultivation including grove land, old fallow and barren waste, remains the same, viz. 10·5 per cent of the total area, and this shows that the pressure of population has not been such as to necessitate the cultivation of old fallow land and *usar* land. The area under new fallow has increased by 3,000 acres, and this increase is possibly due to the extension of sugar-cane cultivation which requires that land should be kept fallow preparatory to a crop of sugar-cane in the succeeding year.

JAUNPUR

In Jaunpur, another representative district of this region, the average density of population increased from 659 persons per square mile to 816 persons per square mile between 1872 and 1891. But later on, there was almost a continuous decline from 816 in 1891 to 775·6 in 1901, to 746 in 1911 and to 745·2 in 1921. During the decade 1921–31 there was a striking recovery and the density of population rose to 797 persons to the square mile, the rural density being 761 to the square mile. The cultivated area had increased from about 60 per cent of the total area in previous times to 66·94 per cent in 1896. In 1906 the average cultivated area was only 64·4 per cent. In 1931 we find a slight increase to only 65·6 per cent. Up to the closing years of the last century cultivation extended, as in Benares, naturally in those portions of the district which possess the best soil. Thus we find that in most of the parganas of Jaunpur tahsil which contain loamy soil, the cultivated area occupied more than 72 per cent of the total area. Elsewhere, cultivation extended by the reclamation of *usar* land on the borders of *jhils*. There was thus an extension of cultivation in the Ungli pargana, and Machlisahr and Mariahu tahsils. But still the cultivated area has not exceeded 66 per cent in these tracts and has mostly been barely 60 per cent. This comparatively low percentage shows that the scope for the extension of cultivation has been limited by the inferiority of the soil as compared with the rich loamy soil of the Gangetic Plain.

Between 1908 and 1926–7 the culturable area including current fallow has not changed. There has been no change in the district area as a result of alluvion or diluvion; nor has there been any change in the area not available for cultivation. The area under new fallow has increased only by 6,000 acres, and this increase is explained by the increased cultivation of sugar-cane which requires that land should be kept fallow preparatory to a crop of sugar-cane.

By 1908 it was found that the area under culturable waste could not be reduced any further as the bulk of this area covered *usar* tracts, or *Dhak* jungle, or else consisted of land of very poor fertility. The largest area under culturable waste was found in the Machlisahr and Mariahu tahsils where, as already said, cultivation extended by the reclamation of *usar* land and the utilization of land of poor fertility. Moreover, the area under pasture had been reduced to a dangerously low proportion. Thus further extension of cultivation either by reclaiming *usar* land or by breaking up pasture land had clearly reached its limit by 1908. The high pressure of the population upon the soil in this district is indicated by the large number of emigrants who probably still form over 10 per cent of the natural population.

BALLIA

Next we shall consider the district of Ballia which, in spite of an abnormal death-rate in previous years, recorded a high average density of 791 persons per square mile in 1901. But in this district there has been a heavy loss of population in recent times, so that the mean density was 742 persons to the square mile in 1931. In the case of this district the changes in density are not clearly reflected in the changes in the average cultivated area. The district seems to have reached its fullest development so far as the extension of cultivation is concerned by 1891, when the highest density of 798 was recorded. Since 1891, the density has gone on continuously diminishing owing predominantly to a high death-rate. But the cultivated area has remained almost stationary at about 67 to 68 per cent of the total area. Within the district, however, the extension of cultivation and density have the closest correspondence. As in other districts, extension of cultivation has been greatest in those portions which possess the best soil. There is a deterioration of the soil from east to west, and the alluvial lowlands of the east are more extensively cultivated than the western uplands. In the eastern portions, especially in the parganas lying in the ancient alluvium, the cultivated area, on the average, exceeds 75 per cent of the total area, whereas in other parts of the district it does not exceed 65 per cent. Population in those parganas is also more dense than in the western parganas.

The area recorded as culturable waste was 127,418 acres in 1901 and 126,097 acres in 1926-7. The percentage of culturable waste is highest in the western parganas which contain vast stretches of *usar* land. This culturable waste includes current fallow, the area under which has increased, as in Jaunpur, by 8,093 acres owing to the increased cultivation of sugar-cane. The increase in the area under current fallow is at the expense of the cultivated area under other crops, which occupy a corresponding portion of the former culturable waste at the expense of old fallow, grass land, or pasture land.

AZAMGARH

The district of Azamgarh maintained a remarkably high density of 804·7 persons per square mile as early as 1891, which is a landmark in the history of the agricultural development of most of the districts situated in the Gangetic plain. After 1891, the density went down to 712·5 in 1901, and then to 675 in 1911. But after this set-back there was again an upward tendency, so that the density was 690·8 in 1921 and 710 in 1931. It would seem that the increase of population had reached its limit by 1891. But it must be remembered that the decline in population in the early years of this century was due partly to excessive rainfall which led to an outbreak of fever, and partly to emigration. Moreover, 848,144 acres of fresh land had been brought under the plough by 1907-8.

Hence, so far as the supply of land is concerned, there was still some scope for further extension of cultivation. By the closing years of the last century the cultivated area had reached about 58 per cent of the total area. But later on owing to the extension of cultivation it reached about 60 per cent by 1908, and in 1931 it was as much as 63·8 per cent. Thus, it seems that the agricultural possibilities of the district in respect of the supply of arable land had not been fully exploited, and the upward movement of density is justified by the circumstances. As in other districts of the Gangetic Plain, land on the old alluvium is more extensively cultivated and densely populated. The percentage of cultivated area is also very high in the alluvial lowlands which are not only more fertile owing to inundations, but are also free from saline efflorescence which is so common in the uplands where the drainage channels take their rise.

GAZIPUR

Lastly, we shall consider the district of Gazipur which, like Azamgarh, had also reached a very high density (737·3) by 1891. In this district, as in Azamgarh, there was a continuous decrease of population after 1891. In 1901 the density was 656·9, and in 1911 there was further decrease to 603. In the case of Gazipur, as also in the case of Azamgarh, the decrease of population must be explained, partly by the abnormal death-rate, and mainly by emigration which has been very strong since 1872. Lastly, like Azamgarh, Gazipur has also begun to recover the lost ground in recent times. The density of population which had been 597·9 persons to the square mile in 1921 was 634 in 1931.

The cultivated area had reached a very high figure, viz. 617,735 acres in 1891, which was the peak year so far as the density of population is concerned. About 1901, the cultivated area had dropped to 591,687 acres, in 1926–7 it was 569,700 acres or 68·36 per cent of the total area, and in 1931 it was still found to be only 68·8 per cent of the total area. The agricultural situation of the district can be realized properly when it is remembered that even as far back as 1879 the cultivated area was 68·15 per cent of the total area. The reason why the extension of cultivation has not proceeded far and does not show any sign of proceeding farther, is that the extent of barren land infected with saline efflorescence is very large in some parts of the district. As a matter of fact we may say that the extension of cultivation in this district is entirely limited by the ability of the cultivators to reclaim *usar* land. Hence it is natural that in the alluvial parganas of the district where there is not much *usar* land, the cultivated area varies from 75 per cent to 80 per cent of the total area; whereas in the northern uplands where, as in Azamgarh, the drainage channels take their rise, and consequently *usar* lands are found in extensive patches, the cultivated area generally does not exceed 68 per cent and is often as low as 56 per cent.

With the decrease in the cultivated area there has been a corresponding increase in the area recorded as culturable waste, including current fallow by 13,841 acres since 1902. The real increase is much more, because the district area has increased by 57,688 acres. The area including old fallow and culturable waste proper has increased by 12,303 acres. This means either that much of the *usar* land brought under cultivation is no longer cultivated now, or that the area of *usar* land has increased as a result of the deterioration of the drainage system. The latter conclusion is probable, as the serious drawback from which the district suffers is over-saturation of the soil due to defective drainage.

SUB-HIMALAYA, EAST

Sub-Himalaya, East, has been one of those agriculturally undeveloped regions in which the density of population has increased in comparatively recent times as a result of extension of cultivation. In this region rainfall is comparatively heavy and reliable, and the high water-level facilitates artificial irrigation.[1] Moreover, there have been extensive undeveloped areas in the northern portion of this region which have attracted settlers from the overcrowded tracts of the south. In 1881 the density of this region was only two-thirds that of the Indo-Gangetic Plain, East, the most thickly populated region in the Upper Gangetic Plain. Now the density of population is 31 per cent higher than what it was fifty years ago, and this phenomenal increase of population has been mainly ascribed to the extension of cultivation into the undeveloped tracts of this region. As Mr. A. C. Turner, I.C.S., observes, even during the decade 1921–31 the higher percentage of the increase of population in this region than in other regions of the Upper Gangetic Plain is due, in no small measure, to the extension of the cultivated area in the northern tracts, 'the pressure on the land in other areas having driven cultivators into hitherto undeveloped tracts. This is specially

[1] *Census Report*, U.P., 1931, p. 67.

noticeable in the north of the Gorakhpur district where many new village sites have sprung up in the past decade, and much virgin soil is being cultivated, more especially with sugar-cane to feed the numerous cane factories that have sprung up towards the end of the decade.'[1]

GORAKHPUR

What distinguishes Gorakhpur, which is one of the representative districts of Sub-Himalaya, East, from other districts situated in the Upper Gangetic Plain, is that almost all the land is cultivable. Hence, so far as the supply of arable land is concerned, there has been no hindrance to the phenomenal increase of density through long periods. Before 1919 the population of the district had increased by 16 per cent during the preceding thirty years, and more than half of this increase had taken place between 1881 and 1891. The result was that the average density of population was 707 per square mile in 1919. In the southern parganas, where there is very little culturable land available, the density of population is as high as 1,000 to 1,100 persons per square mile of cultivated area, or roughly there are 3 persons to 2 acres of cropped land. In the north, however, there is more elbow room and some scope for further extension of cultivation. Statistics of cultivation show that whatever extension of cultivation there has been in this district has taken place mostly in the Padarauna tahsil which recorded a comparatively low density of 657 per square mile even in 1911, and more particularly in the pargana Sidhua Jobna, where culturable waste was still available in the remote *Bhat* tracts of the north. Hence it seems that a further increase of density has been rendered possible by the extension of cultivation into the northern tracts although the extreme north of the district is unhealthy.

Extension of cultivation means a corresponding decrease in the area recorded as culturable. Later statistics, however, reveal a decrease in the area recorded as unculturable. This must be explained by reference to a new principle of statistical classification which was adopted later on and according to

[1] *Census Report*, U.P., 1931, p. 99.

which land which is capable of bearing any vegetation whatever is regarded as culturable and not unculturable. But such a decrease in the unculturable area must mean a corresponding increase in the culturable area. Hence in comparing the culturable areas in former periods with those in later periods we must make allowance for this kind of increase in the culturable area, so that the *real* decrease in the culturable area would be far more than the ordinary difference between the culturable areas in the two periods.

The revision of settlement in 1919 showed that the cultivated area had increased by 1·98 (100 thousand acres), and the real decrease in the culturable area had also been to a corresponding extent; whereas the average density had increased by about 42 persons per square mile. The bulk of the increase in the cultivated area took place in the northern portions of the district where waste land was available. In Sidhua Jobna there was a permanent increase of 40,000 acres, and it is significant that most of this increase had taken place at the expense of old fallow land which usually does not repay tillage. In the eastern tahsils the area under old fallow in 1919 was half of the area recorded as such at the last settlement. This shows clearly the extreme pressure of the population upon the soil. Statistics of cultivation show an increase in the area under groves chiefly in the eastern tahsils. This must be regarded as a redeeming feature because, as already said, the peculiarity of this district is that almost all the land is culturable and practically all of it is cultivated, and this means a corresponding encroachment upon the pasture land with all its dangerous reactions upon the rural economy of the district. Recent statistics show that the limit to the extension of cultivation and the consequent increase of population has not yet been reached. While people have emigrated from the overcrowded tracts in the south of the district in which there is extreme pressure of the population on the soil, in the northern tracts much virgin soil is being brought under cultivation and devoted to sugar-cane to feed the numerous sugar factories that have sprung up during the decade 1921–1931 as a result of the tariff protection granted to the sugar industry.

BASTI

In the neighbouring district of Basti, we find essentially the same tendencies of agricultural development. As in Gorakhpur, the southern portion of this district, which is near the Gangetic Plain, has been more densely populated and extensively cultivated through long periods than the northern portion. In the north, the area of grove land and jungle was disproportionately large, and during 60 or 70 years before 1905 there had been a progressive extension of cultivation, especially in the north-eastern portion of the district where most of the forest tracts are situated. The average density of population has increased from 528 per square mile in 1872 to 737 persons per square mile in 1931, and the cultivated area has also increased from about 62 per cent of the total area to 72·9 per cent of the total area in roughly the same period. The reclamation of the north has been so complete that the cultivated area varies from 71 per cent to 81·4 per cent of the total area in the northern parganas.

Further extension of cultivation as a result of an increase of population, especially in the southern portion of the district, must have taken place, as in Gorakhpur, at the expense of the area recorded as culturable waste, and practically at the expense of the area recorded as old fallow. The area recorded as old fallow has diminished from 200,862 acres at the first settlement to 156,176 acres at the revision of settlement, and then again to 151,249 acres in 1921. This area is mostly uneven land on the banks of the rivers and streams, or land which is too swampy or unfit for cultivation owing to saline efflorescence. Some portion of this area might have relapsed into barrenness, and a part of the decrease in the area under old fallow might be explained in this way. But in fact a large portion of this decrease is explained by the increasing pressure of the population upon the soil, as in the case of Gorakhpur.

The culturable waste including current and old fallow has diminished by 4 per cent of the total area between 1905 and 1926–7, and the unculturable area has also diminished by 2 per cent. Hence the *real* decrease in the culturable area is by more than 4 per cent. This shows that the extension of cultivation has taken place at the expense of both culturable waste proper and old fallow, even in comparatively recent times. Before 1905, a considerable amount of culturable waste proper had been brought under cultivation as a result of increased assessment, and more land has been available for cultivation in the north, especially in Basti and Rasulpur parganas, so that it is natural that the same process should have continued even up to recent times. At the present time the extreme pressure of the population on the soil is indicated by the fact that 81·6 per cent of the total cultivable area is under cultivation, as against 79·8 per cent in the Indo-Gangetic Plain, East, which records the highest rural density in the Upper Ganges Valley. And the most disquieting feature of this district is that the area under groves as well as under pasture is diminishing progressively, and the small area under current fallow shows that the land suffers from over-cropping.

INDO-GANGETIC PLAIN, CENTRAL

We shall now study a natural region which stands third in order of density amongst the natural regions of the Upper Ganges Valley. The districts included in this region are affected, in varying degrees, by both the alluvium of the Ganges and that of the Jumna, which exercise distinct influences on the conditions of agriculture, the extension of cultivation, and the distribution of population. In the tracts mostly affected by the alluvium of the Jumna (the trans-Jumna tracts) the soil is inferior to that usually found in the trans-Gangetic tracts; the greater depth of the water-level has also increased the difficulties of well irrigation, while, at the same time, in spite of the development of canal irrigation, the farmers there have to depend, to a very large extent, on the uncertain natural sources of agricultural water-supply in the absence of wells. Consequently the density of population has been found to be invariably higher in the tracts affected by the Gangetic alluvium than in those affected by the alluvium of the Jumna. Examining the variation of density in the Indo-Gangetic Plain, Central, during the decade 1921–31 Mr. A. C. Turner, I.C.S., concluded in the *Census Report* of

1931 that 'the tahsils lying along the left bank of the Ganges (i.e. north) have, as a rule, increased substantially' in population.[1] For example, 'the three north-eastern tahsils, Handia, Phulpur and Soraon, show considerable increases, whereas the western and trans-Jumna tahsils show small increases.'[2]

ALLAHABAD

Allahabad, one of the typical districts of this natural division, had reached the maximum density of population, like most other districts of the Upper Gangetic Plain, by the year 1891. After that year there was a continuous decrease of population. The density of population, which had been 543·07 persons to the square mile in 1891, fell to 522·05 in 1901, to 513 in 1911, to 491 in 1921, and finally to 457 in 1931. The steady increase of population before 1891 and the steady decrease thereafter were shared equally by the trans-Gangetic region and the Doab region. But the trans-Gangetic tracts contain the rich and well-consolidated alluvium of the Ganges, and consequently are more fertile than the Doab which is affected by the alluvium of the Jumna. The peculiar black soil, the great depth of the water-level, and the thin superstratum of alluvial deposit on sand constitute a great hindrance to the agricultural development of the Doab. Hence we find that the extension of cultivation and the density of population are greater in the trans-Gangetic tracts than in the Doab region. In the former, the density on the total area is 100 per acre more than in the latter, the density on the cultivated area being considerably higher.

The cultivated area in 1931 was found to be the same as it had been as far back as 1873, viz. 56·8 per cent of the total area, and this may be regarded as an evidence of the declining conditions of agriculture. Between 1874 and 1912–16 there was an extension of cultivation only in the trans-Gangetic tracts; but this was mainly due to the increase in the supply of land as a result of the fluvial action of the Ganges. In 1916 it was also found that cultivation had extended in these tracts into the swampy and raviny land, that embanked

[1] *Census Report*, U.P., 1931, p. 90. See also p. 84.   [2] Ibid., p. 86.

squares for the cultivation of rice had been pushed out into the *jhils*, and that natural hollows and reservoirs had been drained off, thus undoubtedly restricting the supply of water otherwise available for irrigation. These facts show that there had already been extreme pressure of the population upon the soil, and the situation becomes all the more alarming when it is remembered that the density per cultivated acre in Allahabad is abnormally high, and, as in Gorakhpur, an acre has to support more than one person.

Cultural waste proper, including current fallow, is naturally more abundant in the Doab region than in the trans-Gangetic tracts. Between 1907–8 and 1931 the cultivated area has diminished from 58·19 per cent to 56·8 per cent of the total area, and the culturable area has also increased proportionately. The area recorded as new fallow has also diminished in the same proportion as the cultivated area, and there has been a corresponding increase in the area recorded as old fallow.

CAWNPORE

In the neighbouring district of Cawnpore, which is another representative district of the southern portion of the central Gangetic Plain, the average density increased from 485 in 1872 to 528 in 1901 which represents the maximum yet recorded. As in other districts, population diminished after 1901, and the density was as low as 482 in 1911 and 485 in 1921. The density of population in 1931 was, however, 512 persons to the square mile. In Cawnpore the soil deteriorates from north to south as in other districts of the central Gangetic Plain, the northern parganas being affected by the alluvium of the Ganges and the southern by the inferior alluvium of the Jumna. Consequently the northern parganas are more densely populated and more extensively and intensively cultivated than the southern parganas. As a matter of fact, in regard to this district as well as other districts of the Doab, we may say that density and extension of cultivation vary directly with the distance from the Jumna and inversely with the distance from the Ganges. But still, as the successive censuses of 1872, 1881, and 1901 indicate, population has gone

2

on increasing in the sparsely populated tracts in the south. A good deal of this increase has been due to the extension of cultivation brought about by canal irrigation. Nevertheless the soil of the southern parganas is inferior, and certain portions of this region cannot do without natural sources of water-supply, with the result that agriculture is distinctly precarious in spite of the canals.

The gross cropped area in Cawnpore increased from 903,915 acres in 1870 to about 959,630 acres in the decade ending with 1906–7, and the double-cropped area increased from 45,215 acres to 124,086 acres in the same period. It is apparent that there has been a decrease in the net cultivated area; but this decrease has been more than compensated by an increase in intensive cultivation which is most remarkable. The percentage of cultivated area is about 60 per cent in the poorest and most precarious tracts, whereas it is barely 53 per cent in the richest tracts of the north. But the proportion of barren waste is less in the southern than in the northern tracts, and the soil of the latter being more fertile, it is natural that there should be a very intensive cultivation of land. Hence, in the case of this district we must consider not merely the area under cultivation, but also the area bearing two crops in a season.

We have seen that the density of population of this district has gone on decreasing since 1901. This is reflected in the changes in the gross cropped area. But it must be remembered that while the net cultivated area shows a decrease of 11,620 acres, the double-cropped area shows a decrease of 46,995 acres, so that the declining conditions of agriculture are reflected more in diminished double-cropping than in the contraction of the cultivated area.

There has been an increase in the area under culturable waste including current fallow. Culturable waste proper excluding grove land consists of either *usar* land or land classified as old fallow. The land recorded as old fallow is either sandy, or raviny, or without means of irrigation, or distant from the village sites. The area under such culturable waste has remained almost the same. The increase in the area under culturable waste including current fallow thus means a very large increase in the area under current fallow which has become almost double. And this increase is the result of the same cause which is responsible for diminished double-cropping, viz. a release of the pressure of the population upon the soil.

FATEHPUR

In the district of Fatehpur the average density of population had, as usual, reached its maximum by 1891, being 428 per square mile in that year, and then it dropped to 420·8 in 1901, to 412 in 1911 and 397 in 1921. At present the rural density is barely 409 persons to the square mile. This district resembles other districts of the Doab so far as physical conditions are concerned, and consequently the density of population and the extension of cultivation vary inversely as the distance from the Ganges. Hence the northern parganas which are affected by the Gangetic alluvium are more densely populated and more intensively and extensively cultivated than the southern parganas which are affected by the alluvium of the Jumna. The density of population and the extension of cultivation have been determined by the varying physical conditions in this district in a very interesting manner. The successive dry and wet cycles have had their unfavourable effects upon the agriculture of the district as a whole. Between 1872 and 1881 the rainfall was lighter; this did not affect the northern parganas which were irrigated from wells; but it seriously affected the southern parganas where irrigation is difficult owing to the great depth of the water-level. In the next decade, the south gained in numbers owing to good rainfall; but the north, which contains many stretches of water-logged depressions, suffered from unhealthiness and lost in numbers. The precariousness of agriculture in the south has, however, been removed to a certain extent by the opening of a branch of the Ganges Canal. But on the whole, the comparatively low density of population in this district is due to the waterlogging of the central depressions and the great depth of the water-level in the south.

The cultivated area in Fatehpur had been only 54 per cent of the total area in 1905 and was found to be still 54·7 per cent in 1931. This is a very low figure, and the reason why it is so low is the presence of a very large area of barren land and extensive tracts of grove land and waste. There has been only an increase of 5 per cent in the cultivated area between 1870 and 1915, and this increase has been due to the extension of cultivation in the Jumna tracts as a result of the development of the irrigation system. In 1915 the area under old fallow amounted to 117,513 acres, and that under culturable waste proper was only 59,158 acres. Some portion of the area under old fallow was reserved for grazing purposes, and another portion, situated in the Jumna tracts, was alternately cultivated and kept fallow. Thus it seems that little land was available for further extension of cultivation. So far as the present conditions are concerned, we find that the net cultivated area has remained almost stationary.

SITAPUR

Lastly, we shall take up the district of Sitapur, which is still one of the most backward districts of the United Provinces of Agra and Oudh, and which, although it lies in the Central Gangetic Plain and exhibits the characteristic physical features of this region, cannot be regarded as a representative district of this region. The upland plain of this district is a level tract with slight undulations, and the land between the streams in this tract is liable to over-saturation. Moreover, the growth of grass jungles has always been a serious hindrance to the extension of cultivation. The lowlands, unlike those in other districts of the plain, are liable to violent floods which render cultivation entirely precarious. The district enjoys but little facilities of irrigation, and there are large tracts which suffer from uncertainty of rainfall. The result has been that the standard of cultivation is low and the population also is sparse. The average density of population increased from 425·6 to 476·9 between 1881 and 1891, which was a period of prosperity in almost every district of the United Provinces of Agra and Oudh. In the succeeding decade the increase of population was maintained in spite of the famine of 1897, and in 1901 the average density rose to

582·8, which was the maximum ever recorded. After 1901 there was a progressive decline, the average density being 506 in 1911 and 484 only in 1921. An increase of population was recorded at the census of 1931, and the density of population was found to be 520 persons to the square mile.

The proportion of cultivated area to total area in this district has always been very high owing to the fact that, although much of the land is poor and its cultivation precarious, yet there is but little land which is absolutely unproductive. We find a gradual increase in the cultivated area corresponding to a progressive increase in the density of population. By 1884, the cultivated area had increased by over 17,000 acres. During the next decade again there was an increase. In the famine year of 1897 there was a contraction of the cultivated area, but in 1898 a further increase of 80,000 acres was recorded, and in 1901 there was another increase of 56,000 acres. In 1903–4 the cultivated area was thus 72·2 per cent of the total area. At present 64·8 per cent of the total area is cultivated, and it is obvious that this district has not regained the position which it occupied in 1901 in point of the extension of cultivation and the density of population. But still the pressure of the population on the soil is sufficiently high, and fully justifies the considerable increase in emigration in recent times. As Mr. A. C. Turner observes, 'an outlet is evidently imperative for such a rapidly increasing population'.[1]

Culturable waste is naturally small, considering the enormous extent of the cultivated area and the extensive precarious tracts to be found in this district. Between 1864 and 1904 the area under culturable waste diminished from 19·68 of the total area to 14·45 per cent. This decrease was due mainly to the extension of cultivation by the reclamation of forests. The area under old fallow is large, because land which might be cultivated in a good season is kept fallow in a bad season.

[1] *Census Report*, U.P., 1931, p. 88.

OUDH

The districts of Oudh fall within the Central Gangetic Plain and exhibit, no doubt, the characteristic physical conditions obtaining in this natural region. But these conditions are somewhat different from those found in Allahabad, Cawnpore, and Fatehpur which constitute the typical Doab region of the Central Gangetic Plain, and hence the districts of Oudh deserve a separate study.

PARTABGARH

In Partabgarh, a representative district of this region, the average density of population had reached its maximum by 1891, in common with many other districts of the Gangetic Plain, there being a remarkable increase of density between 1881 and 1891 from 589·6 to 624. In 1901 there was a slight increase to 626·1, and in the next decade there was a slight decrease to 624. Hence the average density remained practically stationary between 1891 and 1911. At the census of 1921 the average density was 593, the district thus sharing a general decline of population which took place in the whole of the Gangetic Plain. But during the next decade the density of population increased to 628 persons to the square mile with the result that the position reached towards the end of the last century was regained.

The district, considered as a whole, is a fairly level plain of which nearly every part is equally fertile and well cultivated, and the physical conditions favour a very high average density of population. The changes in density are clearly reflected in the extension of cultivation. At the settlement of 1863 the cultivated area was 448,648 acres or 48·76 per cent of the total area. The settlement was immediately followed by an extensive clearance of jungle and waste land, and much land that was regarded as barren was soon bearing rich crops. Large stretches of waste land were sold out to the highest bidders; moreover, clearance leases were given and a nominal rent was charged for at least three years. In this way about 18,000 acres were brought under cultivation within five years. By 1892 the cultivated area was 498,916 acres or 54·03 per cent of the total area, thus showing an increase of 50,000 acres. A large portion of this increase was due to Capt. Chapman's reclamation of the Benti Lake by means of embankments, by which more than 3½ square miles were available for cultivation. In 1902 the cultivated area was 514,615 acres or 55·7 per cent of the total area. Since then there has been very little increase, and even in 1931 the cultivated area was only 56·1 per cent.

Corresponding to an increase in the cultivated area there has been a decrease in the area recorded as culturable waste. In 1863 this area was 14·79 per cent of the total area, but by 1892 it was reduced to 11·03 per cent, but since then there have been little variations. The area under new fallow increased remarkably from 803 acres in 1863 to 20,265 acres in 1902, as a result of the increase in the cultivated area. But this area has also remained the same since 1902. The figures for 1926–7 show an increase in the area recorded as culturable waste including old fallow from 14·39 per cent in 1902 to 16·89 per cent. But there has been also a corresponding decrease in the area recorded as barren waste, which shows that the area which was regarded as barren waste is now recorded as culturable, so that the increase in the area recorded as culturable waste including old fallow can be explained in this way. The declining conditions of agriculture are, however, indicated by the decrease in double-cropping, the double-cropped area having diminished from 33·5 per cent of the cultivated area in 1902 to 19·8 per cent in 1931.

SULTANPUR

In the district of Sultanpur the average density of population had reached almost its maximum by 1901, having increased from 561·1 in 1881 to 629·2 in 1891, and to 637 in 1901. After 1901 there was a decrease to 612 in 1911, and to 586 in 1921. The decade 1921–31 witnessed a remarkable increase of population, the density of population having increased from 586 persons to the square mile to 614 persons to the square mile. Thus the population in Sultanpur regained during this decade the position it had reached in 1911. Between 1881 and 1891, a period of great prosperity, the increase of population had been, as usual, very rapid, but the census of 1901 recorded a comparatively small increase. Later enumerations show that there was a release of the high pressure of the population upon the soil.

These tendencies are reflected in the statistics of cultivation. The cultivated area had increased from 52·8 per cent of the total area in about 1870 to 55 per cent in 1895, and in 1901 it was 58 per cent. After 1901 there was no further increase, and even in 1931 the cultivated area was only 58·2 per cent. This somewhat low percentage is due to the fact that lands in the central belt, both in the north and in the south of the Gumti, suffer from oversaturation due to defective drainage; moreover, the riparian tracts as well as lands in the lake belt of the district are liable to excessive flooding. There seems to have been very little change in the normal cultivated area from 1902 up to very recent times. Hence, there has not been any change also in the area recorded as culturable waste. But some portions of barren waste have been cultivated and regarded as old fallow, so that these must have been recorded as culturable waste later, and it is in this way that the increase in the area recorded as culturable waste can be explained. But, as in Partabgarh, the declining conditions of agriculture in this district are reflected in diminished double-cropping (the double-cropped area having decreased by 4 per cent since 1902) rather than in any decrease in the cultivated area.

FYZABAD

In Fyzabad the average density had reached its maximum by 1891, having increased from 640 in 1881 to 703·7 in 1891. In 1901 there was an increase, but this increase was fictitious owing to the presence of a large number of temporary visitors. The density dropped to 666 in 1911 and rose again to 677 in 1921, and to 699 in 1931. There is thus a tendency for the population to increase further up to the maximum reached in 1891. The remarkable increase of population in this district between 1881 and 1891 is common to other districts of Oudh, and, as in Partabgarh and Sultanpur, there is also a tendency for the population to recover the position which it had reached towards the beginning of the present century.

These tendencies are reflected in the extension of cultivation in this district. The cultivated area increased from 56 per cent in 1865 to 62·83 per cent in 1904. This is certainly a very high figure, considering the large areas of unculturable waste to be found in Fyzabad. Moreover, agricultural security in this district is very much affected by rainfall, because agriculture depends so largely upon tanks and *jhils* for irrigation in normal years, or else upon wells in years of drought. Up to 1895 agricultural insecurity was very great owing to the deficiency of well irrigation. But later on, although well irrigation developed and agricultural insecurity diminished in consequence, yet there was still a good deal of agricultural insecurity which operated as a drag upon the increase of population and the expansion of cultivation. In fact the normal cultivated area has increased but little since 1904; even in 1931 it was barely 63·7 per cent.

Culturable waste, including old and new fallow, has remained almost the same. The decline of agriculture is also indicated strikingly by the diminution of double-cropping which was so very extensive in the rice-lands of the district.

BARA BANKI

In the district of Bara Banki the average density of population had reached its maximum by 1901. The period between 1881 and 1891, which was one of great prosperity, witnessed a remarkable increase in the density of population from 580·6 to 649·9. So far as the rural density was concerned it exceeded that in Fyzabad and even that in Lucknow. In the next decade there was a further increase of density till it was 692·5 in 1901. It was thought at that time that the contraction in the area of pasture land, with its consequent reactions upon the number and breed of cattle and the supply of manure, was a warning which could not be ignored. The later censuses, however, recorded a decrease of population. In 1911 the average density was 616, and in 1921 it was only 586. But during the last decade the density of population increased to 606 persons to the square mile, so that there seems to be a tendency for the population to reach once more the high density recorded in 1911, as in the district of Sultanpur.

These tendencies are reflected in the expansion of cultivation. The cultivated area was 60·32 per cent of the total area in 1872. By 1892 it had become 64·5 per cent, and in 1902 it was 67·5 per cent. In 1902 it appeared that owing to the comparative absence of barren land and the small area recorded as culturable waste no further expansion was possible; rather there was an actual contraction of the cultivated area in subsequent years. In fact the cultivated area was only 61·4 per cent of the total area even in 1931.

The area recorded as culturable waste was 22·96 per cent of the total area in 1872. Since then it decreased, owing to the expansion of cultivation, to 21·95 per cent in 1899 and to 14·8 per cent in 1902. The small decrease in the area recorded as culturable waste between 1872 and 1899 is explained by a large increase in the area recorded as old fallow which forms a part of the culturable waste. This increase in the area under old fallow was due to large tracts of land being thrown out of cultivation as a result of water-logging and flooding during the wet cycle of years. Moreover, new land that was taken up was mostly land in the neighbourhood of tanks and *jhils*, and this was the land which suffered most from the floods, so that a decrease in the area under culturable waste proper was compensated by an increase in the area under old fallow.

Since 1902 there has been an increase in the area under culturable waste together with a contraction of the cultivated area. The real position of the district is also indicated by the diminution of the double-cropped area by 4 per cent.

LUCKNOW

In Lucknow the average density had reached its maximum by 1901. There was a remarkable increase of population, as usual, between 1881 and 1891, the average density having increased from 721 in 1881 to 800·6 in 1891. The increase was maintained up to 1901, when it was 811·9. This unusually high density was, of course, due to the presence of the city. During the next two decades there was a great loss of population, till at the end of this period the density of population was 749 persons to the square mile. But the density recorded at the last census was 814 persons to the square mile, which exceeded the highest density recorded so far in 1901.

The cultivated area increased by more than 10 per cent between 1881 and 1902, and in the latter year it occupied 60 per cent of the total area. In 1931 it was 57·3 per cent. The percentage that was reached in 1902 was already very high, considering that the average size of the holding was less than in any other district of Oudh. And it is significant that the percentage of cultivated area in 1931 did not come up to the high figure which had already been reached in 1902.

The area recorded as culturable waste was 172,500 acres in 1866. By 1893 it had been reduced by 21,000 acres, and in 1899 it amounted to only 100,000 acres. But it was considered doubtful whether the existing culturable waste would repay cultivation. As in Bara Banki, the decrease in the area under culturable waste had been accompanied by an increase in the area under old fallow, because fresh land that was taken up owing to the pressure of the population upon the soil was often given up and regarded as old fallow. The area under old and new fallow has increased by 11,000 acres, and it is likely that much of this increase has been due to this sort of shifting cultivation.

The most extensive reclamations have taken place in this district after 1893. By 1902 one half of the area recorded as new fallow had again been brought under the plough, and the area under old fallow had been reduced to a large extent. This shows clearly the extreme pressure of the population upon land. The culturable land that was available at that time was either sandy or *usar* land. Moreover, as in Bara Banki, the area of pasture land had become dangerously small, and the cattle were fed on juar and other fodder crops. All these facts show that the limit to the utmost expansion of cultivation and the increase of density had already been reached by 1902.

INDO-GANGETIC PLAIN, WEST

We shall now take up a natural region which stands fourth in order of mean density amongst the different natural regions of the Upper Gangetic Plain. The districts included in this region show considerable diversity in physical conditions. The inherent differences of physical conditions have mani- fested themselves in the settled and intensive agriculture in some of the districts, and in the shifting, precarious, and careless cultivation in other districts. Consequently, we find considerable variations in density and the extension of culti- vation amongst the districts included in this natural region. But it must be noted that the development of canal irrigation has mitigated, to a large extent, the rigours which nature has imposed upon the agriculturist in many of these districts, and has stimulated the growth of population by increasing both agricultural productivity and agricultural security. In fact, in summing up the account of the variations of population in the different tracts of this region during the decade 1921– 1931, Mr. A. C. Turner, I.C.S., observed in the *Census Report* of 1931 that the population increased in this region during this period by the provincial average. The main factor to which this increase has been attributed is 'the protection afforded to the western districts of Muzaffarnagar, Meerut, Bulandsahar, Aligarh, Muttra, and Agra by the Ganges and Jumna Canals'.[1]

MEERUT

Let us take up the district of Meerut in which the high proportion of cultivated to total area has always been a re- markable feature of agriculture. This district, unlike the districts of Oudh, has not lost its population since 1901. There was, as usual, a remarkable increase of population between 1881 and 1901, the average density having increased from 551·9 in 1881 to 587·2 in 1891 and to 652 in 1901. In 1911 a decrease was noticed, but by 1921 the density rose again to 652. During the decade 1921–31 the population

[1] *Census Report*, U.P., 1931, p. 83.

increased still further and the present density is 699 persons to the square mile.

The rapid development of canal irrigation gave a great impetus to the extension of cultivation in this district. In 1836, when there was only the Jumna canal, and the Ganges canal and the Anupsahar branch did not exist, the cultivated area was only 57 per cent. But after the full development of the irrigation system it was as much as 69 per cent. Since then there has been only a slight increase. In 1895 the cultivated area was 70 per cent, and finally in 1902 it was 72 per cent. A part of this increase had been due to reclamation of land in the neighbourhood of *jhils* and depressions and clearance of *Dhak* jungles. This shows that the limit to further expansion of cultivation had almost been reached.

In fact, the percentage of cultivated to total area in 1902 was already remarkably high. At present the high percentage of cultivated area is hardly exceeded in other districts of the United Provinces of Agra and Oudh. The cultivated area is 73·7 per cent of the total area, and this is natural because the density of population now is higher than in 1901. The scarcity of cultivable land and the increasing pressure of the population on the soil are evidenced by increased emigration. As Mr. A. C. Turner, I.C.S., observes: 'There has been increased emigration into Delhi and the towns of the Punjab during the past decade, specially from tahsil Baghpat. The pressure of the population on the soil has demanded an outlet.'[1]

BULANDSAHAR

In the neighbouring district of Bulandsahar we find the same facts and tendencies. The average density of population in this district increased from 497 in 1891 to 596·48 in 1901. During this period ten persons were added to the population in each year per square mile. The density dropped to 590 in 1911, and 560 in 1921. In 1931 the density rose to 599, there being thus a recovery of the position reached in 1901.

The cultivated area increased from 64 per cent of the total area in 1853 to 69 per cent in 1890. In 1902 this area was as

[1] Ibid., p. 77.

much as 73 per cent. This high percentage was regarded as marking the final stage of the utmost expansion of cultivation, and it was feared that a further increase in the cultivated area would be accompanied by a disproportionate decrease in the necessary land required for fodder crops and pasture. The development of the canal system had already been completed, as in Meerut, and further extension of cultivation had been at the expense of inferior land including land covered with saline efflorescence. The extreme pressure of the population upon the soil was manifested in a minute subdivision of holdings, and it was calculated that 10 per cent of the cultivators were well able to manage, and indeed desired to possess, more land. After 1902 the cultivated area has, on the whole, not exceeded 73 per cent. In fact, even in 1931 it was found to have been only 71·6 per cent.

MORADABAD

Next, we shall take up a number of districts which suffer from serious natural limitations in one respect or the other and do not enjoy the stable agricultural conditions of the Central or the Eastern Gangetic Plain. In the district of Moradabad the average density of population increased slightly from 440·9 to 446·5 between 1881 and 1891. But during the next decade the increase of population was more rapid, so that the density rose to 469·1 in 1901. In the succeeding decade the increase was still more rapid, and the density rose to 553 in 1911. The population increased still further during the next two decades, and the density of population in 1931 was found to be 561 persons to the square mile.

The average cultivated area in the decade ending with 1892–3 was 70·4 per cent of the total area, whereas in 1870 it was only 64·4 per cent. The percentage that was reached was already high, considering the agricultural possibilities of the district. In the next decade there was a substantial increase of density. But there was a marked decline in the cultivated area owing to successive bad seasons and two years of drought, so that the average cultivated area during the decade ending with 1902–3 was only 71·4 per cent, which means an increase of only 1 per cent. This percentage was remarkably high in a district which contains so large an extent of sandy soil. As a matter of fact, in the fertile and well-irrigated portion of the district situated in the uplands, the cultivated area already occupied about 83 per cent to 86 per cent of the total area, the area recorded as culturable waste was insignificant, and there was a scarcity of pasture land. It is thus apparent that most of the area recorded as culturable waste and old fallow was situated in the precarious tracts which suffered from either excessive or deficient rainfall. In 1902 out of the total culturable area covering 114,332 acres 64,284 acres were situated in Hasanpur, a precarious tract. The bulk of the remainder was situated in the Thakurdwara tahsil which is another precarious tract. A good deal of old fallow also was situated in the *Khadir* tract of these two precarious regions. This area under culturable waste and old fallow was employed as pasture land owing to the unstable conditions of agriculture. All these facts point to the conclusion that the limit to the utmost expansion of cultivation had already been reached by 1902–3, and there was no further scope for an increase in the cultivated area. Moreover, it must be remembered that the high percentage of cultivated area to total area which had been reached by 1902–3 could be maintained only in favourable seasons, and that agriculture in this district is very much affected by drought, against which it has very little protection. In view of these considerations a further increase of population between 1901 and 1911 was sufficiently alarming. During the decade 1921–1931 the density of population increased to 561, thus exceeding the density reached in 1911, while the cultivated area remained the same as it had been in the early years of the present century. But it must be remembered that during this decade there was an increase of 34 per cent in the population of the Moradabad municipality, so that the increase in the mean density of the district was, to a large extent, due to this enormous increase in the population of the Moradabad city.

ETAH

Like Moradabad, the district of Etah, too, is liable to suffer from unstable agricultural conditions produced by fluctuations of rainfall. But whereas the former is liable to suffer from drought, the latter has a tendency to suffer from excessive rainfall, and a wet cycle of years is accompanied by serious agricultural distress. Both density and expansion of cultivation are determined by this peculiarity of the physical conditions. Thus the population decreased between 1881 and 1891 owing to the wet cycle of 1885–9, and increased by 23·1 per cent between 1891 and 1901 during the dry cycle which commenced after 1896. By 1911 the density had increased to 504 but had again dropped to 483 by 1921. During 1921–31 there was again a recovery, and the density of population was 501 persons to the square mile in 1931, so that the population recovered the position it had reached in 1901. But it was thought that the limit to further increase of population had already been reached by 1901, when the mean density was 499·1 per square mile, the density per square mile of cultivated area being as high as 784, and there were 1·2 persons per cultivated acre. The soil deteriorates from west to east. Moreover, the eastern portion of the district gets more rain, and the agricultural conditions there are less stable. Consequently the population of the eastern portion is sparse as compared with that of the western portion of the district.

As a result of the wet cycle of 1885–9 there was a very large contraction of the cultivated area between 1881 and 1891, the contraction of this area being as much as 36 per cent in the central Doab. In the next decade, owing to the dry cycle, the deficiency was almost entirely made up, and by 1905 the cultivated area was 705,867 acres. This was regarded as the maximum after making allowance for the diluvion of the rivers. As a matter of fact, on the whole, the district had been losing its population since 1905, and the normal cultivated area in 1921–2 was considerably less than the average reached in 1905.

The extension of cultivation in this district has corresponded with a decrease in the area under culturable waste including old fallow. Culturable waste consists mostly of *usar* lands, so that this decrease implies mainly a decrease in the area recorded as old fallow. The area under old fallow had also diminished by 10,861 acres, and a further diminution was dangerous as the land of the district is light and sandy and requires rest. These facts show that further expansion of cultivation and a consequent increase in the density of population were not warranted by the agricultural possibilities of the district.

MUTTRA

The district of Muttra, too, suffers much from the niggardliness of nature and unstable conditions of agriculture, as a result of which the density of population is low. The average density in this district increased from 462 in 1881 to 524 in 1901, and after that there was a decline, the density being 453 in 1911 and 421 in 1921. During the decade 1921–31 the density of population increased to 461, but it was still less than the density recorded in 1901. The year 1901 thus seems to represent the peak year. The trans-Jumna tracts in the east were served by a canal and numerous wells, the cultivation there reached a high standard, and luxuriant crops and mango groves indicated the high fertility of the soil. The western tracts, on the other hand, suffered from over-saturation owing to a very high spring-level and the absence of good drainage. Consequently the eastern tracts were more densely populated than the western. A succession of dry seasons and the famine of 1897 showed the precariousness of the Jumna tracts. There was a fall of the subsoil water-level, the supply of water in the canal was short, and the well water, too, became brackish. Moreover, the tracts were overrun by a weed called *Bhaisuri* which has become a regular scourge in years of drought. In the western tracts, on the other hand, the development of irrigation and extension of drainage works have resulted in an increase of population.

The extension of cultivation in this district had proceeded very far even in early times. By 1879 the cultivated area had been 83·5 per cent of the total area, the trans-Jumna

3

tracts having on the average about 85 per cent of cultivated land. This percentage was abnormally high and can be explained by the fact that in the statistics of cultivation the area under current fallow might have been included in the cultivated area. But still there is no doubt that there had been much extension of cultivation in previous years. The average cultivated area between 1903 and 1907 was 711,875 acres, or 77 per cent of the total area, while at the present time it is 70·9 per cent.

The area under culturable waste is mostly situated in the lowlands, where the soil is poor and cultivation precarious. In the uplands the culturable waste is nowhere extensive and exists only in patches. Thus in Sadabad the cultivated area amounted to 84·6 per cent in 1903–7 and the culturable waste was only 4·20 per cent. Moreover, in spite of the development of irrigation the area under culturable waste has not shown any sign of diminution. Hence it is apparent that the extension of cultivation had clearly reached its limit by 1903–7.

JHANSI

Lastly we shall take up the district of Jhansi, in which the influence of unfavourable natural conditions upon the density of population is seen to best advantage. Jhansi does not fall within the Gangetic Plain, but it borders on it and exhibits by contrast the characteristic natural conditions which govern the density of population in a river valley.

In this district the rocky soil, the deep water-level and the consequent difficulty of irrigation, deficient rainfall, and rapid drainage have combined to produce unstable conditions of agriculture, and the result has been that the density of population is low and has not increased at the same rate as in the Gangetic Plain. The average density increased, as elsewhere, from 212 in Jhansi, and 128 in Lalitpur in 1881 to 234 in Jhansi, and 141 in Lalitpur in 1891. But thereafter it decreased to 219 in Jhansi, and 128 in Lalitpur by 1901. In the next decade the density increased further to 187, but in 1921 it was only 166. The decrease of population after 1891 has been due to the famines of 1896–7 and the drought of 1900. The drought of 1918–19 was possibly responsible, to a large extent, for the decrease of density recorded in 1921.

The standard of cultivation in this district is very low, and a large portion of the cultivated area is in the hands of non-resident tenants. The cultivated area had reached 42 per cent of the total area by 1892, but after that year, which was also a peak year in regard to the density of population, there seems to have been a decline. At the revision of settlement in 1903–6 the cultivated area was only 33 per cent. The variations in the percentage of cultivated area are due to the fluctuations of rainfall, which affect very much the agriculture of this district, but there is no doubt that the normal cultivated area has gone on diminishing since 1891.

One of the most remarkable features of agriculture in this district is the presence of an unusually large area under culturable waste, including land classified as old and new fallow. In 1902–3 the culturable waste including old and new fallow amounted to 27 per cent of the total area in Jhansi and 37 per cent of the total area in Lalitpur. The presence of such a large area of culturable waste can be explained by the fact that the inferior red soil as well as the lighter soils of the district absolutely requires fallowing. Moreover, a margin has always to be kept for the possible spread of *kans* grass which is a scourge of the district. Hence most holdings contain a portion of the area recorded as culturable waste, and this area is cultivated in good seasons and kept fallow in bad seasons. Consequently, changes in this area are a very fair index of the fluctuating conditions of agriculture in different seasons in districts like Jhansi.

During the decade 1921–31 the population of Jhansi increased in spite of the vicissitudes of the seasons in the last three years of the decade. The density of population in 1931 was 191 persons to the square mile and surpassed the density recorded at the end of the last century. Owing to unfavourable natural conditions, only 37·8 per cent of the cultivable area of the district is cultivated, and the cultivated area forms only 30·2 per cent of the total area even at the present time. During the decade 1921–31 except in the Mau tahsil, in which there was less scope for expansion of cultivation, there was an increase of population through the extension of cultivation into tracts where the density had been low. In Mau the pressure of the population upon the soil had already been great and consequently bad seasons caused much emigration from this locality.[1]

CONCLUSION—INFERENCES AND TENDENCIES

Certain broad facts emerge from the foregoing study of agricultural development in the different natural regions of the Upper Gangetic Plain. The most significant factor governing the balance of rural economy in these regions is scarcity of cultivable land, which is a fundamental limiting factor of the growth of population. Such scarcity has manifested itself very strikingly in the very large percentage of the area under cultivation which has made dangerous encroachments upon the reserve necessary for fodder and pasture. In some regions this percentage has not been high because over-saturation of the soil as a result of defective drainage has always been a hindrance to the expansion of cultivation. In other dry regions, where the soil is light and sandy and absolutely requires rest and there are extensive barren wastes, the percentage of cropped area has also been comparatively low. But such regional differences must be attributed to peculiar advantages or limitations characteristic of the physical conditions governing agriculture rather than to the adequacy or inadequacy of agricultural enterprise. In fact, as we have shown above in the case of every district, expansion of cultivation has been greatest and the density of population highest in those tracts which possess good soil and are favoured by facilities of natural and artificial irrigation.

Considering the problem of the scarcity of cultivable land from a historical point of view, we find that the period 1881–91, which was characterized by very great agricultural prosperity, was particularly a period in which intensive agricultural development by means of extension of cultivation synchronized with a rapid increase of the density of population. But the expansion of cultivation and the consequent increase of the

[1] *Census Report*, U.P., 1931, p. 91.

density of population gradually approached their final limits
in almost all the natural regions by the closing years of the
last century or by the beginning of the present century. In
subsequent decades the density of population has gone on
increasing, but the expansion of cultivation has not kept pace
with it. What may naturally be expected in a situation like
this is that the entire system of rural economy will be subject
to extreme stress and strain which can only be relieved by
counteracting forces. This aspect of the problem has become
very important in recent years, and it will be worth while to
survey the situation with particular reference to the facts
revealed by the *Census Report* of 1931, which are given in the
following statistical table.[1]

Regions	Variation in density, 1921–31	Variation in area under cultivation, 1921–31	Variation in double-cropped area 1921–31
Indo-Gangetic Plain, East (Density, 686)	+6·0%	+2%	−9%
Sub-Himalaya East (Density, 624)	+8·1%	+1%	+9%
Indo-Gangetic Plain, Central (Density, 504)	+5·1%	−3%	−6%
Indo-Gangetic Plain, West (Density, 459)	+6·7%	−3%	−3%

It appears from the statistics that with the increase of
population ranging from 5 to 8 per cent in the different natural
regions during the last decade, the situation as regards the
cultivated area has become distinctly alarming. In the
Indo-Gangetic Plain, Central, and in the Indo-Gangetic
Plain, West, there has been an actual decrease in the percentage of cropped area. In the other two regions, the final
limit to the expansion of cultivation has not apparently been
reached, as the increase in the percentage of cropped area
clearly indicates. But, apart from the fact that the extension
of cultivation in these overcrowded regions has very often

[1] Ibid., p. 37.

been at the expense of the scanty reserve necessary for fodder and pasture, it is abundantly clear that 'if the population continues to multiply at the present rate the time is not far distant when no extension of the cultivated area will be possible to provide for them. Even as it is, we see that a large volume of emigration takes place from these divisions owing to the pressure on the soil.'[1]

Now the question which naturally arises is, how is the economic strain due to the increasing pressure of the population on the soil possibly relieved? It is obvious that when more and more extensive cultivation cannot provide for a rapidly multiplying rural population the farmers have one or more of several alternatives before them. (1) They can supplement their income by more intensive farming in the shape of double-cropping; (2) they can supplement their income by growing more remunerative crops; (3) they can devote their spare time to subsidiary occupations; (4) they can emigrate in search of better employment to other less crowded regions when they find that their holdings are so small that with the existing standard of cultivation they can not get a bare subsistence out of agriculture.

As regards the first of these alternatives, a complete study of the conditions governing double-cropping and of the contribution of double-cropping to agricultural productivity has been attempted in the next chapter. But what immediately concerns us here is the alarming decrease in the extent of double-cropped area during the last decade. In spite of the increase of population, the double-cropped area, or the area which is intensively cultivated, has not only not increased but has actually diminished. How far this phenomenon is due to the already extreme pressure of the population on the soil is a question which will be fully discussed in the next chapter. But the apparent tendency seems to be that with the existing standard of agriculture more extensive double-cropping, which is necessitated by an increase of population, has become almost an impossibility.

So far as the second alternative is concerned, it also appears that under the static conditions of farming in our country

[1] *Census Report*, 1931.

there has been little change in the matter of growing more valuable crops during the last decade, although, as explained in Chapter IV, we find a remarkable change in the choice and combination of crops in the direction of more intensive subsistence farming during previous decades. It remains for us now to consider how far subsidiary occupations and rural emigration tend to relieve the increasing economic strain of over-population.

The extent to which subsidiary sources of income in the different natural regions of the Upper Gangetic Plain release the pressure of the population on the soil is indicated by the following statistical tables taken from the *Census Report* of 1931.[1]

Regions	Density	Those who returned subsidiary occupations per mille of earners
Indo-Gangetic Plain, East .	686	209
Sub-Himalaya, East . .	624	182
Indo-Gangetic Plain, Central .	504	141
Indo-Gangetic Plain, West .	459	104

Regions	Density	CULTIVATING TENANTS Number per mille earners (principal occupation) who have		
		No subsidiary occupation	An agricultural subsidiary occupation	[2] A non-agricultural subsidiary occupation
Indo-Gangetic Plain, East	686	803	108	89
Sub-Himalaya, East	624	818	66	116
Indo-Gangetic Plain, Central	504	857	54	84
Indo-Gangetic Plain, West	459	897	41	62

The figures given above show a striking positive correlation between the number per mille of workers who have subsidiary

[1] Ibid., 1931, pp. 415–6.   [2] Two main heads recorded.

occupations and the density of population. This tendency merely confirms the thesis that, when the growing population can no longer depend on an increase of the net cropped and the double-cropped areas and on increasing cultivation of more paying crops, their agricultural holdings become too uneconomical even for the maintenance of a very low standard of living and they have to supplement their incomes by agricultural and non-agricultural subsidiary occupations. Indeed, there are reasons to suppose that subsidiary occupations enable the farmer not only to make both ends meet in spite of uneconomic holdings, but also positively to improve his economic position. For example, it has been found that the proportion of indebted tenants is higher in the Indo-Gangetic Plain, West, in spite of the fact that the pressure of the population on the soil is much less intense and the average holding is above the economic level. The explanation is that subsidiary occupations are far less frequent there than in the eastern regions. On the other hand, in the Sub-Himalaya, East, where there are as many as 116 per mille of cultivating tenants who have non-agricultural subsidiary occupations, rural indebtedness is smaller in extent in spite of non-economic holdings created by the increasingly intense pressure of the population upon land.[1] It appears from the table given above that in this region while the population has increased by 8·1 per cent, the net cultivated area has increased by only 1 per cent. This means that the higher density of population can be maintained only by increased double-cropping (which is 9 per cent more than in the previous decade) and by greater reliance on subsidiary sources of income.

Another important subsidiary source of income in the densely populated regions of the Upper Gangetic Plain is the remittances sent home by emigrants who have been obliged to leave their uneconomic holdings and settle in other localities. Indeed, it is these remittances from emigrants which make it possible for the rural population in the Sub-Himalaya, East, in the Indo-Gangetic Plain, East, and in the Indo-Gangetic

---

[1] 'The chief non-agricultural subsidiary occupations in Sub-Himalaya East are: Blacksmiths and carpenters, barbers, washermen, oil pressers, stockraising, general labourers, potters, grain dealers and other traders, weavers, fishermen and boatmen.' (*Census Report*, 1931, p. 417.)

Plain, Central, to make both ends meet in spite of the large size of their families and their uneconomic holdings. As Mr. Turner observes in the *Census Report* of 1931, the total sum paid out on money orders in the United Provinces of Agra and Oudh was Rs1,385 lakhs, of which 69 per cent was paid out in districts from which emigration is known to be considerable. These statistics are very significant as they give us an idea of the extent to which the rural population in the densely populated tracts supplement their income by remittances from emigrants.

As regards the extent of emigration, census statistics show that there is considerable semi-permanent, if not permanent, emigration, from the densely populated regions of the Upper Gangetic Plain. We have shown that during the last decade population has increased in all the natural regions, and that there would have been serious economic maladjustment but for certain counteracting tendencies which have maintained the balance of rural economy. Greater emigration of labour is one of such tendencies. It appears that taking the United Provinces as a whole, the loss of males by emigration has increased by 200,000 since 1921, and the bulk of it represents semi-permanent emigration of labour.[1] The Indo-Gangetic Plain, East, as a whole, has, if anything, lost on the balance of migration during the last decade, and, of course, the total emigrants in 1931 outnumbered the immigrants by more than two to one. The Sub-Himalaya, East, has lost on the balance of migration 151,000 persons; the loss includes a larger proportion of semi-permanent labour migration to Assam and Bengal. The Indo-Gangetic Plain, Central, has lost on the balance 267,000 persons in the decade, while the Indo-Gangetic Plain, West, has lost 458,000 persons in a similar manner.[2]

---

[1] *Census Report*, 1931, p. 201.   [2] Ibid., pp. 103, 99, 90 and 83.

CHAPTER II

DOUBLE-CROPPING AND DENSITY

THE correspondence between a high density of population and extensive double-cropping is one of the remarkable features of the rural economy of the Upper Ganges Valley. Mr. Blunt, superintendent of the census operations of 1911 in the United Provinces of Agra and Oudh, discovered a close correspondence between the density of population and the gross cultivated area in this region, and the results which he obtained were stated in the following table.[1]

Regions	Order according to density	Order according to gross culti- vated area
Indo-Gangetic Plain, East . .	1	2
Sub-Himalaya, East . . .	2	1
Indo-Gangetic Plain, Central .	3	3
Indo-Gangetic Plain, West .	4	4

It appears from the table that generally speaking while the density of population increases from west to east, the gross cultivated area also similarly increases from west to east. What is called the gross cultivated area includes not only the net cultivated area, but also the double-cropped area, and hence the fact that the gross cultivated area increases from west to east signifies that both the net cultivated area and the double-cropped area are much more extensive in the eastern and the central portions of the Plain than in the western portion. The reason why this is so will be considered later; but first let us observe, in the following comparative table, the regional variations in the extent of the double-cropped area.[2]

[1] The different regions mentioned in the table are the natural regions or the rainfall tracts included in the Upper Ganges Valley.
[2] *Census Report*, U.P., 1931, p. 110.

Regions	Double-cropped area (in percentages of the culturable area)
Indo-Gangetic Plain, East .	20·3
Sub-Himalaya, East . .	28·3
Indo-Gangetic Plain, Central .	16·8
Indo-Gangetic Plain, West .	13·5

It must be noted that the double-cropped area has fluctuated from one period to another, and usually fluctuates also from year to year. As already said in the last chapter, in this region there has everywhere been an increase, not only in the net cultivated area, but also in the double-cropped area as a result of the increasing pressure of the population upon land, and there has been a progressive decrease in the area recorded as recent fallow. On the other hand, the release of this pressure has manifested itself in a decrease in the double-cropped area. But it must also be remembered that the fluctuations in the double-cropped area from one period to another are also due to the nature of the seasonal cycles. A dry cycle of years is unfavourable to double-cropping while a wet cycle is favourable to it. So far as the annual fluctuations in the double-cropped area are concerned, they are due to annual variations in the amount and distribution of rainfall.

But in order to understand the significance of the correspondence between the density of population and double-cropping, it is necessary to inquire into the various physical causes which determine the extent of double-cropping, because, as we shall see later, it is these causes which ultimately govern the agricultural factors of the density of population. It is obvious that the *kharif* crops cannot be followed by a second crop of *rabi* if there is not sufficient moisture in the soil. Whether there will be sufficiency of moisture or not depends, first, upon the amount and distribution of rainfall in a particular tract. If the amount of rainfall in the *kharif* season is insufficient, then, in the absence of artificial irrigation, double-cropping would be an impossibility. On the other hand, if the rainfall is over-abundant then the soil might suffer from water-logging and over-saturation, and a second crop of *rabi* cannot possibly be grown. Secondly, whether there will be sufficiency of moisture or not depends upon the facilities of artificial irrigation. In spite of the natural facilities for the supply of moisture in a particular tract, the cultivators cannot do away with *Do-Fasli* irrigation, except where they have the advantage of possessing *Karail* lands. Hence, we may say that both rainfall and irrigation (or, briefly speaking, agricultural water-supply) determine whether there will be sufficient moisture necessary for double-cropping. Thirdly, whether there will be sufficiency of moisture or not as a result of a given rainfall, whether artificial irrigation will be successful or not, and whether the land will have sufficient plant-food or not, depend upon the texture and fertility of the soil. The *karail* soil has a wonderful power of retaining moisture long after the *kharif* rains and can grow excellent *rabi* crops after *kharif* even without irrigation. The ordinary light *Dhumat* soil, consisting of a large proportion of clay and a small proportion of sand, has also the power of deriving the greatest advantage from a given amount of rainfall. But if the soil is stiff clay, the land will be simply water-logged without retaining sufficient moisture and will be fit only for bearing a single crop of rice. Moreover, well irrigation also depends upon the nature of the soil. In the districts affected by the Gangetic alluvium well irrigation is facilitated by the greater height of the water-level, whereas in the districts affected by the alluvium of the Jumna well irrigation is hampered by the great depth of the water-level.

Thus, so far as the physical causes which determine the extent of double-cropping are concerned, we can lay down two very important propositions, viz.:

(1) That the extent of double-cropping depends upon the *normal* agricultural water-supply in a particular region.

(2) That the extent of double-cropping depends upon the nature of the soil.

Our next problem will be to illustrate these two propositions by facts relating to the various natural regions of the Upper Gangetic Plain.

INDO-GANGETIC PLAIN, EAST

In the districts of the Eastern Gangetic Plain the influence of seasonable and sufficient rainfall upon the extent of double-cropping is very great. On the one hand, the annual inundations in normal years supply the moisture necessary for a second crop of *rabi*, and, on the other hand, the tanks and the *jhils* which are full are fully utilized for double-cropping. In the district of Benares most extensive double-cropping is found in the parganas of Dhus and Majhwar. In Majhwar 31·6 per cent and in Dhus 36·4 per cent of the net cultivated area are twice-cropped. Here rainfall is heavy, and the country is liable to inundations, and so we find a fairly close correspondence between the irrigated area and the twice-cropped area. The figures for the irrigated area are 13,061 acres and 7,046 acres respectively, whereas the figures for twice-cropped area are 11,283 acres and 7,364 acres respectively. In the district of Jaunpur the Jaunpur tahsil showed the highest percentage of twice-cropped area, viz. 32 per cent in all the parganas, whereas the percentage for the whole district was only 26. Here also we find a correspondence between the irrigated and the twice-cropped areas. 71,168 acres were irrigated and 39,230 acres were twice-cropped in this tahsil in 1908. In Azamgarh the influence of rainfall upon double-cropping is observed in a striking manner. The year 1907–8 was a year of deficient and ill-distributed rainfall, and in that year the twice-cropped area was only 163,270 acres, whereas in 1910–11, which was a year of heavy rainfall, the twice-cropped area was 260,968 acres.

If we observe the classes of soil on which double-cropping is extensive in the Eastern Gangetic Plain we get an illustration of the second proposition, viz. that the extent of double-cropping depends upon the nature of the soil. We find that double-cropping is very extensive in the alluvial lowlands, which are subject to annual inundations, but which do not consist of stiff and heavy clay fit to bear a single crop of *kharif* rice; e.g. Chandausi tahsil in Benares, Jaunpur tahsil in Jaunpur, Ballia tahsil in Ballia and Gazipur, Saidpur and Karanda parganas in the district of Gazipur. Then again, double-cropping is extensive in Muhammadabad and Zamaniah parganas in Gazipur and Narwan pargana in Benares owing to the presence of *karail* tracts, over which the current is not very strong during the inundations, and which contain a good deal of alumina, and have the property of retaining moisture long after the rainy season.

SUB-HIMALAYA, EAST

In the districts of Sub-Himalaya, East, also, double-cropping is extensive because of the annual inundations in the alluvial lowlands locally called *Kacchar* lands. In the district of Basti, double-cropping is very extensive in Bansi East and Binayak-pur owing to this natural supply of moisture, and the double-cropped area is as much as 39·7 per cent of the net cultivated area in the former and 50·2 per cent in the latter. In Gorakhpur the twice-cropped area was found to be 6·75 (100 thousand acres) and the irrigated area to be 7·21 (100 thousand acres) in 1919; and this indicates a close correspondence between the agricultural water-supply and the extent of double-cropping.

Taking the soils of the twice-cropped areas, we find that double-cropping is least in the heavy clay lands and the sandy or raviny tracts, and is most extensive in the light, but rich, alluvial *kacchar* lands liable to inundations, in which clay and loam are combined in equal proportions. We also find extensive double-cropping in those tracts in which there is a fertile silt called *bhat*, which, like the *karail* soil in the Gangetic Plain, has a wonderful moisture-retaining property, and extensive double-cropping in Bansi East and Binayakpur is obviously due to the presence of the *bhat* soil.

INDO-GANGETIC PLAIN, CENTRAL

In the districts of the Central Gangetic Plain we find the same correspondence between the available agricultural water-supply and the extent of double-cropping. Here artificial irrigation consists wholly of well irrigation in the absence of the development of canal irrigation. It is a significant fact that well irrigation is particularly facilitated everywhere in the trans-Gangetic parganas owing to the greater height of the water-level; whereas, in the Doab regions, particularly in the south, the peculiarity of the alluvium of the Jumna is that water-level is deep and highly inaccessible. Hence double-cropping is always more extensive in the tracts affected by the Gangetic alluvium.[1] In Allahabad the area under the *rabi* crops has increased in the trans-Ganges from 170,218 acres in 1874 to 203,761 acres in 1916; whereas in the Doab we find an actual decrease. This increase in the *rabi* area is an evidence of more extensive double-cropping, and is, to some extent, explained by an increase in the area under gram and barley, the two leguminous crops which are sown as second crops after *kharif* rice. In Cawnpore, too, we find the same correspondence between the twice-cropped area and the irrigated area.

Parganas	Percentage of twice-cropped area	Percentage of irrigated area
Sheorajpur . . .	29·88	50·77
Bilhaur	25·88	41·77
Bhognipur . . .	11	27·15
Ghatampur · · ·	11	21·28

It must be noted that in Cawnpore, as in every other district of the Doab, there is a marked contrast between the tracts affected by the alluvium of the Ganges, and the tracts affected by the alluvium of the Jumna in the matter of the facilities of agricultural water-supply. Thus Sheorajpur and Bilhaur, which are affected by the Gangetic alluvium, show higher percentages of irrigated area, and it is significant that the double-cropped areas are also remarkably extensive. In Bhognipur and Ghatampur, on the other hand, the irrigated and the double-cropped areas are both considerably less because these parganas are affected by the alluvium of the Jumna.[2]

[1] As pointed out in the last chapter, the density of population is always higher in the tracts affected by the Gangetic alluvium than in the tracts affected by the alluvium of the Jumna.

[2] It is remarkable that double-cropping has become more extensive owing to the extension of canal irrigation in the Jumna tracts. In 1922 the twice-cropped area was as much as 14·5 per cent of the net cultivated area.

In Fatehpur double-cropping is extensive in the Central *Dhumat* tract. But here, although owing to defective drainage (as in Hathgaon, Haswa and Kutila parganas which also show high percentages of double-cropped areas) land is liable to water-logging, yet the conditions are not altogether unfavourable for double-cropping. As a matter of fact, we find that *Birra* or mixed crops, which are sown as second crops after rice, constitute 50 per cent of the area under the *rabi* harvest.

Now if we observe the nature of the soil in the twice-cropped areas of this region we find that double-cropping is extensive in the tracts composed of the rich Gangetic alluvium which contains clay and sand in almost equal proportions, and which is not only absolutely more fertile, but has also a considerable moisture-retaining property.

OUDH

In the densely populated districts of Oudh the extent of double-cropping is also dependent upon the available agricultural water-supply. But here the cultivators are faced with the problem of water-logging and over-saturation due to defective drainage.[1] Hence we find that double-cropping is least in the rice tracts of the district which lie amidst tanks and *jhils* and are intersected by rivers and streams which have a tendency to flood the countryside. In Partabgarh double-cropping is very extensive in the Partabgarh tahsil where the proportion of heavy rice land is the smallest. In Sultanpur double-cropping is extensive in the higher lands of the Musafirkhana and Sultanpur tahsils, and is least in extent in the Amethi tahsil where, owing to the existence of Naiya Jhil and Raja-ka-Bandh, the single-cropped rice lands are found in abundance. In Fyzabad, on the other hand, the land does not suffer from excess of moisture after the *kharif* harvest owing to better drainage, and hence most of the ricelands are twice-cropped, and early rice can be followed by gram or peas in winter. This is the case in the Akbarpur tahsil, where early rice occupied 66 per cent of the *kharif*

---

[1] Where the drainage is not defective the inundations are favourable to double-cropping. This is the reason why double-cropping is extensive in the *Tarai* tracts of the Sai and the Ganges in the district of Partabgarh.

area in 1904, and most of the rice-lands were double-cropped. This is also the case in Pacchimrath and Khandausa where about 50 per cent of the cultivated area was recorded as twice-cropped. In Bara Banki, we find extensive double-cropping in the rice lands. We also observe the influence of annual inundations upon the extent of double-cropping, specially in the *Tarai* lands in the valley of the Gaghra. But in Bara Banki the extent of double-cropping also depends upon the extent of well irrigation. In the Nawabgunj and Hyder-garh tahsils there is extensive double-cropping, which is mainly dependent upon wells that are very numerous in the trans-Gumti parganas. In Nawabgunj 59,561 acres were irrigated in 1902, and 53,232 acres were twice-cropped. In Hydergarh the irrigated area was 46,533 acres in 1902, and the twice-cropped area was 49,307 acres; and in the same year there were 4,368 masonry wells and 8,183 unprotected wells in this tahsil. In Lucknow, too, we find that the extent of double-cropping mainly depends upon well irrigation, and up to recent times the area irrigated from tanks and *jhils* was found to be diminishing and that irrigated from wells was found to be correspondingly increasing.

Now if we observe the nature of the soil in the twice-cropped areas we find that double-cropping is extensive as usual in the *Matyar* soils which are not stiff and heavy and are capable of being ploughed up for a second crop in winter. It is also extensive in the *dhumat* soils and the *Bhur* soils which are light and contain a small proportion of *kankar* or sand.

INDO-GANGETIC PLAIN, WEST

In the Western Gangetic Plain the recent increase in the extent of double-cropping in some of the districts has been mainly due to the extension of canal irrigation. This is obvious from the following figures for the district of Meerut:

	1860	1890
Irrigated area .	580,005 acres	607,647 acres
Twice-cropped area .	46,000 acres (5%)	232,000 acres (22%)

4

In the case of irrigated land the general rule followed is that the land must lie fallow for at least one harvest in three years. But if the land depends for irrigation entirely upon rainfall, only one crop is annually produced. Such a practice indicates that extensive double-cropping is found mainly in the irrigated tracts. The increase in the double-cropped area as a result of the development of canal irrigation is noticeable also in Bulandsahar, in which formerly the *kharif* was the predominant harvest, but now the *rabi* harvest predominates owing to more extensive double-cropping. Similarly in Etah, which is another typical canal-irrigated district of the Western Gangetic Plain, there has been a remarkable increase in double-cropping during the last fifty years. The double-cropped area in this district has increased from 2·2 per cent of the net cultivated area in 1872 to about 20 per cent in 1904–5, as a direct result of the extension of canal irrigation. On the other hand, in the unprotected districts, where canal irrigation has not yet developed, the extent of double-cropping depends upon the natural sources of irrigation, and consequently the double-cropped area is liable to very wide fluctuations from year to year.

Now when we consider the classes of soil on which there is extensive double-cropping we find that they are usually the loamy soils of the canal-irrigated districts. In Meerut, for example, it is very extensive in the north-western tract which consists of a fine, black loamy soil that has rendered the parganas included in this tract the richest in the district. It is also extensive in the land to the east of the Hindan which is a continuation of the north-western tract. In the unprotected districts, where rainfall is ample, double-cropping is extensive in the rice-lands; whereas in the arid districts of the south it is confined to fields where early millets and *Zaid* crops are grown with the help of irrigation.

The descriptive survey of the relation of double-cropping to favourable conditions of soil, rainfall, and irrigation (such as annual inundations, presence of moisture-retaining *karail* soil, or rich and light loamy soil in which the proportion of clay is considerable, and an efficient system of well irrigation) shows the clear significance of the statistics given on page 42.

The statistics show that the double-cropped area as well as the density of population increases from west to east. As already explained, in the eastern and the central portions of the Upper Gangetic Plain the more favourable conditions of soil, rainfall, and irrigation are primarily responsible for the more extensive subsistence farming in the shape of double-cropping; whereas, in the western portion of the Plain the extent of double-cropping is smaller owing to natural disadvantages in respect of soil, rainfall, and irrigation. Moreover, so far as more extensive double-cropping coexists with higher agricultural productivity (or greater agricultural security) it is natural to expect a correspondence between the regional variations in the density of population and the extent of double-cropping.

We shall now examine an interesting question which has an important bearing on the relation of double-cropping to the density of population. It was pointed out towards the end of Chapter I that double-cropping is one of those factors of agricultural economy which counteract the serious maladjustment between the increase of population and the extension of cultivation. When the population multiplies and there is extreme scarcity of good arable land which can be brought under the plough, one of the alternatives before the farmer is to supplement his income by more extensive double-cropping. Now does this mean that the farmer has recourse to increased double-cropping as a last resort, and that double-cropping serves simply as a safety valve which relieves the economic pressure exerted by the growth of an already dense population? Is it then a sign and symptom of economic stress?

An important consideration which has a direct bearing on the present discussion is that double-cropping is often regulated by intelligent methods of agriculture and does not necessarily mean predatory cultivation. In the first place, it is practised on lands which are called *Gauhan* or *Goind* lands according to the conventional classification of soils. *Gauhau* or *goind* lands consist of the highly manured soil adjoining the village site, and the area of such lands depends on the number of hamlets, the cultivating castes, and the number of cattle and the means of irrigation. The next class of soils is called the *Manjha* soil adjoining the *gauhan* soil. According to revenue classification the *manjha* soil has been sub-divided into *manjha* I and *manjha* II. The soil of the *manjha* II type bears *rabi* and *kharif* harvests alternately and thus forms the bulk of the cultivated area in most villages; while the *manjha* I soil is the highly manured soil adjoining the *gauhan* soil but inferior to it. It is this highly manured *manjha* I land which contains a considerable proportion of double-cropped fields. Hence, so far as double-cropping is practised on highly manured and well-irrigated lands near the village sites and thus depends on the energy and enterprise of the cultivators, it is really a sign of the high standard of cultivation which ensures the raising of a variety of crops without exhausting the fertility of the soil.

That extensive double-cropping is often due to agricultural skill and enterprise is indicated by the fact that wherever the so-called lower classes of the rural population, such as Muraos, Kurmis, Ahirs and Jats, who possess greater skill and enterprise as cultivators than the higher castes, have taken up their abode, there is extensive double-cropping, while at the same time the standard of cultivation is high. For example, in Fatehpur the Kurmis have occupied the Kutila and Hathgaon parganas which are the most fertile, the most densely populated and the most intensively cultivated parganas in the district. In the Dheta pargana they form 29 per cent of the population, cultivating 62 per cent and owning 83 per cent of the cultivated area. If we examine the extent of double-cropping we find that these are the very parganas in which it is very extensive, and as a matter of fact this is mainly due to the agricultural enterprise of the Kurmis.

The influence of agricultural enterprise upon the extent of double-cropping is seen to best advantage in some of the districts of Oudh and the Western Gangetic Plain. In Partabgarh the Kurmis formed 13·6 per cent of the Hindu population in 1903. Here there are more Kurmis than in any other district of U.P. with the exception of Bara Banki, and this accounts for the agricultural prosperity of this district. The Kurmis are chiefly found in the Partabgarh tahsil, and this is mainly the reason why double-cropping is

most extensive in this tahsil. In Bara Banki, too, cultivation
has reached a high standard owing to the presence of the
Kurmis. We have seen that in this district double-cropping
is mainly dependent upon well irrigation. This is natural, as
it is merely an evidence of the agricultural enterprise of the
Kurmis. In the district of Sultanpur we find that 43 per cent
of the cultivated area is double-cropped in the pargana of
Musafirkhana. Here, also, one of the main reasons why the
percentage is so high is the existence of Muraos, Kurmis and
Ahirs who are the chief cultivating classes.

Like the Kurmis in Oudh, the Jats are the most skilful and
enterprising cultivators in the Western Gangetic Plain. For
instance, in the Meerut and Bulandsahar districts the high
standard of intensive cultivation is mainly due to their enterprise. In Meerut the Jats occupy a quarter of the entire
cultivated area, and in all the parganas they have succeeded
in occupying the most fertile lands. We have seen that
double-cropping is most extensive in the north-western tract
of the district, and it is a significant fact that the north-western
tract is the homeland of the Jats.

Let us now turn to the other side of this question concerning
the relation of double-cropping to agricultural productivity.
It is true, no doubt, that double-cropping is an index of agricultural prosperity when it is associated with agricultural skill
and enterprise and is practised on highly manured land of
superior fertility in such a way that it does not exhaust the
fertility of the soil. But in regions of dense population double-
cropping is commonly associated with improvident husbandry.
The system of double-cropping modifies the ordinary standard
rotation of *rabi* and *kharif* alternately by which the *rabi*
is followed by nearly three months' rest and the *kharif* by
nine or ten months' rest. In regions of dense population,
where the average size of the holding is very small and the
cultivator does not willingly leave land fallow for successive
seasons, these lengthy periods of rest give time for fresh
supplies of mineral plant-food to become available and for
the bacteria in the soil to develop. Thus, it is apparent that
double-cropping involves a wasteful utilization of land. There
is a downright robbery of the soil as a result of the extreme

pressure of the population on land, and very often it is the
bounty of nature which prevents the utter exhaustion of the
fertility of the soil. Moreover, the sowing of second crops
just after the harvesting of the *kharif* crops means undue
haste and necessarily imperfect tillage which, as Mr. Moreland
points out, is the worst feature of double-cropping. Thus, it
would appear that double-cropping very often means predatory
farming, and is commonly a sign of economic stress in the
densely populated regions of the Upper Gangetic Plain.

It is necessary for us now to consider the whole question
from the point of view of the effect of the increase of population upon the utilization of land. As a result of the increase
of population there has been an extension of cultivated area
in the densely populated tracts of this region, partially by
taking up old fallow land or land in the ravines, swamps, or
sandy tracts, or land distant from the village and imperfectly
irrigated, the cultivation of which is distinctly precarious.
For instance, in Gorakhpur the area recorded as old fallow in
1919 was exactly one-half of the area recorded at the last
settlement, and this was due to the increasing cultivation of
land recorded as old fallow. In Allahabad and Bara Banki
cultivation has extended by bringing under cultivation the
poor soils of the raviny or swampy tracts. In Bulandsahar
land of poor fertility, including that covered with saline
efflorescence, has been brought under cultivation. Moreover,
the resumed cultivation of land recorded as old fallow and
the decrease in the area recorded as culturable mean a corresponding reduction in the area of pasture land with all its
prejudicial effects on the number and breed of cattle. Hence
the intensive cultivation of land of superior fertility by the
increasing adoption of the system of double-cropping shows
how agriculture reacts to the economic maladjustment
created by the scarcity of cultivable land. This phenomenon
has been strikingly observed, for instance, in the district of
Cawnpore. In Cawnpore the gross cropped area increased
from 903,915 acres in 1870 to 959,630 acres in 1907; but during
the same period the double-cropped area increased from
44,215 acres to 189,507 acres. This means an actual decrease
in the net cultivated area. Thus, in spite of the increase of

population there was not only no increase, but there was an actual decrease in the net cultivated area. This shows how extensive double-cropping might operate as a safety valve under the economic pressure exerted by the increase of population. Again in Allahabad, the average size of the holding in 1916 was calculated to be ·85 acre per head in the trans-Gangetic parganas. Here also one of the main reasons why one acre of land can support more than one person is extensive double-cropping.

It is interesting to consider a little more closely this tendency to have recourse to more extensive double-cropping as a result of the increasing pressure of the population upon land. In the eastern and the central portions of the plain there has been a remarkable increase in the double-cropped area in every district. Thus, in Ghazipur the average double-cropped area has increased from 97,604 acres in 1885–6 to 149,175 acres, or 24·25 per cent of the net cultivated area, in 1908. In Benares the average double-cropped area has increased from 78,102 acres, or 18·8 per cent of the net cultivated area, in the decade ending 1896, to 109,239 acres, or 25 per cent of the net cultivated area, in the decade ending in 1904–5. In Jaunpur the average double-cropped area has increased from 142,192 acres, or 22·4 per cent of the net cultivated area, in the decade ending in 1896, to 180,003 acres, or more than 28 per cent of the net cultivated area, in the period 1902–6. In Azamgarh the average double-cropped area has increased from 161,143 acres in 1885–95 to 194,824 acres in 1905–8. In the Central Gangetic Plain also there has been a similar phenomenal increase in the double-cropped area. Thus, in Partabgarh the average double-cropped area was 111,180 acres, or 22·28 per cent of the cultivated area, in 1892; but after that this area has increased to an average of 164,742 acres, or 33·5 per cent of the cultivated area. In Sultanpur the double-cropped area was only 4·5 per cent of the cultivated area in 1864; but in 1902 it was as much as 35·4 per cent. In Fyzabad the double-cropped area was 194,000 acres in 1885, but in 1904 it was as much as 298,945 acres, or 42 per cent of the net cultivated area. In Lucknow the double-cropped area was as much as 26 per cent of the net

cultivated area in 1893; and Mr. Hooper, writing about this
district in 1898, made the following observation which applies
equally to all other districts situated in the eastern and the
central portions of the plain: 'The striking feature is the great
increase in the area under rice and the coarser grains on which
the people chiefly subsist. These crops have not, as in some
districts, taken the place of the more valuable products which
are grown for the market.[1] The increase in the production
of the commoner food grains appears from the statistics to
have been obtained by a great expansion of the system of
double-cropping.' In the southern portion of the central
Gangetic Plain we find a similar remarkable increase in the
double-cropped area. For example, in Allahabad the double-
cropped area was only 5·7 per cent of the net cultivated area
in 1873; whereas the average area for the five years ending in
1907–8 was 23·29 per cent. In Cawnpore the average double-
cropped area was 44,815 acres in 1870; while the average for
the five years ending in 1907 was 139,507 acres. In Fatehpur
the average double-cropped area was only 8·7 per cent in
1870, but in 1904 the average area was in the neighbourhood
of 12 per cent.

The same sort of increase in the double-cropped area is
noticeable also in the districts belonging to the Indo-Gangetic
Plain, West. Thus, in Meerut the double-cropped area was
4·5 per cent of the cultivated area in 1860, but in 1902 it was
as much as 21 per cent. In Bulandsahar, too, there has been
an enormous increase in the double-cropped area during the
same period, and in 1902 it was as much as 24 per cent of
the net cultivated area. In Etah the double-cropped area
has increased from 15,987 acres in 1872 to 148,531 acres in
1904–5. In Muttra, where the practice of double-cropping
is not followed to the same extent to which it is followed in
other canal-irrigated districts, the double-cropped area has
increased from 61,913 acres in 1885–8 to 107,728 acres in
1897–8. Even the unprotected districts of the western
portion of the plain have not lagged behind in the matter of
intensive subsistence farming by means of double-cropping.

[1] The substitution of heavy-yielding food crops in place of valuable commercial crops is another remarkable feature of intensive subsistence farming
which has been studied in chapter IV.

Thus, in Jhansi the average double-cropped area was only 3 per cent in 1892; but in 1902–3 it was as much as 5 per cent. But it must be noted that, whereas in the eastern and the central portions of the plain double-cropping means the production of the cheaper varieties of *rabi* grains, in the western portion of the plain extensive double-cropping has enabled the cultivators to raise the cheaper varieties of *kharif* grains, such as maize.

The facts set forth above reveal the nature of double-cropping as generally associated with the increasing pressure of the population upon land in the Upper Gangetic Plain. It is clear that more extensive double-cropping in this region signifies a more widespread tendency to resort to more intensive subsistence farming which has been forced upon the cultivators by the growth of population. The cheaper varieties of *rabi* and *kharif* food-grains which are essential for the subsistence of the cultivator and his family are commonly raised by means of double-cropping. Thus double-cropping does not commonly mean raising a variety of crops by careful manuring and irrigation on highly fertile lands near the village sites, and, therefore, it usually implies imperfect tillage and wasteful cultivation. This aspect of the system of double-cropping assumes a special importance when we try to explain the significance of a decrease in the double-cropped area almost throughout the Upper Gangetic Plain, in spite of an increase of population during the last decade—a remarkable phenomenon to which the attention of the reader was drawn in Chapter I. Double-cropping is obviously limited by the capacity of the soil. It is highly probable that intensive subsistence farming has reached its limit, and improvident husbandry and over-cropping have all but exhausted the reproductive capacity of the soil, so that the need for increased fallowing has become so urgent that it can no longer be safely ignored. Thus it is very likely that the recent decrease in the double-cropped area is a symptom of over-population producing its dangerous reactions on the stability of rural economy.

CHAPTER III

AGRICULTURAL WATER-SUPPLY AND DENSITY

In the first two chapters we have reached the following important conclusions:

(1) There is a two-fold tendency of agricultural development in the densely populated districts of the Upper Ganges Valley, viz. a tendency to the extension of cultivation sometimes beyond the limits of safety and a tendency to resort to more extensive double-cropping.

(2) Intensive cultivation in the shape of double-cropping has been a safety valve which has come into operation under the pressure exerted by the increase of population.

(3) On the whole, the tendency is that as the density of population increases there is more and more extensive as well as intensive cultivation of land.

(4) This is true not only when we study the agricultural development of a particular district due to an increase of population, but also when we compare the agricultural situation of districts having a low density of population with that of districts which maintain a high density of population.

The underlying causes behind these tendencies have already been indicated. In Chapter I we showed that cultivation has extended most in tracts which possess good soil and excellent facilities of natural and artificial irrigation. In Chapter II it was similarly explained that the extent of double-cropping depends upon the nature of the soil and the adequacy of agricultural water-supply. Hence it follows that in tracts which enjoy inherent advantages in respect of soil and natural irrigation and acquired advantages in respect of artificial irrigation, cultivation is both highly extensive and intensive, and the population also highly dense.

This conclusion points to the overwhelming importance of soil and agricultural water-supply as determining factors in the problem of the density of population. When we speak of agricultural water-supply we think not only of natural irrigation which depends upon climatic factors, and ultimately on rainfall, but also of artificial irrigation, the aim of which is to modify the unstable agricultural conditions produced by deficient or uncertain rainfall. Whether artificial irrigation has given real protection against the niggardliness and caprice of nature, or whether the climatic, or ultimately the meteorological, factors are those which really count is a part of the broader problem of man's control over his environment. We shall answer this question as we proceed; but we shall begin by discussing the relative importance of the two obviously uncontrollable factors of our environment, viz. soil and rainfall.

The efficiency of rainfall is profoundly influenced by the structure or the texture of the soil. The upper soil particles constituting the surface of the soil are exposed to the air, so that there is an evaporation of moisture on the surface particles, and a movement of water upwards to the surface against the force of gravitation. Wind and high temperature increase the evaporation from the soil and the rate of transpiration from the plant. Rainfall, on the other hand, not only supplies to the soil moisture, and with it the soluble plant food, which are absorbed by the roots of the plants, but also reduces the rate of water-loss from vegetation by rendering the air humid. The point at which a plant will wither away will, therefore, be determined, on the one hand, by the rate at which the area covered by the root hairs is absorbing moisture and, on the other, by the rate at which the surface of the soil is losing water by evaporation. Moreover, the roots of the plants go deeper and deeper into the soil with their gradual growth and development, so that the intensity of absorption of moisture and plant food becomes greater and greater. Such intense absorption is possible during the rainy season when the air is humid and there is a sufficient supply of moisture to the soil, and that is why this season corresponds with the period of highest growth and development of plants in the tropics. But the absorption of moisture by the plants on which their life and development so largely depend is obviously conditioned by the texture of the soil. The facility of percolation will be different according to the differences of soil structure. Black cotton soil, for example, expands as soon as it receives rain, expelling the interstitial air and leaving it in an impervious condition which renders percolation slow. Moreover, such dark soils become strongly heated and there is an intense evaporation of rain as it falls on them. On the other hand, the *karail* soil, which is found in the Indo-Gangetic Plain, has a wonderful power of retaining moisture long after the rains. Ordinarily the facility of percolation will depend upon the relative proportions of sand and clay, the two ingredients which are found in varying combinations in the different natural regions of the Gangetic Plain.[1]

Just as the efficiency of rainfall depends upon the structure of the soil, so also the efficiency of the soil in respect of its physical and chemical conditions and in the matter of the supply of sufficient plant-food depends upon rainfall and temperature. Most agricultural plants require a supply of oxygen in order that the living matter of the cells of the root might function properly, and the healthy growth of plant life depends upon this normal functional activity.[2] Except rice, which draws oxygen dissolved in water, other plants absorb oxygen from the gases contained in the interstitial spaces of the soil. 'An excess of rainfall leads to too great a reduction of the interstitial gases, and so leads to asphyxiation through lack of sufficient supply of oxygen.'[3] Such a danger arises in years of excessive rainfall, especially when there is continuous and heavy rainfall for a pretty long time. Such a danger of excessive moisture in the soil also arises in the low-lying tracts which serve as the drainage outlet of the surrounding country. There are extensive tracts in some portions

[1] The efficiency of rainfall is also conditioned by the slope or conformation of the land. For instance, the efficiency of rainfall in South Bihar has been much reduced by the rapid drainage of this region.

[2] Soil aeration is also essential for (i) the respiration of plant roots, (ii) the growth of aerobic micro-organisms in the top layers of the soil, and (iii) the conversion of ferrous salts into ferric salts in those soils which are rich in iron.

[3] Martin Leake, *Bases of Agricultural Practice and Economics in U.P.*, ch. xv.

of the Gangetic Plain which suffer from oversaturation due to defective drainage, and which consequently depend only on rice, because it is only the rice plant which is able to draw oxygen dissolved in water.

The efficiency of the soil in respect of its physical and chemical conditions and in the matter of the supply of plant food is also very much affected by high temperature caused by the deficiency of rainfall. We have seen that the healthy growth of plants depends upon the rate at which moisture and, with it, the soluble plant-food reach the roots and the rate at which there is water-loss from foliage due to evaporation. The rate of diffusion of moisture in the intercellular spaces to the external atmosphere will depend upon the humidity of the air and the temperature. In a dry atmosphere the water-loss tends to become more rapid than the absorption of moisture through the transpiration current. In such circumstances nature provides a check to such an excessive outflow; the stomata located in the lower surface of the leaf, which serve as a channel for the evaporation of water, will close. But this closing of the stomata due to high temperature has a very important effect upon the physical and chemical conditions of the soil which regulate the supply of plant food. The guard-cells of the stomata, as already explained, regulate the access of air into the intercellular spaces; but while doing so, they also regulate the supply of carbon-dioxide contained in the air. This carbon-dioxide diffuses into the intercellular spaces, is then absorbed, built up into starch, and subsequently converted into sugar and, in this form, is carried throughout the plant wherever the living matter of the cells requires food for its activity. The closing of the stomata, therefore, not only stops the access of air, but also prevents assimilation in the formation of starch, and hence retards the growth of plants. Hence, so long as the stomata are closed owing to high temperature the growth of plants will be checked even when ample moisture is supplied to the roots by artificial means. The sugar-cane plant, for example, gets ample water throughout the summer months for the necessary supply of oxygen, hydrogen, and mineral salts, and enjoys the warmth and light necessary for assimilation. But still 'growth cannot take place because the stomata are, for the most part, closed and access of carbon-dioxide prevented'.[1] But with the arrival of the monsoon there is a sudden stimulus to growth, because the humidity of the outer atmosphere is not much greater than the humidity of the air in the intercellular spaces, and consequently the water-loss does not exceed the water-income, the stomata do not close, the formation of plant food is not prevented, and there is very rapid growth. It would appear, therefore, that air moisture has a very direct effect upon plant-life, and when temperature conditions are unfavourable, artificial irrigation will be of very little avail in fostering the growth of plants. This scientific conclusion is of very great significance which we shall realize fully at a later stage of our enquiry.

Certain important conclusions follow from the above discussion on the relation between soil and meteorological conditions. We started with the question of the relative importance of soil and meteorological conditions which are the uncontrollable factors of our environment. We saw that the efficiency of rainfall depends upon the texture of the soil. Secondly, it was explained that the efficiency of the soil, also in respect of the physical and chemical conditions and the supply of plant food, is determined by rainfall and temperature. Hence there seems to be no sharp line of distinction between the physical and chemical conditions of the soil and the meteorological conditions, although the distinction is clearly marked. These two sets of conditions constitute what we understand by environment. But on the whole, the importance of soil is overshadowed by the importance of the climatic factor when we study the geographical distribution of species, or when, as in India, the uncertainty of rainfall has such far-reaching consequences on agriculture and, hence, on the movement of population.

In fact the climatic factor is a factor of fundamental importance which determines the geographical distribution

[1] Martin Leake, *Bases of Agricultural Practice and Economics in U.P.*, Ch. xii.

of population.[1] It is one of the basic facts of Human Geography that the fullest and best development of humanity is confined to regions lying between the extremes of rainfall.[2] The great centres of dense population are located in these intermediate zones. As La Blache says, the distribution of the early centres of dense population 'seems to be confined, approximately, to a zone bounded by the Tropic of Cancer and the fortieth parallel of latitude.'[3] Here 'the climate is warm enough, so that many plants can quickly complete their cycle of growth and take advantage of the interval between periods of seasonal rainfall or river floods. Fresh water in the form of springs, lakes, underground water or streams, collaborates with tropical or sub-tropical climates. The great rivers, in particular, descending from the high Asiatic massifs and fed by seasonal rainfall not only bring waters impregnated with soluble substances, but they also deposit much alluvial material. One is almost tempted to guess that in the beginning the largest human settlements must have been located in the section of the lower valley where the overburdened stream succeeded in depositing its load.'[4]

Let us now consider how the geographical distribution of population in the Upper Gangetic Plain corresponds with the amount and distribution of rainfall in each of its natural regions. The table on page 64 shows this general trend in a striking manner.

The table reveals a striking tendency for both rainfall and population density to decrease from east to west. Let us note briefly the climatic features of the different natural regions in order to realize the significance of this tendency. In the eastern portion of the Gangetic Plain the climate is generally more moist and the temperature more equable than in other portions. In summer the maximum temperature varies from 100 to 110 degrees, and the minimum rarely falls

---

[1] How the chief types of vegetation correspond roughly to the amount and distribution of rainfall is a broad question with which we are not directly concerned; but some aspects of this question which have a direct bearing on the problem of the density of population will be considered in the next chapter.

[2] Brunhes, *Human Geography*, p. 67.

[3] P. Vidal De La Blache, *Principles of Human Geography*, p. 75.

[4] Ibid., pp. 75-6.

below 75 degrees. The rainfall also is higher than in other regions in the north or in the west. The danger of drought is very little in this portion of the Gangetic Plain; on the other hand, it is liable to suffer from excessive rainfall. What is of vital importance to the agricultural security of this region is, however, the seasonable distribution of rainfall rather than its total amount which is rarely if ever deficient. There is a large area under rice in this region, and famines here are the result of an early cessation of the monsoon, which damages all the *kharif* crops generally and creates a danger of fodder famine due mainly to the failure of the fodder crops, juar and bajra. Moreover, the winter rains also must be moderate, otherwise excessive dampness will injure the *rabi* harvest.

AVERAGE NORMAL AMOUNT AND DISTRIBUTION OF RAINFALL IN THE DIFFERENT NATURAL REGIONS OF THE GANGETIC PLAIN

Regions	Order according to density	Average total amount	Average from April 1 to August 31	Average from Sept. 1 to Oct. 31	Average from Nov. 1 to March 31
Indo-Gangetic Plain, East	1	41·77	28·87	9·66	3·24
Indo-Gangetic Plain, Central	2	36·80	26·61	8·24	1·95
Indo-Gangetic Plain, West	3	29·62	21·46	5·89	2·27

The central portion of the Gangetic Plain also exhibits the same essential climatic characteristics. Considered as a whole it receives less rainfall than the eastern portion. None of the districts shows a tendency to suffer from drought, except Sitapur and Hardoi, where there is a deficiency of the permanent water-supply as there are no tanks or canals. On the other hand, in Fyzabad the rainfall is distinctly heavy when compared with that in the rest of Oudh, and there is a danger of excessive rainfall. On the whole, as in the eastern portion of the plain, a poor monsoon or its early cessation becomes disastrous in its effect on the *kharif* harvest, and excessive winter rains also have a deleterious effect on the *rabi* harvest. The range of variation of temperature in this region is wider than in the eastern portion, and is less wide than in the western portion. In the Doab region the heat is greater than in the northern portion, and the violent and hot westerly wind, the chief characteristic of the hot weather in the Western Gangetic Plain, blows in summer.

In the western portion of the Gangetic Plain the annual rainfall is scanty, and this region is liable to suffer from unseasonable distribution of rainfall. So far as the total amount of rainfall is concerned we find a well-marked difference between the northern and the southern portions of this region, the rainfall being generally heavier in the north than in the south. But an important meteorological peculiarity which we find in this region is that rainfall is susceptible to sharp deviations from the normal. In Moradabad, which lies in the northern part of this region, the remarkable feature is the unusually large rainfall outside the regular season, and some portions of the district, which are outside the limit up to which the south-easterly monsoon can reach, receive much smaller rain than other portions. Similarly, Etah is susceptible to deviations of rainfall from the normal, particularly to deviations towards excess, and a wet cycle of years is always accompanied by a shrinkage of cropped area and agricultural distress.[1] Then again in Sahajanpur, where we find a damp climate characteristic of the Sub-Himalayan regions, there are not only sharp variations in the distribution of rainfall in the different portions of the district, but there are also very wide annual fluctuations which produce unstable conditions of agriculture. In the south, where the amount of rainfall is less, the deviations of rainfall from the normal are no less sharp, and the most noticeable departures are towards deficiency. A striking characteristic of climate in the Western Gangetic Plain is that violent and dry westerly winds blow in the summer months, and these combined with high temperature spell ruin to agriculture in years of drought.

The uncertainty of rainfall with all its concomitant

---

[1] It is interesting to note that during the last three years of the decade 1921–31, which were characterized by failure of rainfall, there was a considerable increase in the migration of population from this district.

reactions on the agricultural economy is observed in a striking manner in another region which, although it lies in the Central India Plateau, exhibits the essential climatic features of the Western Gangetic Plain, particularly of its southern portion. This region receives on the average an annual rainfall of 34·85 inches, which is distinctly above the average for the Western Gangetic Plain, which is only 26·62 inches. Still the density of population in this region is considerably smaller than in the Western Gangetic Plain. The reason is not far to seek. Out of the four districts of the United Provinces of Agra and Oudh included in this region, Hamirpur and Banda lie in what the meteorologists call the 'monsoon trough of low pressure', which is affected sometimes by the Arabian sea monsoon current and sometimes by the Bay current. Consequently they are exposed to variable winds, the rainfall is capricious and irregular, and heavy floods alternate with long breaks of widespread failure of the monsoon. Stable agriculture is impossible under these uncertain meteorological conditions, and it is natural that the density of population should be low. On the other hand, in Jhansi and Jalaun not only is the rainfall variable and uncertain, but its efficiency is also less owing to the unfavourable conditions of soil and drainage. The black soil of this region becomes strongly heated in summer and absorbs much radiant energy, so that it requires a good deal of preliminary watering before it is fit for cultivation. On the other hand, excessive rainfall on this class of soil becomes disastrous to agriculture. Moreover, in Jhansi the rapid drainage of the country interferes with the proper absorption of moisture by the soil, and thus reduces the efficiency of rainfall.

Having observed the climatic peculiarities of the different natural regions of the Gangetic Plain we shall study broadly the manner in which the fluctuations of rainfall affect the *kharif* and the *rabi* harvests in these regions. Excessive rainfall, provided it is sufficiently general and is not ill-distributed, has an injurious effect upon the *kharif* harvest; but it has a compensatory effect in increasing the area as well as the outturn of the *rabi* crops. In 1922–3, which was a year of excessive rainfall, the full normal *kharif* area could not be sown owing to heavy and incessant rain from July to September, the area under the *kharif* crops was the lowest if we take the preceding decade into account, and the crops failed over about 5 per cent of this area. But the winter rains were moderate and well distributed, and the sufficiency of moisture in the soil had the effect of increasing the area as well as the yield of the *rabi* crops. The area under such crops was 5·6 per cent above the normal, and was the largest if we take into account the preceding quinquennium. It is interesting to note that the districts of the Central India Plateau, which, as we have seen, are most susceptible to fluctuations of rainfall, exhibited the effects of excessive rainfall in a most striking manner. In Banda and Jalaun, for instance, the decrease in the *kharif* area amounted to 22 per cent and 84 per cent of the normal area respectively, whereas the average decrease in the provincial acreage was only 7·2 per cent of the normal. The increase in the *rabi* area in these two districts was also most marked; there were increases of 26 per cent and 24 per cent respectively in these two districts, whereas the provincial figure was only 5·6 per cent.

But when the rainfall is not only excessive but also ill-distributed we observe far more disastrous effects upon the harvests. The year 1924–5, for instance, was one of excessive and ill-distributed rainfall. But whereas in 1922–8 the *kharif* sowings were retarded by incessant and excessive rainfall, in 1924–5 the defect of the total amount of rainfall from the normal during the sowing season, ranged from 52 to 96 per cent, and consequently the agricultural operations were retarded by insufficient moisture. During the rainy season, however, the monsoon was strong but the rainfall was ill-distributed, so that in the arid districts of the Western Gangetic Plain, which badly require the full amount of the scanty rainfall which they normally receive, the rainfall was below normal; while other portions of the Plain, where there is a danger of excess, received abnormally excessive rainfall, and in some twelve districts more than 20 inches of rain were recorded in July. The excessive rains continued till the middle of August, and after a short break there was again general and heavy rain in September. Owing to these abnormal weather conditions there was a decrease in the area and outturn of the *kharif* crops. The decrease in the *kharif* area was 10·5 per cent of the normal and was the lowest if we take into account the preceding 12 years, in the districts of the Central India Plateau the deficiency being nearly 21 per cent. The *rabi* area in the United Provinces as a whole increased by 6·6 per cent. This increase was mainly due to the fact that excessive rainfall had not been sufficiently general. As a matter of fact we find a decrease in the *rabi* area owing to excessive moisture in many districts. But although there was an increase in the *rabi* area, the deficiency of the winter rains, particularly in the Western Gangetic Plain, had an unfavourable effect upon the outturn of the *rabi* crops. Hence the outturns of almost all the *rabi* crops were distinctly lower than in 1922–3.[1]

Excessive or ill-distributed rainfall is a contingency over which man has little or no control, and the resulting scarcity becomes almost a dispensation of nature. Even in normal years the agricultural problem in certain districts of the Eastern Gangetic Plain is no doubt essentially the problem of water-logging and over-saturation. But the fundamental agricultural problem in a tropical region like the Gangetic Plain is not normally, as in England, the problem of reducing the water content of the soil, but that of retaining every drop of moisture in the soil.[2] The eastern and central portions of the Gangetic Plain receive more rainfall than the western portion. But still the former regions do not get so much rainfall as to do without artificial irrigation, and in the latter region, where the total amount of annual rainfall is much less, artificial irrigation is still more essential for the necessary supply of moisture to the soil. Hence it is that in normal years artificial irrigation is a factor of considerable importance

[1] The effects of ill-distributed rainfall upon the harvests were seen to best advantage in the year 1915–16. The eastern portion of the Gangetic Plain suffered from excessive rainfall and the western portion from drought combined with failure of winter rains. The effects on both *kharif* and *rabi* harvests were consequently disastrous.

[2] Martin Leake, *Bases of Agricultural Practice and Economics in U.P.*, p. 163.

in the rural economy of the Gangetic Plain. Moreover, the
deficiency of rainfall in abnormal years is a calamity, the
severity of which man can mitigate to some extent, and the
manner and extent of man's control over his environment in
this respect is a question of far-reaching importance.

But the question as to how far artificial irrigation has
succeeded in modifying the effects of drought upon the
harvests, and how far the extent of agricultural security
due to artificial irrigation has varied in the different natural
regions, cannot be considered properly unless we study the
nature of artificial irrigation in the different portions of the
Gangetic Plain.

It is a significant fact that the nature and development of
artificial irrigation have been conditioned by the peculiarities
of natural environment in the different regions. In the
eastern and the central portions of the Gangetic Plain the
main sources of artificial irrigation are wells, supplemented
by tanks and other natural sources; whereas in the Upper
Gangetic Plain the development of canal irrigation has
revolutionized agriculture, and although well irrigation is
common in those tracts which are out of reach of the canal
system, yet wherever possible it has been largely superseded
by canal irrigation. As already said, in the eastern and the
central portions of the Gangetic Plain there is little danger
of a total failure of the monsoon, these regions being liable
to suffer rather from an early cessation of the monsoon, or
an unseasonable distribution of rainfall, or a failure of winter
rains. An early cessation of the monsoon has the direct effect
of damaging the *kharif* crops generally. But it has also an
indirect effect of restricting the area sown under the *rabi*
crops, because after the *kharif* harvest there is very little
moisture left in the soil to permit of preliminary agricultural
operations connected with the *rabi* harvest. In these
circumstances the wells constitute an effective protection
against an early cessation of the monsoon and prevent a
restriction in the area sown under the *rabi* crops. Secondly,
the wells also mitigate the effects of unseasonable rainfall
by supplying the natural deficiency of moisture at the proper
times during the different stages of the growth and maturity

of the crops. Lastly, well irrigation has been a great protection to the rice crop (late rice) and the *rabi* crops in general in the event of a failure of winter rains which prejudicially affects the outturns of both these crops. Moreover, the soil and the water-level in these regions have particularly favoured the development of well irrigation, and have increased the efficiency of wells as sources of artificial irrigation. In the Gangetic Plain as a whole the soil in the neighbourhood of the rivers is sandy and porous, but the proportion of clay in the soil increases as we go farther inland, till in the depressions beyond the old alluvium the soil stiffens into clay. Hence, in the neighbourhood of the rivers wells cannot be sunk owing to the sandy nature of the soil and the great depth of the water-level, and we invariably find unstable conditions of agriculture in such riverain tracts. But in the old alluvium, which, as a rule, is densely populated and both extensively and intensively cultivated, not only is the water-level within twenty or thirty feet from the surface, but the soil also is of such consistency as to obviate sometimes the necessity of providing masonry linings in the wells. In the depressions no artificial irrigation is necessary, and the ample supply of moisture and the clay soil favour the cultivation of rice, which is one of the most important crops grown in the eastern and central portions of the Gangetic Plain.

Thus, the facility with which wells can be constructed in the eastern and the central portions of the Upper Gangetic Plain, and the protection which they provide in abnormal years, are such as to encourage a remarkable development of well irrigation. A striking tendency that we observe in the statistics of irrigation is that well irrigation has superseded irrigation from tanks and other natural sources. The most serious disadvantage of tank irrigation as well as irrigation from other natural sources is that these sources of irrigation absolutely fail in a year of deficient rainfall, whereas the wells not only provide greater resistance against drought, but also constitute a highly elastic source of agricultural water-supply. It is, no doubt, true that deficient rainfall causes a fall of the water-level in the wells, and a succession of dry seasons leaves them in a more or less unserviceable condition.

For instance, in some of the districts of Oudh there had been a gradual fall of the water-level for some years before 1913, till in that year it became so pronounced as to cause misgivings about the security provided by well irrigation. But as a result of heavy rainfall in 1916 and 1917 the water in the wells rose to its normal level, so that in the dry seasons of 1918 and 1919 the wells could perform their function in a perfectly normal manner. The fall of the water-level in certain districts of the Lower Gangetic Plain is also due to the draining of *jhils* which act as surface reservoirs. We have shown that, as a result of the increasing pressure of population, cultivation has extended in many districts by draining off these surface reservoirs; but it is interesting to observe that such agricultural enterprise has not been an unmixed blessing in view of its dangerous reactions on the sub-soil water-level. But, on the whole, it is true to say that well irrigation has established its inherent superiority over irrigation from tanks and other natural sources.[1]

This process of change in the character of irrigation in the Eastern and the Central Gangetic Plain through the development of well irrigation commenced, properly speaking, after the famine of 1896, which established the superiority of well irrigation over irrigation from tanks and other natural sources. Since then there has been a remarkable development of well irrigation which has continued up to very recent times. Let us examine this change in the nature of irrigation in some of the typical well-irrigated districts of the Central Gangetic Plain. In the district of Sultanpur there were only

[1] In 1931 the average irrigated area in the United Provinces of Agra and Oudh was estimated to be about 9¼ million acres, of which 5 million acres were irrigated from wells, 2¼ million acres from canals and 2 million acres from other sources. The area irrigated from canals, reservoirs, and wells depends upon the price of agricultural produce and the extent to which other sources of irrigation are available. When crops sell at very low prices it does not pay to take water from the canals or reservoirs. For example, in 1931–2 while the area irrigated from canals, reservoirs, and wells fell by 7·0, 8·3 and 3·4 per cent respectively, that irrigated from other sources rose by 11·2 per cent (*Season and Crop Report, U.P.*, p. 3). Again in 1928–9, which was one of the worst years of drought, there was an increase of 145 per cent in the area irrigated from other sources. It is only when other sources fail on account of scanty rainfall that farmers have recourse to wells and canals. For example, in 1932–3 there was little water in *tals* and ponds, and so, while the area irrigated from canals, reservoirs, and wells increased by 14·8, 6·5, and 8·2 per cent respectively, that irrigated from other sources fell by 37·5 per cent.

8,992 wells at the time of the first settlement; in the following thirty years 1,461 more wells were constructed. In 1902 there were 42,349 wells, and in the dry season of 1913–14 there were 42,956 wells available for use. In Fyzabad, another typical well-irrigated district, the tank-irrigated area was 54 per cent of the total irrigated area in 1865. In 1895 it was still 53 per cent. In the famine year of 1896, although there was a large contraction of the cultivated area, yet only 44 per cent of this area was irrigated, so that since then the percentage of tank-irrigated area had been gradually reduced, till in 1902 it was only 34 per cent. Similarly in Bara Banki the tank-irrigated area was 57 per cent of the total irrigated area at the time of the first settlement; but by 1902 it was reduced to 52 per cent. In 1902 there were 1,821 masonry wells and 23,553 non-masonry wells available for use; but in 1921–2 the numbers of such wells available were 13,719 and 24,079 respectively. In Lucknow the area irrigated from tanks and *jhils* gradually decreased from 72·5 per cent in 1866 to 60 per cent in 1893 and 35·5 per cent in 1902. The same tendency to a gradual shrinkage of the area irrigated from tanks and other sources and a corresponding development of well irrigation is also observed in the Doab region of the Central Gangetic Plain. In Allahabad the area irrigated from sources other than wells diminished in the trans-Gangetic tracts from 110,931 acres to 61,773 acres between the year of the first settlement and 1916; in the rural Doab this area diminished from 50,470 to 30,579 acres in the same period. In Cawnpore this area diminished from 41,351 acres to 35,724 acres between 1872 and 1903. Similarly, in Fatehpur this area decreased from 85,523 acres in former times to 36,954 acres in comparatively recent times. At the present time, except in Cawnpore and Fatehpur where the canal-irrigated areas are 76 and 31 per cent of the total area respectively, the area irrigated from wells varies from 65 to 84 per cent in years of drought as the first table on p. 73 clearly demonstrates.

In the eastern portion of the Gangetic Plain as well as in Sub-Himalaya, East, there has been a similar development of well irrigation which has continued even in comparatively recent times, as the second table on p. 73 clearly shows.

	Percentage of well-irrigated area in the Central Gangetic Plain in 1928-1929—a year of drought
Allahabad	74·6
Cawnpore	19·6
Fatehpur	52·2
Lucknow	71·8
Fyzabad	76·1
Sultanpur	75·4
Partabgarh	83·8
Bara Banki	65·8

Regions	Number of wells available for use in 1913–14	Number of wells available for use in 1932–33	Percentage of well-irrigated area in 1928–29 —a year of drought
Indo-Gangetic Plain, East . . .			
Benares . . .	22,705	24,681	96·5
Azamgarh . .	41,559	48,495	79·1
Jaunpur . . .	50,956	52,701	97·5
Ghazipur . . .	22,474	22,121	82·2
Ballia . . .	23,912	26,661	93·5
Sub-Himalaya, East			
Gorakhpur . .	84,497	103,532	64·2
Basti . . .	49,383	53,893	47

In order to realize the exact significance of the remarkable predominance of well irrigation in these regions we must take into account two important facts. In the first place, the wells constitute a highly elastic source of agricultural water-supply. For example, 'the well-irrigated area in 1928–9 doubled itself as compared with that in the previous year; on the other hand, the area irrigated from tanks and reservoirs, wherein there was a shortage of water owing to drought, decreased by 7 per cent.'[1] It is obvious that such an elastic source of irrigation is of very great economic advantage in

[1] *Season and Crop Report, U.P.*, 1928–9, p. 7.

these regions in which artificial irrigation has not the same importance in normal agricultural seasons as it has in years of drought. In the second place the real significance of the increase in the number of wells in these regions is greater than what is revealed by the statistics given above. The wells taken into account include not only the masonry wells which represent permanent sources of supply, but also the non-masonry and unprotected wells which constitute a temporary source of supply and are sunk in large numbers in abnormally dry seasons. The unprotected wells have a small water-bearing capacity, and, in a year of drought, yield only enough water to permit of land being sown with crops, so that naturally the utility of these wells as means of effective protection against drought is extremely limited. The masonry wells, on the other hand, have a large capacity, are more or less permanent sources of supply, and in the event of an early cessation of the monsoon, or failure of winter rains, enable the farmer not only to sow the *rabi* crops at the proper time, but also to irrigate them properly at the different stages of the growth and maturity of these crops. It is thus obvious that an increase in the number of masonry wells is a fair index of the increasing protection against drought which a particular district is able to secure by means of well irrigation, and just as there has been a change in the character of irrigation in the Central and the Eastern Gangetic Plain by the elimination of the uncertain natural sources of supply, so also has there been a further striking change in comparatively recent times in the direction of substituting permanent and more reliable sources of supply in the shape of masonry wells in place of the temporary and insufficient sources of supply represented by the non-masonry wells. The statistics given above show a remarkable increase in the total number of wells. But it is the improvement in the *quality* of irrigation, through the construction of a larger number of masonry wells, rather than an increase in the total *number* of wells, which is of greater significance.

It would be instructive in this connexion to study this process of change in the character of well irrigation a little more closely. It has been estimated that during the decade

1921–31 the number of masonry wells in the United Provinces of Agra and Oudh increased by as much as 11 per cent, the total number of new wells sunk being 150, 314. The following table shows the number of new wells sunk in recent years in the well-irrigated regions of the Upper Gangetic Plain:

NEW MASONRY WELLS SUNK IN RECENT YEARS

Regions	1928–29[1]	1929–30[2]	1930–31	1931–32	1932–33
Indo-Gangetic Plain, Central	4,459	4,488	2,339	1,869	2,211
Indo-Gangetic Plain, East	3,383	3,718	2,481	2,358	2,246
Sub-Himalaya, East	4,507	3,486	2,775	2,217	1,849

It appears from the statistics that in recent years there has been a regular addition to the total number of masonry wells in these regions. Many of these new wells simply replace the old wells which have fallen into disrepair and become useless. But there is no doubt that every year there is a net addition to the total number of masonry wells. It will be observed that the largest number of new masonry wells were sunk in the abnormally dry seasons of 1928–9 and 1929–30. It is obvious that when all other sources of irrigation fail, the farmers naturally have to rely on an unfailing source of agricultural water-supply which saves the *kharif* harvest, or, at least, ensures the success of the following *rabi* harvest. But the new masonry wells that are sunk render unnecessary the sinking of a large number of unprotected wells in future years of drought, and, at the same time, ensure a better and more reliable agricultural water-supply

[1] The districts which showed an appreciable increase in the number of their existing wells during the year are Gorakhpur (2,578), Azamgarh (942), and Allahabad (666).

[2] The district of Gorakhpur was responsible for the largest number of new masonry wells, the number being 2,213, followed by Allahabad with 1,503, and Basti with 1,273. The districts which show an appreciable increase in the number of their existing wells are Gorakhpur (1,405), Jaunpur (1,236), Basti (814), Azamgarh (789), Cawnpore (572), and Sultanpur (520). It should be noted that the Sub-Himalayan districts of Gorakhpur and Basti, which are liable to suffer extremely from an early cessation of the monsoon and a failure of winter rains, have definitely fallen back upon well irrigation in recent times.

in any future emergency. Thus, every dry season leaves a legacy of new defences which increase the power of resistance against drought. But, as the statistics clearly show, the construction of these defences is not confined to abnormally dry seasons. As a matter of fact, wherever the soil is favourable to the sinking of masonry wells, and the water-level is easily accessible, such wells are sunk in increasing numbers even in years of excessive rainfall.

The effect of this remarkable increase in the number of masonry wells has been that in recent years of drought the area irrigated from wells has reached a high percentage, and the position of the farmers has gradually become much stronger than what it used to be in earlier years of drought, as the following comparative table clearly shows. Indeed, as Mr. Turner observes in the *Census Report* of 1931, the recent increase in the number of masonry wells is clearly 'a sign of agricultural prosperity' and 'means added security for the future.'[1]

MASONRY WELLS IN DROUGHT YEARS

Regions	1913–14	1928–29	1929–30
Indo-Gangetic Plain, Central	129,696	180,894	182,985
Indo-Gangetic Plain, East	121,947	143,842	145,821
Sub-Himalaya, East	86,505	107,626	109,845

Thus we see that the districts situated in the Eastern and the Central Gangetic Plain have shown a remarkable resourcefulness in developing the means of artificial irrigation. The inelastic and unreliable sources of irrigation are being gradually replaced by the permanent, reliable, and elastic sources, and a study of successive famine years reveals an increasing power of resistance against drought.

Next we shall study the problem of artificial irrigation in the Western Gangetic Plain. It is interesting to observe how the character of irrigation in the Western Gangetic Plain has been determined by the nature of the soil and the depth

[1] *Census Report, U.P.,* 1931, p. 32.

of the water-level. As already said, this region, as a whole, is liable to suffer from drought, and the agricultural conditions are very much susceptible to fluctuations of rainfall. Hence, it may be presumed that just as the creation of the permanent sources of irrigation has been an effective means of protection against drought in the Eastern and the Central Gangetic Plain, so also the construction of masonry wells will ensure agricultural security in this region too. But in many districts of this region construction of such wells has been rendered difficult and costly, because the soil is not so good or the water-level not so easily accessible as in the Eastern and the Central Gangetic Plain. In the northern portion of this region the construction of masonry wells presents considerable difficulty; but the water-level is not very deep and consequently non-masonry wells can be constructed to meet an emergency. In the extreme north, which, like the Sub-Himalayan regions in the east of the United Provinces of Agra and Oudh, suffers extremely from fluctuations of rainfall, non-masonry wells are constructed in abnormal years only, and, moreover, such wells are confined only to the upland tracts. In Agra and Muttra districts, on the other hand, the water-level is generally deep, and not only is the construction of wells expensive, but the results also are uncertain; moreover, there is a tendency for water to become more brackish after the wells have been in use for some time. Similarly, farther south in the districts of the Central India Plateau the water-level is highly inaccessible, and the construction of wells has been found to be too expensive to be a business proposition.

In view of these adverse natural conditions which have prevented the development of well irrigation on the same lines as in the Eastern and the Central Gangetic Plain, the phenomenal development of canal irrigation in the Western Gangetic Plain has been a factor of great importance so far as the productivity and the security of agriculture are concerned. In fact, canal irrigation has revolutionized agriculture in various ways. There has been a remarkable increase in the irrigated area in all the districts which have been brought within the canal system. In Meerut, for instance, there was an increase of 150 per cent in the irrigated area between 1836 and 1860 as a result of the opening of the Ganges Canal, and the total irrigated area increased from 27 per cent of the cultivated area in 1836 to 60 per cent in 1895. In Buland Sahar where the canal-irrigated area constituted 50 per cent of the total irrigated area, the total irrigated area increased from 41·1 per cent in 1871 to 60·6 per cent in 1890, and the canal-irrigated area increased by 565 per cent in the same period. Such a remarkable expansion of the irrigated area obviously meant that extensive areas of dry waste land were brought under cultivation, and the tracts indifferently served by wells began to be intensively cultivated owing to a plentiful supply of canal water. Moreover, the development of canal irrigation has increased agricultural productivity, not only by calling forth the full powers of the soil and supplying sufficient moisture to it, and thus increasing the outturn of the crops, but also by leading to a substitution of valuable *rabi* crops like wheat, maize, and sugar-cane for the inferior *rabi* crops like barley, juar, bajra, and gram. Thus, naturally, there has been a phenomenal increase in the density of population in the Western Gangetic Plain as a result of this rapid development of canal irrigation.[1]

A striking tendency which must be noted in connexion with the development of canal irrigation is that it has not been confined to the arid tracts which had no means of irrigation, but that it has also extended into the tracts served by wells, thus superseding well irrigation to a very large extent. For example, the extension of canal irrigation in Allahabad, Cawnpore, and Fatehpur has no doubt increased both agricultural security and agricultural productivity in the tracts affected by the alluvium of the Jumna where the construction of wells was extremely difficult; but here canal irrigation has also superseded well irrigation. Thus, in Allahabad we find a decrease in the well-irrigated area in the Doab region, as a result of canal development. In Cawnpore the well-irrigated area diminished in this way from 178,722 acres in 1872 to 162,555 acres in 1903. In Fatehpur this area decreased from 168,565 acres to 137,158 acres in roughly the

[1] See Ch. IV.

same period. Similarly, in Meerut the well-irrigated area diminished by 65,500 acres. In Etah this area has become half of what it was before the introduction of canal irrigation. In view of the fact that it costs Rs. 4 per acre to irrigate land from the canal and about double this amount to irrigate it from the wells, such a replacement of well irrigation by canal irrigation is perfectly natural. Moreover, there has been a rise of the spring level as a result of the canal development, because water has percolated from the canal and the various distributaries and other streams, and such a rise of the spring level has been greatest in the tracts intersected by large and constantly flowing high-level canals. This has naturally created difficult problems of over-saturation and drainage, but what is more important is that the over-saturation of the sub-soil has rendered the construction of masonry wells still more difficult, and has led to a collapse of the unprotected non-masonry wells.

But it must be remembered that canal irrigation has not developed on such an extensive scale as to be regarded as the only source of artificial irrigation in the Western Gangetic Plain. There are large arid tracts in this region which are still out of reach of the canal system, and in which the wells are the only source of irrigation in normal as well as in abnormal years. In these tracts the percentage of irrigated to total cultivated area is much lower than in the Central and the Eastern Gangetic Plain, and the number of acres served by a masonry well is also considerably larger.[1] Thus, in such tracts the natural difficulties in the way of artificial irrigation have not been overcome, and consequently they have shown far less power of resistance against drought. Even in those districts which have been brought within the canal system, well irrigation is indispensable in the case of lands near the village sites as well as in outlying tracts. But the rise of the spring level has, to a great extent, increased the difficulty of constructing masonry wells. Hence it is obvious that canal irrigation would have produced the most desirable results and ensured greater agricultural protection on the whole, if

[1] See *Season and Crop Report of the United Provinces of Agra and Oudh*, 1921-2, p. 5.

it had supplemented well irrigation and developed mainly in the arid tracts where the agricultural water-supply derived from wells and other sources is totally deficient. But this principle has not been followed, and the mere replacement of well irrigation by canal irrigation has been clearly an economic waste.

We are now in a position to consider the important question from which we started, viz.: how far well irrigation in the eastern and central portions of the Upper Gangetic Plain, and canal irrigation in the western portion, have modified the effects of drought upon the harvests. The best way of answering this question is to study the relative deficiency of rainfall and the relative decrease in the area under the *kharif* and the *rabi* crops in these two regions in the two typical drought years, viz. 1913–14 and 1918–19. The relevant facts are embodied in the following comparative tables:

DEFICIENCY OF THE KHARIF AREA IN PERCENTAGES OF THE NORMAL

(Figures for the normal are those for the normal agricultural season 1921–22)

Well-irrigated Districts			*Canal-irrigated Districts*		
Districts	1913–14	1918–19	Districts	1913–14	1918–19
Benares .	—6·3	—1·5	Etawah . .	—13	—10
Jaunpur .	—1	—1	Farukhabad .	—8	—10
Azamgarh .	—2	—3	Saharanpur .	—5	—21
Partabgarh .	—2	—4	Muzaffernagar .	—1	—21
Sultanpur .	—2	—1	Meerut . .	—2	—6
Fyzabad .	—1	—2	Bulandsahar .	0	—5
Cawnpore .	1—5[1]	—1	Aligarh . .	—2	—4
Fatehpur .	2—14[2]	—11	Muttra . .	—5	—11
			Mainpuri . .	—6	—7
			Jhansi [3] . .	—17	—10
			Jalaun [4] . .	—14	—37

[1] and [2] The comparatively large deficiency was due to the fact that although the extension of canal irrigation has given a certain amount of protection to the unprotected tracts along the Jumna, yet there are places which depend wholly upon rainfall because wells cannot be constructed easily in these Jumna tracts. This is also why there was a similar large deficiency in the area under the rabi crops. (See table on p. 82). [3] and [4] Unprotected districts.

DEFICIENCY OF RAINFALL FROM THE NORMAL IN INCHES

(Figures for the normal are those for the normal agricultural season 1921–22)

Regions	In 1913-14				In 1918-19			
	Average Total	Average April 1 to August 3	Average Sept. 1 to Oct. 31	Average Nov. 1 to March 31	Average Total	Average April 1 to August 31	Average Sept. 1 to October 31	Average Nov. 1 to March 31
Indo-Gangetic Plain, East	—·48	—2·71	—·56	—1·73	—9·03	—3·97	—4·49	—·57
Indo-Gangetic Plain, Central	—10·86	—4·83	—5·28	—·25	—14·86	—9·74	—5·10	—·02
Indo-Gangetic Plain, West	—12·31	—6·12	—5·15	—1·04	—18·21	—12·97	—5·44	—·20

DEFICIENCY OF THE RABI AREA IN PERCENTAGES OF THE NORMAL

(Figures for the normal are those for the normal agricultural season, 1921–22)

Well-irrigated Districts			Canal-irrigated Districts		
Districts	1913–14	1918–19	Districts	1913–14	1918–19
Benares .	−5	−6	Saharanpur .	−20	−33
Jaunpur .	−1	−9	Muzaffernagar .	−22	−38
Azamgarh .	−7	−12	Meerut . .	−30	−38
Partabgarh .	−2	−8	Bulandsahar .	−19	−33
Sultanpur .	−4	−15	Aligarh . .	−11	−30
Fyzabad .	−10	−15	Muttra . .	−39	−49
Cawnpore .	−21	−34[1]	Mainpuri . .	−10	−24
Fatehpur .	−26	−20[2]	Etawah . .	−16	−29
			Farukhabad .	−14	−39
			Jhansi[3] . .	−53	−42
			Jalaun[4] . .	−66	−58

A careful study of these statistics points to certain well-defined tendencies, the importance of which can scarcely be exaggerated. In the first place, in the eastern and the central portions of the Upper Gangetic Plain not only is the normal total amount of rainfall greater than in the western portion, the deficiency of this amount from the normal in years of drought is also less; whereas, in the western portion not only is the total normal amount less, the deficiency in years of drought is also greater. In the second place, it is significant that the decrease in the area under the *kharif* crops was greater in the western portion of the Upper Gangetic Plain than in the eastern and the central portions. The sowing of the *kharif* crops depends essentially upon the early rains, and the greater decrease of the *kharif* area in the Western Gangetic Plain, both in 1918–19 and 1913–14, was due to the greater deficiency of rainfall between April 1 and August 31 in both these years. The deficiency of early rainfall was, however, greater in 1918–19 than in 1913–14 in both these

[1] [2] [3] [4] *See* Footnotes, p. 80.

regions, and consequently we find a greater restriction of
kharif sowings in 1918–19 than in 1913–14. Hence whether
we consider the two regions with reference to the same year,
or the same region with reference to the two drought years,
the restriction of the *kharif* area corresponds closely with the
deficiency of early rainfall. In the third place, the decrease
in the area under the *rabi* crops was considerably greater in
the canal-irrigated districts of the Western Gangetic Plain
than in the well-irrigated districts of the Central and the
Eastern Gangetic Plain. The sowing of the *rabi* crops in
years of drought depends wholly upon artificial irrigation,
and every available source of irrigation is utilized in these
years to counteract the effects of drought. Hence the restriction of the area under the *rabi* crops is a fair index of the
extent of protection against drought which a certain region
enjoys as a result of artificial irrigation. Both in 1913–14
and 1918–19 there was a general failure of the winter rains,
the deficiency being a little more pronounced in the western
portion of the Gangetic Plain. But the restriction of the
area under the *rabi* crops was considerably greater in the
western portion of the Upper Gangetic Plain than in the
central and the eastern portions.[1] The obvious inference is
that the phenomenal development of canal irrigation has not
succeeded in ensuring protection against drought. As a
matter of fact in 1913–14 and 1918–19 the increases in the
irrigated area were 17 and 13 per cent of the normal respectively. But the canal-irrigated area remained substantially the same in these two years as in a year of normal
rainfall, and thus proved to be an inelastic source of supply.
Hence, it is the source of supply represented by wells which
showed the degree of elasticity which we observe in years of
drought. Again, it must be remembered that in dry seasons
much of the available canal water is required for the preliminary watering of the soil which becomes strongly heated
due to the deficiency of rainfall, so that there is insufficient
moisture for the maturing of the *rabi* crops. Hence, in the
canal districts we find a tendency, not only to a very large

[1] The higher percentage of deficiency in the rabi area in 1918–19 was to a large
extent due to the influenza epidemic, which hampered not only the sowing
operations but also the construction of temporary wells.

restriction of the area under the *rabi* crops, but also to a considerable diminution in the outturns of these crops in years of drought.

What has been said just now makes it abundantly clear that in the Western Gangetic Plain the tendency should be to rely more and more on well irrigation. But we have already seen that the sinking of masonry wells in this region presents considerable difficulty. Moreover, there are tracts in which the difficulties of sinking wells, whether masonry or unprotected, are insuperable. And the most important natural limitation, which cannot be overcome even when the agricultural water-supply derived from artificial sources is ample, is that the high temperature in a year of drought retards the growth of plant life by preventing the access of carbon dioxide into the intercellular spaces.[1] Thus it appears that the natural advantages or disadvantages in respect of meteorological conditions, and the physical and chemical conditions of the soil (which, as we have seen, are so largely determined by the meteorological conditions), are factors which ultimately determine, not only the agricultural productivity, but also the agricultural security, of the different natural regions of the Upper Gangetic Plain. The eastern and the central portions of this region enjoy inherent natural advantages which have increased agricultural productivity and have created more stable conditions of agriculture by facilitating the development of elastic and unfailing sources of artificial irrigation. The western portion of this region, on the other hand, is more susceptible to fluctuations of rainfall, and the natural disadvantages from which this region suffers have hampered the development of well irrigation on sound lines. The canals have, no doubt, increased the agricultural productivity of certain portions of this region. But there are extensive tracts which are out of reach of the canal system, and, moreover, the canals represent a very inelastic source of agricultural water-supply. Lastly, as we have explained, even if ample moisture is supplied to the roots of the plants by means of artificial irrigation in years of drought, it cannot prevent a failure of crops if the temperature conditions are

[1] See above, pp. 61–62.

unfavourable. All these facts point to the irresistible conclusion that the geographical distribution of population in the Upper Gangetic Plain depends essentially upon the facilities of agricultural water-supply, and these are, again, determined by the meteorological conditions and the physical and chemical conditions of the soil.

CHAPTER IV

CROPS AND DENSITY

IN the last chapter we explained how the agricultural security enjoyed by the different natural regions of the Upper Ganges Valley depends so largely on the physical and chemical conditions of the soil and, above all, on the varying meteorological conditions. In a country where the inadequacy and uncertainty of rainfall have such far-reaching consequences on agriculture, agricultural security is an important factor which controls the movements of population. In this chapter an attempt will be made to examine the problem of the density of population specifically from the point of view of agricultural productivity. As we shall see presently, it is the environmental factors, viz. the physical and chemical conditions of the soil and the meteorological conditions, which also determine the high or low agricultural productivity of the different natural regions by determining the geographical distribution of crops.

Every crop has its own particular range of environment. It finds the most favourable environment in a particular region, and in such a region a comparatively large area sown under this crop, as well as its high yield, shows that it is an important crop characteristic of that region. But its importance diminishes as the environment becomes less and less favourable until it ceases to be grown. Thus, we observe the varying importance of different crops according to variations in the peculiar conditions of soil and rainfall which constitute the most favourable environments.

But it must be remembered that the distribution of soil shows much less regional variation than the amount and distribution of rainfall. The nature of the soils and their distribution do not differ appreciably from one natural region to another. The natural regions are essentially the different rainfall tracts, and within each tract, different classes of crops are grown in the different soil regions. But these soil regions are arranged in an almost similar manner in each rainfall tract, and although it is no doubt true that the predominance of a particular variety of soil in a certain natural region increases the importance of a certain class of crops, yet, on the whole, the importance of different crops in different natural regions is predominantly due to the climatic factors. Thus, throughout the Gangetic Plain loam is the predominant soil. In the neighbourhood of rivers sand predominates, whereas in the depressions the soil stiffens into clay. Each of these soil regions has its own characteristic crops. In the water-logged region the principal staple is rice and the main *rabi* crops are usually gram, peas, and barley. On the dry lands between the rivers and the depressions the usual crops such as cereals, pulses, millets, cotton, sugar-cane, and oil-seeds are grown. The river valleys have their distinctive series of crops characteristic of lighter soils, such as bajra, cotton, and hemp. The arrangement of these soil regions and the characteristic crops grown in each do not vary much from one natural region to another. Hence it is rainfall and temperature which really explain the importance of a crop in a particular region, its diminishing importance in other regions, and its maximum range of environment. Hence a study of the geographical distribution of crops from this point of view is more likely to reveal the varying agricultural productivity of the different natural regions.

Let us observe the range of environment and the varying importance of the main crops characteristic of the Upper Gangetic Plain. Rice, one of the most important staples, requires a mean summer temperature of more than 75 degrees. The largest rice regions have an annual rainfall of 50 inches and a rainfall of 5 inches a month during the growing season. It would appear, therefore, that the eastern portion of the Upper Gangetic Plain which receives, on the average, an annual rainfall of 41·77 inches is not so favourably situated in regard to the cultivation of rice as the Middle Ganges Valley or the Gangetic Delta, but the natural conditions there are not very much unfavourable to rice farming and, as a matter of fact, the rice crop makes a valuable contribution to the agricultural productivity of this region. But the importance of rice diminishes from east to west as the annual rainfall becomes scantier, and as the period of high temperature becomes longer, until the climatic limit is definitely reached in the southern portion of the middle Doab and the Central India Plateau which is a neighbouring region. In Agra and Muttra, for example, the areas under rice are only 84 acres and 15 acres respectively, and in Jalaun, a typical district of the Central India Plateau, the area is only 297 acres. In Jalaun the cultivation of rice is rendered impossible as much by the black cotton soil as by the deficiency of rainfall. But in Agra and Muttra the annual rainfall is not more than 25 inches, and the rainfall during the growing season is not more than 8 inches, so that it appears that rainfall should be at least more, in order that the cultivation of rice may at all be possible.

Wheat, another important staple, has an altogether different range of environment. A temperature of 50 degrees for four months is regarded as sufficient for wheat cultivation. In the temperate belt the temperature ranges between 50 degrees and 68 degrees for four months and wheat is grown. 'In India the soil temperature at seeding time is very important in the production of winter wheat. When sown too early while the ground is warm plants may start well but will soon decay and be attacked by white ants. It is considered safe to seed when the temperature of the soil has fallen to about 77 degrees, but not when it is as high as about 86 degrees.'[1] In the Upper Gangetic Plain the required temperature conditions are satisfied normally. But the moist regions in the eastern portion of the plain cannot be regarded as wheat-growing tracts, because the crop is liable to suffer from rust owing to excessive moisture. Most of the important wheat regions of the world have an annual precipitation of less than 30 inches. In America the successful growth of wheat is not limited by heavy rains, but other crops are usually found to be more profitable in regions where the rainfall is heavy. But where the rainfall is 45 inches or more rust and fungus diseases are prevalent. Moreover, a hot and dry climate produces a fine-stemmed plant, the grain of

[1] J. Warren Smith, *Agricultural Meteorology*, p. 183.

which is hard, glossy, and rich in nitrogen, while a moist climate produces a coarser-stemmed plant with the grains relatively soft and mealy, and poor in nitrogen.[1] In the Upper Gangetic Plain, therefore, the importance of wheat diminishes from west to east with an increase in annual precipitation. But the climatic limit is not reached in the Indo-Gangetic Plain, East, or Sub-Himalaya, East, the rice-growing areas, in which the annual rainfall is 45 inches or a little more. As a matter of fact, wheat is grown even in some of the districts of North, East, and West Bengal where the annual precipitation is much greater. But the yield is poor because the grain is soft and poor in nitrogen owing to excessive moisture, so that other valuable crops are grown in preference to wheat. This is the reason why the importance of the wheat crop diminishes with an increase in the annual precipitation. It seems, therefore, that the Indo-Gangetic Plain, West, which receives an annual rainfall of less than 30 inches, is the typical wheat-growing tract in common with similar regions in America or Australia, while in the central and the eastern portions of this region where the rainfall is heavier wheat is not grown under the most favourable conditions. In fact, whatever wheat is grown there is not pure wheat but is mixed with barley in order to guard against a total failure of crops.

Barley, another important *rabi* staple, has a very wide range of environment. In the U.S.A. most of this crop is grown in cool regions. During the growing season the mean temperature never exceeds 75 degrees, and it is grown in regions with an annual rainfall of less than 35 inches. In the tropics it is grown in regions where the temperature is higher and the annual precipitation also greater. Although there is a danger of rust wherever the rainfall is very heavy, yet this crop has a remarkably wide range of environment. It is the characteristic crop of the uplands and is grown on the light and poor soils. But its importance is greater in the eastern than in the western portion of the plain, because it is the chief *rabi* staple in the moist rice-growing regions where wheat cannot be raised under favourable conditions.

[1] Ibid., p. 185.

Maize, another important crop in the *kharif* harvest, 'so readily adapts itself to its surroundings that it is successfully grown over wide climatic ranges.'[1] The great corn regions of the world are areas of continental climate characterized by a wide range of temperature. Except where irrigation is practised corn is mostly grown in regions having an annual rainfall of over 20 inches and a summer temperature averaging about 75 degrees. In America the most intensive cultivation of maize is found in the region where the mean temperature varies from 70 to 80 degrees, and the annual precipitation varies from 25 to 50 inches. In the Upper Gangetic Plain, as a whole, the rainfall is more than 25 inches and less than 50 inches, the average summer temperature exceeds 75 degrees, and the climate, too, is a continental climate marked by a wide range of temperature. Hence, as this crop has a very wide range of environment its importance, unlike that of rice, wheat or barley, has a correspondingly wide range in the Upper Gangetic Plain.

In the case of cotton, which is another valuable *kharif* crop, the conditions of rainfall predominantly affect its geographical distribution in the Upper Gangetic Plain. The climate limit of this crop is generally determined by the rainfall line of 35 inches, as the regions which receive an annual rainfall of more than 35 inches are rather unsuitable for cotton cultivation.[2] Thus, little or no cotton is grown in Indo-Gangetic Plain, East, Sub-Himalaya, East, Oudh, Central India Plateau, and the East Satpuras. These regions have a moist climate, and the soil also is heavy and clayey and unsuitable for the cultivation of cotton. Moreover, 'light frequent showers with plenty of sunshine between' represent the best conditions for the growth of cotton; but such conditions are found generally in the western portion of the Upper Gangetic Plain. Lastly, a wet autumn is most favourable for the growth of cotton, and a rainfall of 6 inches in

[1] J. Warren Smith, *Agricultural Meteorology*, p. 145.
[2] The reason is that 'An over-supply of moisture causes too rank a growth at first, deferring the fruiting, and causing a development of vegetable limbs instead of the fruiting branches. In the humid regions, too much moisture interferes with the development of the plant either by stunting its growth or by causing the shedding of the buds and young bolls.' (*Agricultural Meteorology*, J. Warren Smith, p. 111.)

September and October sets the limit to the range of importance of cotton.

The cultivation of sugar-cane, which is another important *kharif* crop, requires a high temperature and a constant supply of moisture. It is thus grown in all parts of the Gangetic Plain, its importance varying with the facilities of natural as well as artificial irrigation. In Lower Doab and the Central India Plateau little or no sugar-cane is grown. Its importance is also very small in Middle Doab. The varying importance of this crop in the regions of the Upper Gangetic Plain is explained primarily by the deficiency or adequacy of agricultural water-supply.

Just as barley is the main *rabi* crop in the eastern portion of the Gangetic Plain, where rice is the main *kharif* crop, so also juar is the main *kharif* crop in regions where wheat is the main crop in the *rabi* harvest. Hence the distribution of juar corresponds generally with the distribution of wheat; but where either rice or wheat or both are relatively unimportant crops, juar together with gram, becomes the most important crop. Juar is grown neither on the heavy clay land nor on the lightest soils. Loamy soil, and soil composed of light clay are suitable for this crop. Hence in the eastern portion of the Upper Gangetic Plain barley, which is a more valuable crop, is grown in preference to juar on these better classes of soil.[1]

Bajra, which is the least valuable of the *kharif* crops, is usually grown on poor and sandy soils. The importance of this crop, therefore, gives a very good idea of the extent of the inferior grades of land which a particular tract possesses, and it is significant that its importance is very great in only two agricultural regions of the Gangetic Plain, viz. South Rohilkhand and Middle Doab.

Gram, another important crop in the *rabi* harvest, can be grown successfully on various classes of soil. It is sown on heavy clay land; and it can also be sown on light sandy soils. Hence the range of environment of this crop extends over the whole of the Upper Gangetic Plain. Its importance is

[1] Both barley and juar form the cheap food-grains consumed by the poorer classes. In the Indo-Gangetic Plain, West, juar is sometimes sown alone and cut green, and forms the main fodder crop.

smaller in the eastern portion of the plain, because the land is devoted to better classes of crops. In this region it is usually sown as a second crop on the rice-land. But its importance is considerable in the drier regions of the western portion of the plain. In Middle Doab gram is as important as wheat; and in Lower Doab and the Central India Plateau, where the wheat crop is of smaller importance, gram is the principal crop in the *rabi* harvest.

It is apparent, therefore, that the choice as well as the combination of crops in any region which determines its agricultural productivity, is itself conditioned by the climatic factors which determine the range of environment of crops and their varying importance. But, as already said, there are crops like gram, juar, and maize which have a very wide range of environment. Whether the contribution of such crops to the agricultural productivity of a particular region is relatively large or relatively small, depends on the possibility of selecting other more valuable crops which can be grown under the same climatic conditions. Hence the importance of a crop depends, not only upon its own range of environment, but also upon the range of environment of other more valuable crops which may be grown in preference to it.

Thus, it is important to examine more precisely the varying importance of different crops in the different natural regions. More particularly, it is necessary to fix our attention, not only upon the variety of crops grown in any region, but also upon the choice of more or less valuable staples, and their varying importance as regards area and yield in different regions. Out of those crops which are common to all the natural regions we shall choose the principal crops to the exclusion of the minor ones. Thus, the representative crops selected will be rice, wheat, barley, juar, bajra, maize, gram, sugar-cane, and cotton. The area under these crops forms more than 75 per cent. of the total gross-cropped area, and, therefore, comparisons based on the relative importance of these crops will be, for all practical purposes, sufficiently significant. The reason why it has not been possible to take into account all the crops is that the returns of yields per acre which are, as we shall presently see, the primary basis of our comparisons, are not available for all the crops which are common to all the districts.

The method by which we can construct indices of the contribution of different crops to the agricultural productivity of a natural region, may be explained as follows:

First, we take the area under any crop, say, *a*, in a particular district belonging to a certain natural region. This area is expressed as a proportion of the cropped area under all the representative crops selected.

Secondly, we obtain the index number of yield. This is found out by dividing the yield per acre of the crop *a* in that district by the corresponding yield per acre for the whole province as the standard. Now, the district yield may be expressed as a percentage and this percentage may be regarded as the index number of yield.

Thirdly, the results are multiplied. In multiplying the proportion of the area under *a* and the corresponding index number of yield we take into account:

(1) The relative importance of the crop *a* in that district (as indicated by the proportion of the cropped area which is under *a*), and

(2) The yield of the crop *a* in comparison with the provincial standard.

The product which we get is, therefore, an index of the contribution of the crop *a* to the productivity of the district which we are considering. In this way, we obtain similar indices of the contributions of other crops to the total agritural productivity of the district. Next, by taking an average of the indices of the respective contribution of the same crop to the productivity of the different districts belonging to the same natural region, we get an index which represents the contribution of that crop to the productivity of the entire region. The same process is repeated in the case of other crops, and the results obtained may be tabulated as on p. 94.

We have already said that rice and wheat, the two important food crops of the Upper Gangetic Plain, and sugar-cane and cotton, the two important non-food crops, have distinct ranges of environment which depend upon the climatic factors. It is interesting to observe in the table of indices given below

TABLE OF INDICES OF THE CONTRIBUTIONS OF
DIFFERENT CROPS TO THE PRODUCTIVITY OF
DIFFERENT REGIONS

(The Regions are arranged in order of density)

	Indo-Gangetic Plain, East	Indo-Gangetic Plain, Central	Indo-Gangetic Plain, West
Rice	30·65	28·66	2·50
Barley	24·86	14·20	11·64
Wheat	8·39	17·74	21·95
Juar	3·57	10·73	10·70
Cane	7·19	2·07	3·47
Cotton	—	1·30	6·60
Maize	5·89	8·60	8·48
Gram	13·73	20·00	17·88
Bajra	3·38	7·61	16·15

the varying importance of these crops from east to west. The
contribution of rice to agricultural productivity diminishes
from east to west, and its importance is insignificant in the
Indo-Gangetic Plain, West, where the conditions of rainfall
and temperature are unfavourable. The contributions of
wheat and cotton increase from east to west for the same
reason for which the index for rice is low, viz. the comparative
aridity of the western portion of the Upper Gangetic Plain.
The contribution of sugar-cane also diminishes generally from
east to west because the facilities of natural and artificial
irrigation are greater in the east than in the west. The contribution of barley diminishes, whereas that of juar increases,
from east to west. As already pointed out, barley is the main
rabi crop in the eastern portion of the plain where rice is
the main crop in the *kharif* harvest; and juar is the main
kharif crop in the western portion of the plain where wheat
is the main crop in the *rabi* harvest. Thus, it is obvious
from the table given above that the importance of barley
varies directly as the importance of rice, and the importance
of juar varies directly as the importance of wheat. But it
must be remembered that juar can be grown with as much
facility as barley in the eastern portion of the Upper Gangetic

Plain, and the fact that the contribution of juar to its agricultural productivity is small merely shows that barley, which is a more valuable crop, is grown in preference to juar. Like juar and barley, maize is a subsidiary crop which serves as the cheap food of the poorer classes. As it ripens in a very short time, 'it is of peculiar value as being one of the first crops to come in for food'.[1] And, 'as it is ready for eating early in September, when the stock of food saved from the previous *rabi* is running low, its success is a most important matter'. As we shall see later on, maize has gradually come into importance as a food crop, and as it can be grown successfully over wide climatic ranges it is natural that its importance should be as great in the western, as in the eastern, portion of the plain. From the table given above, however, it appears that the contribution of maize to agricultural productivity is greater in the western than in the central, or the eastern, portion of the Upper Gangetic Plain. This is explained obviously by the fact that in these regions more valuable food crops like barley, or wheat, can be grown in preference to maize. The importance of gram seems to be greater in the western and the central portions of the Upper Gangetic Plain than in the eastern portion. As already noted, it can be grown as well on the heavy clay land as on the lighter soils. In the eastern portion heavy clay-land is devoted mainly to rice, and gram and barley are grown as second crops on the rice-fields. In the western portion gram is grown on the lighter soils which cannot be devoted to any other crop which is more valuable. Moreover, gram is the most important crop in those arid tracts of the western portion of the Upper Gangetic Plain where other valuable crops like wheat are of small importance. Hence, on the whole, it may be said that gram is an important crop in those regions, where, as in the central and the western portions of the plain, either rice or wheat or both are of smaller importance. Lastly, the importance of bajra also increases from east to west. It is decidedly an inferior crop which is grown on the worst class of soils, and the increasing importance of bajra from

[1] Moreland, *The Agriculture of the United Provinces*, p. 179. Maize is also a staple cereal in Rumania, Italy, and Mexico, and in U.S.A. and South Africa a certain amount is used for human food.

east to west merely shows that there is a deterioration of the soil from east to west.[1]

The nature of the geographical distribution of crops just described reveals the relative importance of the three natural regions from the point of view of agricultural productivity and density. It will be observed that the predominantly rice-growing tracts are also the centres of dense population; whereas, the Indo-Gangetic Plain, West, where wheat is the main crop, has a relatively low density of population. We shall show presently that in the rice-growing tracts the combination of crops is such that the more valuable or heavy-yielding crops contribute, to a large extent, to agricultural productivity and can, therefore, support a comparatively high density of population. But apart from the particular combination of crops which one finds in the rice-growing tracts as distinguished from the wheat-growing tracts, there are several reasons why the predominance of rice cultivation co-exists with a high density of population, while the predominance of wheat cultivation co-exists with a comparatively low density of population. In the first place, 'wheat grows in many climates in almost any soil, with varying rainfall and with but little cultivation after the seed is once sown. It is, therefore, eminently suited to extensive agriculture, particularly in regions of moderate rainfall.'[2] It is obvious that while extensive agriculture always implies a low density of population, a high density of population is always characterized by intensive subsistence farming. But, as Professor Carver says, 'While wheat is an important crop in the world's commerce, it is a poor one from the point of view of intensive farming.'[3] Rice, on the other hand, requires far more careful and laborious cultivation. 'In many regions, for example, the rice seed is sown in prepared beds. Then after five or six weeks it is painstakingly transplanted to the fields which have been carefully ploughed and manured. The rice-fields are surrounded by mud embankments so constructed that water can

[1] It is interesting to observe this sort of deterioration of soil from east to west in the case of individual districts lying in the Upper Gangetic Plain.
[2] *Indian Journal of Economics.* Vol. IV, Pt. I, p. 6. An article on Economic Geography by H. W. Lyons.
[3] Carver, *Principles of Rural Economics*, p. 157.

be held there week after week, not standing perfectly still, but gently moving. The beds are occasionally weeded with care and finally the crop is harvested promptly so that the ripe grains may not fall out and be lost.'[1] In the fertile tracts of the Gangetic Plain and the Gangetic Delta, rice cultivation thus requires a large labour force for the preparation of seedbeds, transplantation, and other agricultural operations incidental to intensive farming. It is significant that transplanted rice, the cultivation of which is more careful and laborious, has a greater importance in the eastern portion of the Upper Gangetic Plain; whereas whatever rice is grown in the western portion is mostly late rice, the cultivation of which is less laborious and requires a smaller labour force. It is, therefore, natural that the predominance of transplanted rice should co-exist with a comparatively high density of population. In the second place, the yield of rice per acre is very high relatively to the yield of any other food crop. 'Under good conditions 50 pounds of rice will furnish seed for an acre of transplanted rice, and the yield will be 2,500 pounds or fifty-fold. This amount, when combined with some beans or meat to furnish protein, is ample food for five adults for a year. Thus a population of 2,000 per square mile is possible. On that basis all the people in the United States could be supported on an area equal to New York State.'[2] In fact, it is the abundant return yielded by the rice crop which accounts

[1] and [2] Ellsworth Huntington and S. W. Cushing, *Principles of Human Geography*, 3rd ed., p. 284. It is interesting to note that it is not a mere accident that the old centres of dense population situated in the rice-growing regions have eventually become centres of civilization. As Huntington and Cushing say, 'Rice culture is a distinct help in promoting civilization. For one thing, a rice farmer can profitably keep cattle, which supply manure and enrich the soil. In the next place, since the enrichment of the soil enables the farmer to devote his energies to one particular piece of land, he is likely to build new rice beds, take care that he has a good supply of water and that all his ditches and dykes are in good order. He finds that the work of one year gives him much benefit the next. Moreover, he cannot go off and leave the rice crop unattended, for a few weeks of carelessness will ruin it. All these conditions cause the careful rice-raising people of India, Java and Indo-China to be more industrious and reliable than other tropical farmers. For the same reasons they are more hopeful and progressive, since they have learned that their efforts are not in vain. Moreover, as the rice-raising population is much denser than elsewhere, wild animals do less damage than in other tropical regions, roads can be maintained and the people get more stimulus and help from one another and from outsiders.' (*Principles of Human Geography*, p. 284.)

7

for a high density of population in such lands as the river plains and deltas of the Ganges, the Yangtse, the Hoang, the Si, the Mekong, etc. In the third place, wheat with its one crop cannot support as many people as rice can with its three possible crops a year. Two or three crops raised on the same land in the same season no doubt put a great strain on the productive capacity of the soil. But in the monsoon regions the fertility of the soil is maintained by the deposition of rich silt carried by the annual floods. Moreover, 'a rice farmer can profitably keep cattle. Even though the animals are small they can plough the soft soil of the weedless rice-fields. As they can be fed on rice straw the scarcity of good grass is not important. They also enable him to use the same fields permanently, for they supply manure and the soil does not become exhausted'.[1] It may be argued that, although the rice crop is an exceptionally heavy-yielding food crop, yet the low food value of a rice diet reduces the utility of rice as a means of subsistence as compared to wheat. 'The great value of wheat lies in the fact that its carbohydrates and proteids are very well balanced, so that even if people have no other food they can live on it a long time.'[2] In this respect wheat is much superior to rice, its nearest rival in importance, which has an excess of starch and a deficiency of protein. Moreover, the well-balanced diet of the wheat regions of Europe, America, or Australia contains not only cereals and vegetables, but also meat which supplies the necessary amount of proteids. Hence land is devoted partly to stock-raising and not exclusively to arable farming. But in the densely populated river-valleys of Asia land has to be devoted exclusively to arable farming, because more food can be obtained from land by concentrating on the cultivation of heavy-yielding food crops like rice and millets, so that land may support a high density of population. As Professor Carver says, 'The nutriment in the grain required to fatten a beef animal under present conditions is usually much larger than that of the beef produced, to say nothing of the other things consumed by the animal. Again, the land required to

[1] Huntington and Cushing, *Principles of Human Geography*, 3rd ed., p. 284.
[2] Ibid., p. 334.

pasture a beef animal for a year would, if put into grain or vegetables, yield a great deal more food than that of the beef which the animal will add to his carcass.'[1] Thus, in the monsoon regions domestic animals have been to a great extent crowded out by human beings. For example, in the plains of Shantung, a typical rice-growing monsoon region in eastern Asia, there is 'no room for nomads and camels, or even for many domestic animals. A cow or a horse needs several times as much land for its support as does a man. So numerous are the villages that there is land enough to raise food for only a very few animals except pigs and chickens, which do not need room for pasture and can be fed on refuse.'[2] In fact there is such a scarcity of animals in the rice-growing regions of China that 'the less expensive meats like pork are too costly for ordinary people except at feasts or other special occasions. That is why the Chinese sometimes eat rats, dogs, and other animals which we despise.'[3] As already said, the only kind of animals which the rice-farmer finds it profitable to keep is the undersized cattle of stunted growth which can plough the soft soil of the weedless rice-fields. These animals can be fed on rice-straw—good grass is not essential for their existence—and, at the same time, they supply manure to the soil. But after all, how, in the absence of stock-farming, has it been possible to solve the problem of the excess of starch and the deficiency of protein in the rice diet? It is interesting to find that a fairly well-balanced diet has been evolved in two ways. In the first place, people in the rice-growing regions have depended upon plants for proteids. As legumes contain more proteids than any other vegetable food, beans and peas have become favourite articles of consumption, in addition to other cereals and vegetables rich in protein. Secondly, the deficiency of protein is also supplied by fish, which is found in abundance in the numerous rivers, water-courses, and tanks in the plains and the deltas of the monsoon regions. Thus, in these regions the high yield of rice, supplemented by the proteids contained in the legumes and fishes,

[1] Carver, *Principles of Rural Economics*, p. 163.
[2] Huntington and Cushing, *Principles of Human Geography*, p. 296.
[3] Ibid., p. 356.

is capable of supporting a high density of population. Hence, no people in the world take more pains than the Chinese to catch fish in the sea and rivers and raise them in ponds. Similarly, the importance of the fishing industry in the rural economy of the Gangetic Delta can scarcely be exaggerated. As an extractive industry it is an important subsidiary source of employment, while at the same time it supplies the much-needed deficiency of the rice diet in protein.[1]

But, apart from these general causes which explain how the density of population varies directly as the importance of rice, the combination of crops in the rice-growing regions is such that the more valuable crops contribute, to a greater extent, to their agricultural productivity. First, it is interesting to observe the relative importance of the eastern and the central portions of the Upper Gangetic Plain from this point of view. We have seen that the importance of barley varies directly as the importance of rice, and that of juar varies directly as the importance of wheat. It appears from the table given above that the combined index for rice and barley is 55·51 in the case of the Indo-Gangetic Plain, East, and only 37·86 in the case of the Indo-Gangetic Plain, Central. But in the latter region wheat and juar are more important crops than in the former region, and naturally the combined index for wheat and juar is 28·47 in the case of Indo-Gangetic Plain, Central, and only 11·96 in the case of the Indo-Gangetic Plain, East. If we take the rice-barley index, together with the wheat-juar index, the two regions obviously stand almost on the same level. But it must be remembered that juar is distinctly inferior to barley and, as already explained, the fact that the importance of juar in the Indo-Gangetic Plain, East, is small only shows that barley, which is a more valuable

[1] It must, however be admitted that the danger of famines is greater in regions that depend on rice or millet with beans or peas. In sub-tropical regions a failure of rainfall causes poor crops, no doubt, but 'the scarcity of pasture, fodder and grain makes it impossible for people to keep all their animals. Therefore, many of them are sold for slaughter; thus, when the carbohydrate supply is short the proteid supply tends for a while to increase. In rice and millet countries the beans and peas are likely to fail at the same time with cereals, since all depend upon the same rains. The failure of both kinds of food produces correspondingly severe famines'. (Ibid., p. 357.) Such a danger, however, rarely arises either in those portions of the Indo-Gangetic Plain, which are protected by an efficient system of well irrigation, or in the Delta region where the rainfall is heavy as well as certain.

and heavy-yielding crop, is grown in preference to juar. Hence, although the index for juar is high in the case of the Indo-Gangetic Plain, Central, yet it is the remarkable importance of barley in the Indo-Gangetic Plain, East, which is of greater significance. Secondly, the contribution of sugar-cane, a valuable commercial crop, to agricultural productivity, is considerably greater in the Indo-Gangetic Plain, East, than in the Indo-Gangetic Plain, Central; and although the latter region has an advantage over the former in respect of cotton, yet, taking sugar-cane and cotton together, the balance of advantage is in favour of the former. Thirdly, maize and barley, which constitute the cheap food-grain of the masses, are more important crops in the Indo-Gangetic Plain, East, than in the Indo-Gangetic Plain, Central. Lastly, gram and bajra, the two inferior crops, make greater contributions to agricultural productivity in the Indo-Gangetic Plain, Central, than in the Indo-Gangetic Plain, East. This is natural in view of the fact that gram, which can be grown on heavy as well as light soils, is substituted by other more valuable crops in the Indo-Gangetic Plain, East, whereas the importance of bajra is a distinct indication of the comparatively large extent of inferior soil in the Indo-Gangetic Plain, Central.

Now, when we compare the eastern and the central portions of the Upper Gangetic Plain with the western portion from the point of view of the choice of more valuable staples, we find that the more valuable cereals contribute, to a smaller extent, to the agricultural productivity of the western portion. The contribution of wheat to agricultural productivity is greater in this region, because, as already explained, the climatic factors are favourable to wheat cultivation. It is also remarkable that the importance of rice is very small as compared to that in the eastern and the central portions of the Upper Plain. But it will be observed that the importance of wheat is not much greater in the Indo-Gangetic Plain, West, than in the Indo-Gangetic Plain, Central; whereas rice makes a very substantial contribution to the agricultural productivity of the Indo-Gangetic Plain, Central. The importance of barley, too, is greater in the central portion of the Upper Plain than in the western portion; while juar is equally

important in both. Thus, on the whole, the predominance
of rice and barley in the central portion of the Upper Plain
is balanced by the importance of wheat in the western portion
only to a very small extent. In respect of sugar-cane and
cotton, the two commercial crops, the Indo-Gangetic Plain,
West, is in a more advantageous position. But this does not
seem to outweigh the advantage which the central and the
eastern portions of the Upper Plain possess in regard to
the important tropical cereals. The predominance of maize
and gram in the western portion of the Upper Plain only indicates that the land devoted to these crops cannot be
devoted to more valuable crops like juar, barley, and wheat.
Moreover, the predominance of bajra, as already explained,
is merely an index of the extent of inferior soil. As a
cheap food-grain it is distinctly inferior to maize, barley,
or juar, and its importance must be regarded as a sign of
agricultural distress.

A study of the problem of the density of population from
the point of view of the choice and combination of crops will
not be complete if we do not consider the reaction of the
increase of population upon the utilization of land. In the
agricultural countries of the West, especially in America, the
choice of crops has been modified by the increasing pressure
of the population upon the soil, and this change has manifested itself in certain well-defined tendencies. Professor
Carver says that 'the growing scarcity of land and the increasing supply of labour have brought about a certain amount
of substitution of heavy-yielding for light-yielding crops'.[1]
Thus, there has been a decrease in the proportion of land
devoted to small grains with the exception of two-row barley
and oats, because the production of small grains is unsuitable
to intensive farming. In America there has been a gradual
shifting of the wheat belt owing to the fact that wheat,
although an important commercial crop, is a light-yielding
crop suited to the requirements of extensive farming. On
the other hand, there is an increasing tendency to devote the
land to the production of not only forage crops for dairy use,
such as hay, grasses, and clover, but also heavy-yielding root

[1] Carver, *Principles of Rural Economics*, p. 158.

crops, such as potatoes, sugar-beets, turnips, stock-beets, etc., which yield a high return per acre to a correspondingly high expenditure of labour and capital. Moreover, there has also been an increase in the proportion of land devoted to truck-farm produce, such as beans, onions, lettuce, tomatoes, and other garden vegetables, because these are all heavy-yielding crops.

It is interesting to observe how far the increasing pressure of the population upon the soil in the Upper Gangetic Plain has also brought about such a characteristic change in the direction of intensive subsistence farming by leading to a substitution of heavy-yielding for more valuable crops. In the Indo-Gangetic Plain, East, the most important crop is rice, which is, *par excellence*, a heavy-yielding crop. It is natural, therefore, to expect that wherever possible there should be an increase in the area under rice. In Chapter I it was shown how cultivation has extended in this region by the reclamation of swamps and *usar* lands. These reclaimed lands have been devoted mostly to transplanted rice. Moreover, the statistics of cultivation also show an increase in the area under early rice which is highly significant. Where the *kharif* is harvested at an early date it is always an easy matter to sow a second crop in good time. Hence intensive cultivation of land by means of double-cropping is possible, in the case of land which is devoted to a *kharif* crop like early rice. Thus, early rice is not only a heavy-yielding crop itself, but it also indirectly contributes to agricultural productivity by making double-cropping possible; and it is but natural that early rice should be largely substituted for other light-yielding crops. Secondly, the development of the practice of double-cropping, as a result of the increasing pressure of the population upon land, has led to an increase in the area under the cheaper varieties of *rabi* grains.[1] Thus, the area under gram and peas shows a remarkable increase in all the districts situated in the Indo-Gangetic Plain, East. In Jaunpur, for example, the area under gram was four times as large in 1908 as in 1841; and that under peas increased from 25,000 acres to

[1] The importance of the leguminous food grains of the rabi harvest in the evolution of a well-balanced diet in these densely populated rice regions can hardly be exaggerated.

81,873 acres or 21·58 per cent of the total cultivated area
between 1841 and 1908. In Benares the area under peas
increased from 18,418 acres in 1878 to 50,476 acres in 1908.
Peas ripen early and the stalks are used for fodder. Hence
they have become an extremely popular staple in the whole of
this region. Thirdly, another remarkable feature of recent
agricultural development has been a rapid increase in the
cultivation of maize. In Jaunpur, for example, the area under
maize increased from 57,000 acres in 1899 to 83,500 acres in
1906. Maize is a valuable crop and, by reason of its early
maturity, tends to increase agricultural security. Moreover, it provides the cultivator with sufficient food till
December, and thus enables him to sell most of the *rabi* crops.
Fourthly, it is also significant that there has been a large
increase in the area under barley, the most important heavy-
yielding crop in the *rabi* harvest. In the Indo-Gangetic
Plain, East, wheat requires a better soil, more manure and
preparation, and more careful attention than barley. Moreover, it is susceptible to rust in the damp weather. On the
other hand, the outturn of barley on average land has been
estimated to be about 25 maunds per acre and that of wheat
to be one-fifth less. Barley has, moreover, been adopted
universally as an article of food and, to the cultivator who
keeps as much food-grain as he can for his personal consumption while he raises money for cash payments from other
commercial crops, a larger outturn is a more important consideration. Hence it is natural to expect that, as a result
of the increasing pressure of the population upon the soil,
barley should substitute wheat, juar, and other light-yielding
crops. Lastly, it should also be noted that this tendency to
grow as much of heavy-yielding food-crops as possible is also
signified by the decrease in the area under sugar-cane until
comparatively recent times. In Gazipur the area under
sugar-cane diminished from 86,196 acres in 1879 to 26,500
acres in 1908. In Benares the area under this crop decreased
from 41,223 acres in 1840 to 20,677 acres in 1907. In Jaunpur
this area decreased from 81,436 acres in 1841 to 40,622 acres
in 1908. This decrease was no doubt due to the relative rise
in the price of agricultural produce and the competition of

beet and other imported sugar. But it must be remembered that the practice of double-cropping which has developed a great deal as a result of the increasing pressure of the population upon the soil also affected the area under this crop. This crop remains on the land for the greater part of the year, and is not reaped till spring. Moreover, it requires that the land should be kept fallow for a long period, while the cost and the risks of cultivation are by no means small. Hence naturally the cultivator preferred to grow maize or rice instead of sugar-cane, and then to sow a *rabi* crop on the same field, thus obviating the necessity of long fallowing. In this way he made a more intensive use of his land, which was necessary in view of the increasing pressure of the population upon the soil. Recently, however, the situation has changed owing to an abnormal fall in the price of agricultural produce and a great demand for sugar-cane to feed the numerous sugar factories which have sprung up as a result of the tariff protection granted to the Indian sugar industry.

The same fundamental tendencies can be discovered in the process of agricultural development in the Indo-Gangetic Plain, Central. Thus, in almost all the districts of Oudh which form the upper portion of this region, we find a remarkable increase in the area under rice. In Partabgarh, for example, the area under rice was 60,706 acres or nearly one-third of the area under the *kharif* harvest in 1863. By 1892 the area had more than doubled itself. In Sultanpur the area under rice was only 133,000 acres in 1864; but by 1893 it had increased by 100 per cent. In Fyzabad the area under rice increased from 107,500 acres in 1865 to 269,315 acres in 1904. In Bara Banki the area under rice increased from 27 per cent of the total cultivated area in 1866 to 48·08 per cent of the total cultivated area in 1904. The increase in the area under rice in these districts has been mainly due to the extension of cultivation into poorer lands which are capable of bearing only a single crop of rice. In Oudh also double-cropping in the rice-lands has become more and more extensive, and there has been a very large corresponding increase in the area under gram and peas, the cheaper varieties of *rabi* grains which are grown on rice-lands in winter. In Fyzabad, for example, the area under these crops has increased by 250 per cent, and now covers 47 per cent of the area under the *rabi* harvest. Again, as in the Indo-Gangetic Plain, East, so also in Oudh, there has been an increase in the area under maize. In some districts, in Bara Banki, for example, this increase is due to the substitution of maize for juar which is an inferior crop. But where this has not been possible juar has maintained its importance as a cheap food of the poor, and the area under juar has increased with the increasing pressure of the population upon the soil. Moreover, in Oudh there has also been an increase in the area under kodon and mandua, two other cheaper food-grains. As already pointed out, the climatic conditions in this region are not unfavourable to the cultivation of wheat, and hence its importance is greater than that of barley. It is natural, therefore, that the area under wheat should have increased since the middle of the nineteenth century. But what is more significant is that while formerly wheat was mostly mixed with either gram or barley, the increasing pressure of the population upon land has led to the substitution of pure wheat for mixed wheat which has always a lighter yield. In Lucknow, for example, the areas under pure wheat and mixed wheat were 64,000 acres and 24,500 acres respectively in 1898; but in 1902 it was found that the area under pure wheat had increased, but that under mixed wheat had remained the same. Lastly, the area under sugar-cane diminished until comparatively recent times, for the reasons explained above. Sugar-cane was substituted by other heavy-yielding or more remunerative crops, and it is interesting to note that there was an increase in the area under cotton which became a more important commercial crop than sugar-cane. Recently, however, the area under sugar-cane has increased as a result of the tariff protection granted to the sugar industry and the abnormal fall in the prices of other alternative crops.

In the lower portion of the Central Gangetic Plain we find similar tendencies of agricultural development. The areas under the *kharif* food crops, such as juar, bajra, and rice, have increased, partly as a result of the extension of cultivation and partly at the expense of sugar-cane and cotton.[1] In Fatehpur, for example, the area under juar increased from 72,991 acres at the time of the first settlement to 110,915 acres in 1915. The area under bajra increased from 22,872 acres to 50,685 acres within the same period. In Fatehpur the area under rice has not increased; but there has been an increase in the area under wheat as a result of the development of canal irrigation in the Jumna tracts. In Allahabad, on the other hand, the area under rice has increased, but that under wheat has maintained itself. But it must be noted that the importance of wheat in this region is small as compared with that of other crops. It is also remarkable that pure wheat has supplanted mixed wheat in this region also. Thus, in Fatehpur the area under wheat has increased from 38,218 acres at the time of the first settlement to 45,707 acres in 1915. The most important crop in the *rabi* harvest is, however, barley, which is mixed with gram or peas. The areas under all these crops have increased remarkably. The increase in the area under gram and peas is obviously due to the development of the system of double-cropping; while the increase in the area under barley has been due to the fact that wheat cannot be grown under favourable conditiions in this region, and barley serves as the food-grain of the masses. It is also significant that the area under cotton, and, until recently, also that under sugar-cane have diminished, and these crops have been substituted by heavy-yielding food crops.

In the Indo-Gangetic Plain, West, the increasing pressure of the population upon land has also been accompanied by an increasing importance of either heavy-yielding food crops or valuable commercial crops or both. This region is predominantly a wheat-growing region, and the development of canal irrigation has led to an enormous increase of wheat cultivation in almost all the districts belonging to this region. In Meerut, for example, the area under pure wheat increased from 270,000 acres in 1860 to 327,500 acres in 1904, whereas the area under mixed wheat also increased from

[1] It is probable that this is a sign of more intensive subsistence farming necessitated by the increasing pressure of population upon the soil.

70,000 acres to 120,650 acres within the same period. In Bulandsahar, another district of Upper Doab, the area under pure wheat did not increase in the same period; but there has been a marked increase in the area under wheat mixed with barley and gram, and this is a sign of intensive farming, because such increase has been at the expense of pure barley which is certainly inferior to wheat. Lower down the Doab region, in the district of Etah, for example, there has also been a very large increase in the area under wheat, because canal irrigation has opened up the precarious tracts, while the wet cycle of 1885–9 also gave an impetus to the increase of wheat cultivation. But it is remarkable that, as in the eastern and the central portions of the Upper Gangetic Plain, the increasing pressure of the population upon the soil has led to more extensive cultivation of the cheaper varieties of *rabi* grain by more and more extensive double-cropping, so also in this region there has been a tendency to raise the cheaper varieties of *kharif* grains in a similar manner. We find in this region an enormous increase in the area under wheat mixed with barley, gram or peas. Now wheat alone is almost invariably sown after a fallow; while a mixed crop, at least in a good irrigated land, is a sure sign of double-cropping. Hence, the increase in the area under mixed wheat clearly indicates the tendency to increased cultivation of the cheaper heavy-yielding *kharif* grains like maize, rice, and other staples which mature early in the year and enable the cultivators to sow a second crop of mixed wheat in the same season. Rice, as we have shown, is an unimportant crop in this region. But its cultivation has increased wherever and whenever the natural conditions have been favourable.[1] There has also been a remarkable increase in the area under maize, as it is the most profitable of unirrigated crops, and is very little affected by the early cessation of the monsoon rainfall. In Meerut, for example, the area under maize increased from 46,680 acres to 129,500 acres between 1860 and 1902. In Bulandsahar the area under maize increased from one-third of the *kharif* area to a quarter in roughly the

[1] In Etah, for example, the area under rice in 1911 was 1½ times as large as it was in 1878. In Meerut, again, the area under rice increased from 17,000 acres in 1860 to 35,000 acres in 1895 as a result of the wet cycle.

same period. In Etah the area under maize was five times as large in 1911 as it had been at the end of the last century. Another remarkable tendency is the increase in the area under juar. The area under juar has increased at the expense of the area under bajra, which is a distinctly inferior crop. Now, although juar is a more remunerative crop, yet it is more delicate, and requires better irrigation or else a better soil. But the development of canal irrigation has made it possible to grow juar in sandy soils where bajra was formerly grown. The area under barley has diminished owing to the increasing substitution of wheat for barley. Where irrigation is possible it is no good sowing a less expensive crop than wheat, and where unirrigated wheat can be grown it is also a bad policy to sow barley. Hence the cultivation of pure barley has diminished a great deal in all the districts of this region. In Meerut, for example, the area under barley diminished from 58,800 acres to 40,500 acres between 1860 and 1902. In Bulandsahar this area shows a decrease of 70,000 acres since 1882. In Moradabad the cultivation of barley is now confined to the arid Bhur tracts which cannot bear any better crop. But the most remarkable tendency in this region is the increase in the area under sugar-cane and cotton, the two valuable commercial crops, as a result of the development of canal irrigation. In Meerut the area under sugar-cane increased from 73,643 acres in 1860 to 115,411 acres in 1902. In Bulandsahar the area under sugar-cane increased from 10,492 acres in 1882 to 33,655 acres in 1901.[1] There has also been an enormous increase in the area under cotton. The increasing cultivation of cotton is significant not merely because it is a more remunerative crop, but also because it has increased the agricultural security of this region. Cotton is less affected by drought than any other crop and is, therefore, a source of agricultural stability. Thus, during the famine year of 1913–14 stress was laid by the District Agricultural Officers of Agra and Muttra on the fact, 'that one of the principal causes that so little signs of distress were shown in these two districts in spite of the

[1] The area has gone on increasing. In 1925 the area was 62,189 acres, almost all of which was irrigated.

failure of food-crops on unirrigated land was the comparative excellence of cotton.'[1] It is, therefore, a sign of agricultural progress that the area under cotton has been increasing in recent times in districts which are outside the regular cotton-growing area.

[1] *Crop and Season Report of the United Provinces*, 1918–14, p. 4.

PART II

TRENDS OF AGRICULTURE AND POPULATION IN THE MIDDLE GANGES VALLEY

EXTENSION OF CULTIVATION AND DENSITY

IN the sheltered valley of the Ganges, which has long been one of the centres of dense population, the conquest of the soil and the consequent expansion of cultivation have since very early times favoured the growth of population. The Middle Ganges Valley, in particular, which lies midway between the dry Upper Ganges Plain and the very wet Delta region, has always constituted an admirable environment for human settlement. But there is no doubt that this region which, at the present time, consists of a level, well-cultivated plain, devoid of hills and natural eminences, and supports a teeming population, was, to a large extent, covered with forests which have been cleared within historical times. Thus, Champaran (*Champaranya*) as its very name implies, was formerly covered with forests. Now it is a flat cultivated expanse supporting a dense population. In fact, agricultural development in the Middle Ganges Valley has been largely determined by the extension of cultivation, and it is through this process of agricultural development that this region has been able to maintain an increasing density of population even in comparatively recent times. We shall study presently how the tracts which have recently been brought under cultivation have offered better economic possibilities to enterprising settlers so as to induce migration of rural population from tracts which have so long been centres of dense population, but in which a further increase of population, under the present conditions, has always involved an extreme economic strain. But at the same time it must be remembered that there is obviously a limit to agricultural development by means of extension of cultivation. In fact such a limit seems to have been reached already, and 'over-population due to the restricted area of land' has threatened the stability of rural economy.

8   113

From the climatic point of view the Middle Ganges Valley is intermediate in character between the dry Upper Ganges Valley and the very wet Delta region. Here the annual precipitation is more than in the Upper Ganges Valley, but less than in the region of the Deltas and, as naturally expected in regions in which the entire agricultural economy depends on the monsoon, the density of population varies directly as the amount of annual precipitation. The river Ganges divides this region into two well-marked natural divisions, viz. North Bihar and South Bihar. On the average North Bihar gets more rain than South Bihar. Indeed, some portions of South Bihar not only receive an annual rainfall of less than forty inches, but are also situated beyond the ancient Gangetic alluvium, and constitute an undulating rocky country covered with brushwood and jungle characteristic of the Chota Nagpur Plateau. Thus, the natural conditions in South Bihar are not, on the whole, favourable to agricultural enterprise and expansion of cultivation, and it is natural that while North Bihar maintains a mean density of 696 persons per square mile, in South Bihar the mean density should be only 565 persons per square mile. In fact, a comparison of the statistics of cultivation shows that the scope for agricultural development by means of extension of cultivation has been relatively less in South Bihar. In North Bihar 69·8 per cent of the cultivable area has been brought under cultivation; while in South Bihar the proportion is as much as 74 per cent of the cultivable area. The figures indicate that South Bihar does not lack in agricultural enterprise. What has really been a hindrance to the growth of population is the limited area of cultivable land. While 89·5 per cent of the total area is cultivable in North Bihar, only 78·4 per cent is cultivable in South Bihar, and it is the comparative scarcity of arable land in South Bihar which explains why the net cultivated area is only 57·6 per cent of the total area, while in North Bihar it is as high as 62·5 per cent of the total area. But while we think of these differences which distinguish the northern from the southern portion of the Middle Ganges Valley, we must remember that in both the density of population is high in the tracts bordering on the Ganges, and that it is found to be diminishing as one travels inland away from the river to the south and the north. The riparian tracts have been occupied from time immemorial and have always been centres of dense population. But in the course of time, as the pressure of the population on the soil has increased, a wave of agricultural enterprise has travelled to the north away from the river Ganges. As we shall see presently, some of these riparian tracts have become decadent within recent times, and the centre of population has shifted, especially in North Bihar, to the rice-growing regions away from the Ganges where cultivation has extended and the density of population has increased in consequence.

NORTH BIHAR—SARAN

We shall now study in greater detail the course of agricultural development as determined by the extension of cultivation in the northern and more densely populated portion of the Middle Ganges Valley, viz. North Bihar. Saran, which is the most densely populated district in the Middle Ganges Valley, except Muzaffarpur and Darbhanga, is a representative district of North Bihar in which over-population due to scarcity of cultivable land has clearly manifested itself. As in the Upper Ganges Valley, so also in the Middle Ganges Valley the period between 1881 and 1891 was a period of great agricultural development which stimulated a growth of population. Thus, the density of population in Saran increased from 859 persons per square mile in 1881 to 923 persons per square mile in 1891. But even in 1931 the density of population in this district was found to be only 927 persons to the square mile. Mr. P. C. Tallents, I.C.S., Superintendent of Census operations, writing in the *Census Report of 1921*, commented that 'the results of the Censuses seem to show that the number which the soil can bear in present conditions was reached some years ago'. In 1921 it was found that the population of this district had increased by 2·21 per cent during the previous decade. Mr. Tallents observed that the decline of emigration more than accounted for the increase in the actual male population, and that the increase had occurred largely amongst the males of the labouring castes from which emigrants are drawn in large numbers. The increase of population did not mean, therefore, that the pressure on the soil had been increasing.[1] Thus, it appears that scarcity of cultivable land has been the most important limiting factor of the growth of population. In fact, even as early as 1901 the cultivated area was 78·6 per cent of the total area, and the area recorded as cultivable was about 11 per cent of the total area. One-third of this cultivable area was under mango-groves and about half of it was recorded as old fallow. Most of the area recorded as old fallow consisted of land infected with saline efflorescence which is found in patches all over the district because it abounds in marshes and low-lying depressions. Such land will grow nothing but inferior grass, and consequently it forms the only real source of pasture in the district except such scanty pickings as the cattle may find on road-sides and field-boundaries or in groves of trees. An idea of the extreme pressure upon the soil may be derived from the fact that as early as the beginning of this century there was an encroachment even upon the mango-groves, and that little more than one acre in every hundred brought under the plough was given rest even for a single year.[2]

During the last revisional settlement proceedings it was discovered that 82·55 per cent of the district was under cultivation, that there had been a great increase in the number of settled and occupancy raiyats, and that fields and holdings had diminished in size. The settlement officer added that 'the craze for extending cultivation is so great that extension has mostly been achieved at the expense of the pasture lands. The area reserved for grazing has accordingly decreased. The cattle have to be maintained in a precarious manner by means of dry stalks of maize and other *rabi* crops for the greater portion of the year. After the crops have

[1] *Census Report, Bihar and Orissa*, p. 22.

[2] It is interesting to note what Mr. L. S. S. O'Malley observed in the district *Gazetteer* in 1908: '30 years ago it was said that people had a passion for planting them (mango trees), so much so that the rainfall at Chapra was increasing owing to the number of groves with which the town was being surrounded. At present the demand for timber on the one hand and for arable land on the other, and the facilities afforded to the cultivators of disposing of their rights in them are gradually leading to a depletion of these orchards.'

been taken off the ground they are frequently let on to it and they live on the stubble as best as they can.'[1] In view of the facts just stated it might appear strange that the population of this district should have increased by 6·26 per cent during the decade 1921–31. But as already explained, the economic strain created by a scarcity of cultivable land is sometimes relieved by certain counteracting forces. In Saran we find two factors which have alleviated economic distress in spite of the scarcity of arable land and the growth of population, viz. cultivation of valuable crops and emigration. In this district the cultivators depend less on rice than on valuable crops like vegetables including root-crops, fruits, and sugar-cane. In 1921 the area under sugar-cane was more than twice the corresponding area in any other district of North Bihar, and the area under vegetables including root-crops was nearly twice as great.[2] Moreover, the people of this district can also supplement their income to a great extent by remittances from emigrants. In fact, it is significant that during the decade 1921–31, 'the only districts whose emigrants have increased in number to any marked extent are Saran, Muzaffarpur and Champaran. All these districts lie in the densely populated tract of North Bihar, and it is not at all surprising that the additional strain imposed on the resources of the soil by the growth of population since 1921 has been in some measure relieved by a quickening of the stream of emigration.'[3]

It is interesting to observe the course of agricultural development in the different sub-divisions of Saran through the successive decades. The Sadar sub-division, which is a trans-Gangetic tract, was the most densely populated sub-division up to 1891. It had a density of 985 persons per square mile; in some of the parganas the density was more than 1,000 per square mile, and in Manjhi it was as high as 1,077 per square mile. In the two northern sub-divisions the

[1] *Census Report, Bihar and Orissa*, 1921, p. 22.
[2] During the decade 1921–31 'there was a good demand for sugar-cane, which stimulated the cultivation of this crop, and each year showed a substantial increase in the area under cultivation'. (*Census Report*, 1931, p. 18.) The recent development of the Indian sugar industry has accelerated this increase.
[3] *Census Report*, Bihar and Orissa, 1931, p. 107.

density was less; in Siwan it was 955 per square mile, and in Gopalganj it was only 806 per square mile. The rent rates also were higher in the southern tracts bordering on the Ganges. A decrease of population was inevitable in the Sadar sub-division which was fast being overpopulated. In fact, a check to the increase of population was first observed in 1891. Whereas the population in this sub-division had increased in the decade ending in 1881 by 11·6 per cent, it increased by only 7·2 per cent in the next decade. The census of 1901 revealed a decrease of 2·2 per cent, and after that the population decreased continually during the succeeding decades. This progressive decrease was shared by all the over-populated thanas of this sub-division. But there was a heavy decrease, especially in Manjhi, Chapra, and Sonpur thanas in which an unusual density of more than 1,000 persons per square mile had been reached by 1891. Thus, between 1891 and 1901 the density of population in Manjhi decreased from 1,077 persons per square mile to 1,051 persons per square mile, in Chapra it decreased from 1,075 persons per square mile to 994 persons per square mile, and in Sonpur it decreased from 1,087 persons per square mile to only 921 persons per square mile. It is true that the ravages of plague have contributed to this heavy decrease of population. But it must not be forgotten that the increasing pressure of the population on the soil had been checked as early as the decade ending in 1891.[1] Moreover, the fact that there was over-population in this sub-division due to the scarcity of agricultural land is indicated by the extent of steady emigration, particularly from Chapra, Manjhi and Sonpur thanas, during the decade ending in 1891. During this decade the proportion of females to males was highest in this sub-division; in Manjhi there were 127·58 females to every 100 males, in Chapra there were 120·66 females to every 100 males and in Sonpur there were 133·12 females to every 100 males. Such disproportion shows clearly the extent of emigration, at least half of which was of a permanent character. The rent rates prevailing in this sub-division were high. Even in 1901 they were higher than the district average of Rs.4–5 as.–4 p. per

[1] Plague in an epidemic form first made its appearance in 1900.

acre, in Sonpur and Chapra the rates being more than Rs.5–6 as. per acre. It is certain that such high rent-rates have driven out people to adjoining tracts where the rent-rates are lower and the land is not much inferior.

The northern parganas of Saran which are situated at a distance from the Ganges were formerly more sparsely populated than the Sadar sub-division. Here the rent-rates were lower and the natural conditions were not favourable to the growth of population. But the agricultural development of these tracts depended upon artificial irrigation, and it is likely that the expansion of cultivation and the increase of population in these tracts were due to well-irrigation which was extensively begun in the closing decades of the last century. The northern parganas depend less upon *Aghani* rice, which is likely to be a poor crop when there is a failure of rains, and more upon the *Bhadoi* and the *rabi* crops. So it appears that the agricultural security enjoyed by these parganas will also enable them to maintain a higher density of population.[1]

CHAMPARAN

The course of agricultural development in Champaran, which is one of the most sparsely populated districts in North Bihar, provides an interesting contrast to what we observe in Saran. In Saran the land has been extensively cultivated from comparatively early times, the limit to the extension of cultivation and the growth of population has been reached early, and over-population due to the scarcity of cultivable land has been relieved by emigration. In Champaran, on the other hand, the density of population has been quite low even in recent times, extensive tracts of land have long waited for the advent of the plough, and the fertile virgin soil has attracted immigrants from the over-populated tracts both within the district and outside it.[2] From 1793 to the Revenue Survey of 1845 agricultural development in this district was

---

[1] The cultivated area in Saran has increased by 14,000 acres since the last settlement, the increase being noticeable in Mirganj and Siwan, the northern parganas.

[2] The pioneers of cultivation in this tract are the Tharus, a very hardy community of farmers.

very rapid. In 1794 the collector of the district reported that 'Champaran is not above a quarter cultivated'. In 1801 it was said that 'where 60 bighas in 100 were in cultivation formerly, 80 or more are now in that state'. About 50 years later Mr. Wyatt, the Revenue Surveyor, observed that whereas the pargana of Majhawa (which covered the greater portion of the district) had been covered with forest, they were at the time of the survey inhabited and 'under beautiful cultivation'. After 1850 the expansion of cultivation was less rapid but was still considerable. In fact, there was still great scope for the extension of cultivation as late as the closing years of the last century. Thus, during the settlement operations of 1892–9 it was found that the percentages of areas recorded as new fallow and old fallow respectively were still high; 3 per cent of the cultivated area in the district, as a whole, was given rest every year, as against barely 1 per cent in the neighbouring over-populated districts of Saran and Muzaffarpur. In the thinly populated northern portion of the district (Bettiah sub-division) the proportion was as high as 4 per cent. The reason why such large areas were kept fallow every year was that the farmers had plenty of land at their disposal, and not that the land required rest. The land recorded as old fallow covered as much as 12 per cent. In Bagaha and Shikarpur (which are still thinly populated and await agricultural development) the proportions were 20 per cent and 15 per cent respectively. Such land was utilized for grazing purposes by migratory herdsmen from over-populated regions. On the whole, between 1874 and 1907 the cultivated area in this district had increased from 67 to 70 per cent, and at the census of 1921 it was found to be 78·3 per cent of the total area. And it is significant that the density of population during this period also increased from 408 persons per square mile to 550 persons per square mile. But even in 1931, while the population was 25 per cent larger than it had been in 1881, there was still room for expansion, particularly in the north-west, where there is a considerable area of grass land at the foot of the hills.

The relation between the extension of cultivation and the density of population is strikingly illustrated in the case of the different agricultural tracts within the district. Generally speaking, the river Sikrana, flowing in a south-easterly direction through the centre of the district, divides it into two characteristic agricultural tracts. The soil of the northern tract is mainly clay, and is especially adapted for rice cultivation. In fact, some of the richest soil in the district is found in this tract. Moreover, it receives a heavier rainfall than the southern tract. Thus, in so far as the natural conditions favour the cultivation of a heavy-yielding crop like rice, the density of population ought to be high.[1] But this region contains a good deal of unreclaimed land and still awaits agricultural development which, though sufficiently rapid in recent times, is still far from complete, the main reason being its insalubrious climate. During the decade 1911–21 there was a great increase of population in Bagaha thana which was ascribed to the increase in the area irrigated from the Tribeni Canal from twenty to ninety-two thousand acres since 1911. But fever, which is endemic in this tract, militates against the increase of population. In fact, as Mr. P. C. Tallents observes in the *Census Report of 1931*, 'the expectation that cultivation would be extended in these tracts has not yet been realized, apparently because of their unhealthiness.'[2] In the southern tract the soil is lighter and grows millets, cereals and oil-seeds. It is in this tract that agricultural enterprise has been active from early times, and consequently it maintains a high density of population. For example, in Adapur, Dhaka and Madhuban, where the cultivated area is over 80 per cent, the density is the highest in the district, viz. over 800 persons per square mile. 'The maximum density (962) occurs in Dhaka revenue thana, where the soil, extremely fertile in itself, is rendered still more productive by a small but valuable system of canals.'[3] In Motihari and Govindganj, where agricultural development has been hampered by the lightness of the soil, and barely 70 per cent of the total area has been brought under cultivation, the density of population is about 750 persons per square mile or even less,

---

[1] It must, however, be noted that a tract which depends exclusively on the single rice crop becomes especially liable to famine. This question is discussed below and also in the last chapter of Pt. II.

[2] *Census Report*, 1931, p. 20.   [3] Ibid., p. 20.

and the rent-rates are also correspondingly lower. In the rice-growing tracts of the north, where, as already said, agricultural development has not been complete, the proportion of the cultivated area was barely 60 per cent towards the close of the last century, and the density of population was also not more than 322 persons per square mile.

As already explained, the natural conditions prevailing in the northern tract are very favourable to the growth of population. As a matter of fact, the trend of agricultural development in recent times has been the extension of cultivation in this tract, the remarkable fertility of which has been attracting a regular stream of immigrants. It is no doubt true that many enterprising immigrants from the neighbouring over-populated districts have been attracted naturally to the easily accessible and more healthy centres of dense population in the southern tract.[1] But the main trend of the migration of surplus population is towards the north. Thus, between 1881 and 1891 in Shikarpur and Bagaha, the sparsely populated parganas of the northern tract, the population increased by 15·2 and 9·4 per cent respectively when the average increase in the district as a whole was only 8·1 per cent. It is remarkable that even during the decade ending in 1911 the population increased by 12·80 per cent in Shikarpur, while the average increase in the district as a whole was only 6·59 per cent. As a matter of fact, within recent times 'a wave of agricultural enterprise starting from the southerly thanas has flowed northwards through the thanas of Dhaka and Adapur drawn by the extraordinary fertility of the soil. Having covered most of this tract it is now spreading to Shikarpur thana.'[2] Those portions of the southern tract which suffer from a light inferior

[1] There are several reasons why Champaran has been attracting immigrants from the neighbouring districts. 'In Champaran the incidence of rent is much less than it is in Muzaffarpur and Darbhanga and less than half of what it is in Saran. There has also been a tendency for land to pass from the possession of landlords into the holdings of the raiyats, while its money value has about doubled. Trade has developed greatly; the proportion of land under the more valuable crops, rice and sugar-cane has increased and so also, thanks to the extension of irrigation, have the average outturn and the twice-cropped area.' (*Census Report*, 1921, pp. 24–5.) There is no doubt that these favourable conditions will encourage immigration and agricultural development in this district in the immediate future.

[2] Stevenson Moore, *Survey and Settlement Report*.

soil have become decadent, because people have been migrating to the fertile tracts of the north, and it was pointed out in the *Census Report of 1921* that in Khesariya, Motihari and Govindaganj where the soil is light and sandy, there has been a large contraction of the cultivated area owing to emigration. But it must not be forgotten that the northern tract has also attracted numerous immigrants from the neighbouring over-populated districts. Apart from the stream of emigration which is flowing northwards within the district, another stream has flowed regularly eastwards from the congested districts of Saran and Gorakhpur and has spread over the thinly settled Bagaha thana situated in the north-west of the district.

MUZAFFARPUR

In the neighbouring district of Muzaffarpur we observe all the signs of over-population due to the scarcity of cultivable land. As in Champaran, so also in this district, agricultural development began in comparatively recent times; but while it is far from complete in Champaran, it has reached its limit in Muzaffarpur. The extension of cultivation and the consequent growth of population in this district have been very rapid, and the final limit to further expansion of cultivation has been reached in the course of a little over a hundred years. It is on record that in 1783 the Collector of Tirhut propounded a project for attracting cultivators from the dominions of the Wazir of Oudh to reclaim the unpeopled wastes of his district. About 1850 Mr. Wyatt, the Revenue Surveyor, found that a large part of the district was under careful cultivation, the density of population being roughly 320 persons to the square mile. By 1872 a considerable proportion of the total area had been brought under cultivation, and the density of population as recorded by the census of that year was as high as 765 persons to the square mile. After 1872 the increase of population was less rapid. The density of population was 867 persons to the square mile in 1881, and then it rose to 906 persons to the square mile in 1891. But the possibilities of further extension of cultivation had been definitely

exhausted by this time.[1] In 1891 it was found that 80 per cent
of the total area had already been brought under cultivation
(in the northern parganas the cultivated area was more than
80 per cent). If we add to this 4 per cent which was under
mango groves, and make allowance for 10 per cent of the total
area which is unfit for cultivation, it is easily seen that there
was little or no room for the extension of cultivation. The
area recorded as current fallow was only ·87 per cent, which
shows that hardly one acre out of every hundred was given
rest for even a single year. Thus, the cultivable land, apart
from the area under mango groves, amounted to less than
6 per cent. This land was absolutely necessary for pasturage.
But such was the extreme pressure of the population upon
the soil that there was an encroachment even upon this area
as well as the mango groves. Thus, in the uplands of the
Hajipur sub-division, which maintained as many as 1,251
persons per square mile of cultivated land, the only available
grazing grounds were the boundary *ails* of fields and sides of
village roads. Moreover, during the settlement operations of
1892–9 an Assistant Settlement Officer reported that 'should
the mango crop be a poor one for two or three seasons in
succession (and this usually happens) they proceed to fell
the offending trees'. It is obvious that these were distinct
signs of over-population due to the scarcity of cultivable
land. As a matter of fact, agricultural development by means
of extension of cultivation had already reached its limit by
1891. Between 1891 and 1921 the cultivated area increased
by only 1·5 per cent, and it is highly significant that while
the density of population was 906 persons to the square mile
as early as 1891, it was only 907 persons to the square mile as
late as 1921.

During the decade 1921–31 there was only a slight increase
in the cultivated area, the net cultivated area having increased from 81·5 per cent of the cultivable area to 82·2 per
cent of the cultivable area. But the density of population

---

[1] The census of 1891 showed an increase of 5 per cent over the population
of 1881. In the adjoining districts of Durbhanga and Champaran the increase
was greater, the figures being 6·4 and 7·09 per cent respectively. But both
these districts were less developed agriculturally than Muzaffarpur. In the
former only 70 per cent of the total area was found to be under cultivation;
whereas the cultivated area in Muzaffarpur was 80 per cent.

increased from 907 persons per square mile to 969 persons per square mile. It is no doubt true that 'the cultivation of sugar-cane was considerably extended and proved to be very profitable,' and thus increased the agricultural productivity of the district. Moreover, as the vital statistics show, the 'balance of migration is still in the outward direction,' so that the district lost a portion of its surplus population in this manner.[1] Nevertheless, the increase of population during the last decade has created an alarming economic situation full of dangerous possibilities.

It is interesting to observe the course of agricultural development in the different agricultural tracts of this district. The river Baghmati, which runs across the centre of the district, divides it into two distinct agricultural tracts with their characteristic natural conditions and systems of farming. The country to the south of the river (which embraces the Hajipur sub-division and a large part of the headquarters sub-division) borders on the river Ganges, contains a large block of upland and is the richest and most fertile portion of the district. Here the characteristic crops are the *rabi* and the *bhadoi* crops. The extent of heavy rice land is the least. Cultivation is consequently intensive, the holdings are small and rent-rates are high. The country to the north of the Baghmati is a marshy plain fertilized by numerous streams. Here people depend mainly on *aghani* rice, the holdings are large and rent-rates are lower. Owing to the bounty of nature there is little attempt at intensive farming, and the crops raised are cheap heavy-yielding food crops. This difference in the nature of farming explains why the southern tract can maintain more people per acre of cultivated land than the northern tract. In fact, in 1891 while the density of population was 1,251 persons per acre of cultivated land in the Hajipur sub-division, it was 1,089 persons per acre of cultivated land in the Sitamarhi sub-division. But it must also be noted that the extension of cultivation has been less in the south than in the north, not only because the extent of un-cultivable area is larger in the southern tract, but also because of the very nature of farming in this portion of the district.

[1] *Census Report, Bihar and Orissa*, 1931, pp. 22 and 23.

As already said, the extension of cultivation in this district has been complete in the course of a little over a hundred years. It is a striking fact that, as in Champaran, cultivation has extended mainly in the marshy plain of the north, where the fertility of the soil and the opportunities for the cultivation of rice and other heavy-yielding food grains have attracted a regular stream of immigrants from the over-populated southern tract as well as from the neighbouring congested districts. The southern tract bordering on the Ganges was the oldest centre of population. As early as 1788 it was highly cultivated, while there was much room for the expansion of tillage towards the north. By the closing years of the last century it was found that in the three northern thanas the proportion of cultivated area had become more than 80 per cent. Indeed, in Sitamarhi, the northernmost thana, the proportion was as high as 86 per cent. Thus it appears that the growth of population in the southern tract was arrested at an early date, while there was a rapid increase of population in the virgin lands of the north. We have no statistics of population for decades preceding 1872. At any rate, after 1872 the population of the Sitamarhi sub-division (the northern tract) increased by as much as 6·73 per cent, and this increase is accounted for by immigrants. At the census of 1891 this sub-division showed the greatest increase of population, viz. 10·4 per cent, and the fact that males and females in this sub-division balanced one another very nearly proves that there was very little emigration from this tract. Indeed, the very large increase of the whole population raised 'a strong presumption of immigration into it'. In fact, the increase of population was due to immigration, many of the newcomers being Nepalis, but many also immigrating from the southern tract. In the Hajipur sub-division, on the other hand, we find a striking tendency to emigration. As early as 1891 there were nearly 100,000 more females than males in the whole district, and this was due to emigration from the south of the district, principally from Hajipur.

The most important effect of the variation in the distribution and movement of population which we have just described has been a shifting of the centre of population.

'From 1881 to 1921 the centre of population shifted persistently towards the north. This process was carried so far that when the 1921 census was taken the total population of the Hajipur sub-division was found to be less by about 75,000 than it had been forty years previously, whereas during the same period the total population of the Sitamarhi sub-division had increased by 214,000.'[1] But it should be noted in this connexion that it is doubtful whether the continuous emigration of people from the overcrowded tracts of the south to the marshy lands of the north is altogether an economic advantage. It is true, no doubt, that there has been great agricultural development as a result of extension of cultivation into the virgin lands of the north, the farmers having been lured by the low rent-rates prevailing there. But by settling there they have exposed themselves to the danger of depending exclusively on the single rice crop which is liable to be destroyed by severe floods. On the other hand, in the southern tract not only is the danger of floods less, but the variety of crops also affords greater agricultural security. Thus it appears that the northward drift of the population in this as well as in the neighbouring districts cannot be viewed with equanimity, in spite of the fact that it has relieved the pressure of the population upon the soil.

DARBHANGA

Darbhanga, with a density of 946 persons per square mile, comes next to Muzaffarpur in order of density. As in Muzaffarpur, so also in Darbhanga, the limit to further extension of cultivation and the consequent growth of population was reached by the closing years of the last century. In fact, the full agricultural development of the district from the point of view of the extension of cultivation was completed in the course of the last century. In the early part of the nineteenth century a very large portion of the district, amounting probably to one-half of the total area, and in the north certainly to more than one-half, was uncultivated. By 1840 the cultivated area had increased to three-fifths of the total area,

---

[1] *Census Report, Bihar and Orissa*, 1931, p. 22.

but in the north the uncultivated area was still more than one-half. During the next decade the cultivated area appears to have increased rapidly, and in 1850 it amounted probably to nearly three-quarters of the total area. In 1875 it was estimated by Mr. A. P. Macdonell to be as high as 79 per cent, and towards the close of the century the proportion was just below 80 per cent. Thus, the cultivated area nearly doubled itself during the nineteenth century, and the greater part of the increase took place in the first half of the century. The whole cultivated area had been distributed more or less evenly over the different portions of the district. The proportion of uncultivated land is higher in the north and the middle of the district than in the south; but this difference is due to the existence of swamps and marshes in the middle and in the north of the district which remain waterlogged for the greater part of the year. In fact, the district had already become over-populated due to the scarcity of cultivable land as early as the beginning of the present century. With 80 per cent of the total area under cultivation, and with 9 per cent recorded as uncultivable land, the area available for cultivation was barely 11 per cent, most of which was land impregnated with saline efflorescence which could grow nothing except long grass, and was the minimum necessary for the needs of pasture. The density per square mile of cultivated area had also reached a very high figure. In the district as a whole there were 849 persons per square mile of cultivated area. Indeed, in the southern sub-division of Samastipur a square mile of cultivated area had to support as many as 1,000 persons. In view of these facts it is not surprising that, as in Mazaffarpur, the population in this district was practically the same in 1921 as it had been in 1901.

During the decade 1921–31 the population of this district increased by 8·67 per cent, while the net cultivated area increased from 85·7 per cent of the cultivable area to 87·6 per cent of the cultivable area. In the *Census Report of 1921* Mr. P. C. Tallents, I.C.S., commenting on the economic situation in Muzaffarpur and Darbhanga observed, 'The population is predominantly agricultural and is likely to remain so, for there is no mineral wealth to attract any industry unconnected with agriculture. In these circumstances it is impossible to suppose that an increase of population is either likely or desirable.'[1] During the decade 1921–31 the slight increase in the cultivated area and the development of the sugar industry must have relieved to a small extent the increasing pressure on the soil. But considering the fact that there was no outward migration of surplus population during this decade, an increase of population by 8·67 per cent seems to have created an impossible economic situation. In fact, one would have no hesitation in agreeing with Mr. W. G. Lacey, I.C.S., when he says that 'it is difficult to view without some apprehension the probable course of events in North Bihar and particularly in Tirhut, in the near future'.[2]

The analogy between the agricultural development in Darbhanga and that in Muzaffarpur becomes all the more striking when we consider the tendency for the centre of the population to be shifted to the north. The northern tract covers a low marshy plain watered by numerous streams, which depends mainly upon the cultivation of winter rice, In the southern tract, on the other hand, there are rich uplands, where the cultivation is more intensive and more valuable crops are grown. It is this difference in the nature of farming which explains why in Samastipur sub-division (lying in the southern tract) a square mile of cultivated area was able to support 1,000 persons in 1901, whereas in the Sadar and the Madhubani sub-divisions (lying in the northern tract) the density was barely about 810 persons to the square mile of cultivated area. Moreover, it is the difference in the natural conditions under which agriculture is practised which also explains why the area recorded as current fallow was larger in the south than in the north. In the uplands of the south it is necessary to keep lands fallow for a season. But in the rice tracts of the north nobody would think of keeping land fallow in a year of good rainfall. Moreover, rice-lands positively deteriorate when left uncultivated. When left fallow they 'are baked and hardened, the *ails* and partitions between fields become broken, and the drains by which the land was irrigated get filled up or obliterated. The cost of

---

[1] *Census Report, Bihar and Orissa*, 1921, p. 33.   [2] Ibid., 1931, p. 31.

9

cultivating such lands is, therefore, large, and the raiyats will not pay anything like the original rent for it.'[1] But it must be remembered that nature is more bountiful in the north than in the south. The soil of the northern tract is extraordinarily fertile and favours the cultivation of a heavy-yielding crop like rice. The natural conditions, therefore, are not unfavourable to the growth of population (although this tract is liable to famine when the rains fail, because people depend too much on the winter rice crop). In fact, it is in the northern tract which has long been very sparsely populated that cultivation has extended so largely during the last century, and it is this tract which has attracted immigrants from the congested localities. On the other hand, in the southern tract, which has long been a centre of dense population, the growth of population has been arrested at a comparatively early date. Thus, in Samastipur the growth of population was suddenly arrested during the decade ending in 1891. During the next decade there was a recovery, but in 1901 the population was less than what it had been in 1881. Later enumerations show a progressive decrease in the density of population. In the Madhubani sub-division, on the other hand, the population increased very rapidly during the decade 1881–91. It continued to increase during the next decade, although the rate of increase fell from 12 to 7·85 per cent. During the next two decades the net increase was as much as 6·43 per cent, in spite of the fact that the population of the district, as a whole, remained practically stationary. These movements of population are such that their significance is not obscured by the short-period effects of epidemic diseases or famines. In Madhubani, for example, the reported death-rates during many years prior to the census of 1901 had been higher than in other parts of the district, and it had also suffered most seriously during the famine of 1897; but still, as already pointed out, the census of 1901 revealed a very large increase of population. These facts illustrate clearly the predominant influence of agricultural factors upon the density of population.

[1] Finucane, *Final Report of Alapur Settlement.*

BHAGALPUR

In the district of Bhagalpur the population has, on the whole, remained stationary since the closing decade of the last century, as in the over-populated districts of Muzaffarpur, Darbhanga and Saran. It is also a striking fact that in this district the immigrants had outnumbered the emigrants up to 1891; but since 1891 the situation has been reversed, and the emigrants have far outnumbered the immigrants throughout the successive decades. At first sight it seems surprising that the extension of cultivation should have been arrested in this district as early as the closing decade of the last century. In Muzaffarpur, Darbhanga, and Saran the limit to further expansion of cultivated area was reached so early because, as already said, more than 70 per cent of the cultivable area had already been under cultivation, and there was little room for further extension of cultivation. But in Bhagalpur the cultivated area was barely 64·7 per cent of the cultivable area in 1921 and 64·2 per cent as late as 1931. In fact, if we leave out Purnea the extension of cultivation in Bhagalpur would be found to be the least in the whole of North Bihar. In 1901 the area recorded as cultivable waste other than fallow had been 396,827 acres, and even as late as 1931 this area remained practically undiminished—a fact which shows that Bhagalpur, with such a large area of cultivable land, has reached a decadent state, in spite of the fact that the mean density is barely 529 persons to the square mile.

The obvious explanation of such a curious phenomenon is that the natural conditions in the district as a whole are such as to hamper the extension of cultivation and the consequent growth of population. Let us consider this point a little more closely. The river Ganges, which flows through the middle of the district, divides it into two distinct agricultural tracts. The portion of the district north of the Ganges forms an eastward continuation of the great alluvial plain of Tirhut as far as the limit of the Kosi floods. A large part of this tract is inundated during the rainy season by many rivers flowing out of the southern ranges of the Himalayas, as well as by the overflow of the Ganges over its northern bank. This tract, therefore, is a low-lying plain, which, except in years of unusually scanty rainfall, never requires artificial irrigation. A considerable portion of it has been brought under cultivation in comparatively recent times. At the revenue survey of 1846–50 Mr. Pemberton wrote that whereas at the time of the Permanent Settlement nearly two-thirds of this northern tract had been grass or tree jungle, by 1850 more than 80 per cent was under cultivation. But this tract is peculiarly liable to the floods of the Kosi and, to a smaller extent, of the Tiljuga.[1] It is cultivated in the intervals between the floods of these rivers, and cultivation has always shifted beyond the reach of these floods.[2] Practically the whole of North Bhagalpur is now a network of river beds, running parallel with one another from north to south; when the monsoon comes, it is sometimes one channel and sometimes another which carries the main stream of this incalculable river (Kosi).[3] The result has been that agricultural conditions here are extremely unstable and are obviously incompatible with the existence of a dense population. It is interesting to observe, however, that population has increased in this tract in very recent times wherever the conditions have been favourable to the extension of cultivation. In the Kishanganj thana, for example, the decrease of population was 7·5 per cent during 1881–91 and 6·9 per cent during 1891–1901, due to the fact that people had been moving north and deserting the water-logged areas subject to the ravages of the river Kosi. But by 1911 the population of this thana had increased by as much as 39·85 per cent because

[1] The peculiarity of the Kosi floods is that the flooded area is overlaid with sand which destroys the productive powers of the land.

[2] Thus the two north-eastern parganas, which in the beginning of the last century constituted one of the most fertile tracts of the sub-Himalayan region, lost considerable portions of their cultivated area in consequence of changes in the course of the Kosi river. 'Large tracts of land in thanas Doparkha, Pertabganj and Bhimnagar in the Supaul sub-division have, on account of the continuous shifting of the bed of the Kosi, been rendered useless by a deposit of sand from the river. Similarly some tracts in the Madhipura sub-division have lost their fertility from the same cause; *per contra* other tracts recently abandoned by the river have now become cultivable and very valuable owing to rich alluvial deposits.' (*Season and Crop Report*, 1914–15, p. 4).

[3] *Census Report, Bihar and Orissa*, 1931, p. 26.

the continued westward movement of the Kosi had permitted a large area of swamp and jungle to be brought under the plough. Similarly, the population of Bihpur thana also increased during the decade ending in 1911 by 14·55 per cent as a result of the extension of cultivation. At present Bangaon is the only thana in North Bhagalpur which is more or less secure against inundation from the Kosi, and this is why the rate of increase of population there during the decade 1921–31 was found to be the highest, viz. 13·20 per cent.

The portion of Bhagalpur south of the Ganges comprises, in addition to alluvium, various geological formations. Here the soil is less fertile than in the northern tract, and 36 per cent of the cultivated area depends on artificial irrigation. The proportion of uncultivable land is also high, and the land recorded as current fallow occupies a very large area, because the soil is poor and the uplands in the hilly area are cultivated only once in two or three years.[1] Thus, obviously the unfavourable natural conditions have hampered the extension of cultivation in this region, so that barely 56 per cent of the total area has been brought under the plough. Hence it is but natural that the density of population in the Banka sub-division in the south should be only 332 persons per square mile.

Thus, river floods in the north and the barren soil and the lack of artificial irrigation in the south are the greatest obstacles in the way of agricultural development in Bhagalpur, and we are not surprised when we find that while 90 per cent of the total area is said to be fit for cultivation only 60 per cent is actually cultivated in any one year. Moreover, as the statistics of cultivation show, 51·6 per cent of the total cultivated area is under rice, as against the average of 41·8 per cent in the whole of North Bihar, and this percentage is the highest in North Bihar except Purnea. The predominance of the rice crop, particularly in the south of the district, has increased economic insecurity, and a failure of rainfall always encourages emigration while it discourages immigration. For example, during the famine of 1919, which had been caused by the failure of rainfall in 1918, 200,000 persons

[1] Ibid., 1921, p. 33.

emigrated from the Banka sub-division in South Bhagalpur between the preliminary and final census enumerations.

PURNEA

The district of Purnea, which lies at the eastern extremity of North Bihar, is next to Champaran the most sparsely populated district in this region. Like Champaran it is a sub-montane tract in which the rainfall is plentiful, the soil is fertile and rent-rates are low. Consequently, like Champaran, it has also attracted a regular stream of immigrants from the over-populated districts of North Bihar. Indeed, it is immigration, and not the natural increase of population, which to a large extent accounts for the increase of population in the last sixty years. At present the immigrants form as much as 10 per cent of the population, and the majority of them have taken up their residence permanently in the district. But in this district cultivation has extended and the population has increased at a very slow pace. According to Buchanan Hamilton's estimate, 67·8 per cent of the total area was under cultivation as early as 1802. In fact, he was impressed by the density of population and the abundant harvest reaped, for he refers to 'the immense population by which the country is overwhelmed'. But during the survey and settlement operations of 1901–8 the proportion of cultivated area was still found to be only 66 per cent. It seems, therefore, that the cultivated area in Purnea during the last century as a whole has been more or less stationary. It is very likely that this was due to unstable agricultural conditions prevailing in the western portion of the district which suffered from the sudden changes in the course of the river Kosi. For example, Damdaha was the most fertile and densely populated portion of the district in the beginning of the last century. But since then it has suffered from the devastations of the Kosi, and by the closing years of the last century it was found to have partially relapsed into jungle. On the other hand, the Korha thana which consisted of waste land, and was covered with scrub jungle in the beginning of the last century, was found to have a density of 344 persons to the square mile in 1891.

But it must be noted that in spite of these unstable agricultural conditions, low rents and the fertile soil were attracting large numbers of immigrants. Between 1872 and 1881 the population of the district increased by 7·8 per cent; between 1881 and 1891 the increase was 5·1 per cent, and the growth was most rapid in the great pastoral thanas of Damdaha and Forbesgunj, which attracted numerous settlers from Bhagalpur, Monghyr, and Darbhanga, and added one-third and one-seventh respectively to their population. But during the next decade there was a severe set-back to agricultural development. Between 1881 and 1891 the density of population had increased from 370 persons to the square mile to 389 persons to the square mile; but during the next decade there was a heavy mortality due to general unhealthiness and two severe cholera epidemics, so that in 1901 the density was only 375 persons to the square mile. Thus, the fact seems to be that agricultural development of the district during the last century was hampered not only by the ravages of the Kosi, but also by the ravages of disease.

But since the beginning of this century agricultural development has resumed its upward tendency. Between 1901 and 1911 the population increased by 5·98 per cent. During the next decade the increase was 1·76 per cent, and the density rose to 405 persons to the square mile. Between 1921 and 1931 the population of the district increased by 8·16 per cent, and the density in 1931 was 440 persons to the square mile. During this decade immigration continued unabated. 'The testimony of the local officers is that since 1921 there has been a steady influx of settlers and persons in search of casual employment.'[1] The full significance of this tendency will be clear to us if we observe the course of agricultural development in the different agricultural tracts. The district may be divided into two portions by a line drawn diagonally from the north-west to the south-east, the country to the east being drained by the Mahananda and that to the west by the Kosi. In the east there is a fertile loamy soil of alluvial deposit which yields rich crops, chiefly rice and jute. The country is marshy and intersected by numerous streams.

[1] *Census Report, Bihar and Orissa*, 1931, p. 30.

The waterways have deteriorated, as in Bengal, and malaria has made its appearance. No jute was grown in this tract before 1867; but since then the cultivation of jute has increased and favoured the growth of a dense population. Consequently, in spite of diseases which levied a heavy toll upon the population between 1891 and 1901, the density in the Kishanganj sub-division was as high as 460 persons to the square mile in 1901, as compared with 826 persons to the square mile and 887 persons to the square mile respectively in the other agricultural tracts of the district. But there was a rapid agricultural deterioration in this tract during the succeeding decades, and the population decreased by 9·63 per cent between 1901 and 1921. The western portion of the district was, during the last century, subject to the ravages of the Kosi, which frequently changed its course and left behind sandy beds unfit for cultivation. There was consequently a large area of uncultivated land which spread out to the north and west, opening out occasionally into fine, grassy, prairie-like plains. Thus, some of the thanas in this tract were pastoral regions in which the density of population was necessarily low. But since the beginning of this century the river Kosi has moved westward and has now swung right across into Bhagalpur. The result has been that cultivation has extended in this tract, and the population has increased in consequence. 'The high grass jungle described in the report of 1891 has now become one of the most fertile and best cultivated areas in the district, and Damdaha is now with the exception of Katihar the most densely populated tract in the sub-division.'[1] In fact, in the Araria and the Sadar sub-divisions (which had been subject to the ravages of the Kosi) the population increased by 19 and 9·6 per cent respectively between 1901 and 1921. In the Damdaha thana (which had partially relapsed into jungle) the increase was as much as 58·23 per cent during the same period. This process of agricultural development continued even during the decade 1921–31. While the Kishenganj sub-division recorded a decrease of population by 0·03 per cent, the population increased by 12·76 per cent in the Araria sub-division,

[1] *Census Report, Bihar and Orissa*, 1921.

and by 10·64 per cent in the Sadar sub-division during this decade.

SOUTH BIHAR

We shall now study the course of agricultural development in South Bihar, which, on the whole, maintains a density of 565 persons per square mile as compared with the density of 696 persons to the square mile in North Bihar. As already pointed out, the lower density of population in South Bihar is due principally to the comparatively large area of uncultivable land. This region receives much less rainfall than North Bihar, and artificial irrigation is the mainstay of agriculture. It is likely that the development of irrigation will convert a good deal of uncultivable waste into cultivable land, as it has done in certain tracts; but under the present conditions only 78·4 per cent of the total area is fit for cultivation, while in North Bihar as much as 89·5 per cent of the total area is cultivable. The scope for extension of cultivation and the consequent growth of population is, therefore, less in South Bihar than in North Bihar.

PATNA

The district of Patna maintains a density of 898 persons to the square mile, as against the average density of only 565 persons to the square mile in South Bihar as a whole.[1] But while in South Bihar, as a whole, barely 57·6 per cent of the total area is cultivated, in Patna as much as 73·5 per cent of the total area is under cultivation. The proportion of cultivated area in Patna is no doubt distinctly less than what we find in the densely populated districts of North Bihar. But it is important to remember that 27·3 per cent of the cultivable area in this district bears more than one crop, as against 23·3 per cent in the whole of South Bihar. Even this figure is less than the corresponding figures for the densely populated districts of North Bihar; but it must be noted that most of the area recorded as double-cropped in Patna bears

[1] The density figure is swelled by the presence of a large urban population. If that is left out the density of rural population would be very much lower.

three or more crops. In 1921 the area recorded as current
fallow was unusually large, viz. about 19 per cent of the total
area, the cultivable waste other than fallow amounted to
about 3 per cent of the total area, and the uncultivable area
was as much as 14 per cent. But it is interesting to observe
that such a situation was reached after the district had lost
its population continuously since 1891. Towards the beginning of this century the extent of cultivated area had already
reached a high figure.[1] 1,686 square miles out of a total area
of 2,075 square miles, i.e. 81 per cent of the total area, had
been under cultivation, while the cultivable and the uncultivable areas had been the same as they were in 1921. The area
recorded as current fallow in the inland and the zamindari
estates had been rather more than 1 per cent, and in the
government Diara estates less than $\frac{1}{2}$ per cent. The cultivable area in the government estates had been 17 per cent
and in the zamindari estates barely $\frac{1}{4}$ per cent. In the district
as a whole nearly the entire area capable of cultivation had
already been brought under the plough and there was little
room for further extension of cultivation. The Bihar sub-
division had the largest area of uncultivated land in proportion to its size, viz. 207 square miles out of a total area of
791 square miles. But it must be remembered that in
Bihar a large tract was covered by the rocky Rajgir Hills,
and only 27 square miles were cultivable waste. These
facts clearly show that there had been intense pressure of
the population upon the soil towards the beginning of this
century.

As already said, Patna had been losing its population rather
heavily since the beginning of this century. Between 1872
and 1881 the density of population had increased from 754
persons to the square mile to 850 persons to the square mile;
between 1881 and 1891 it increased from 850 to 858, and after
that year it dropped to 786 in 1901, to 779 in 1911 and to
763 in 1921. This heavy decrease of population since 1901
has been attributed mainly to epidemic diseases.[2] During
the decade 1921–31, however, not only was the process of

---

[1] The high percentage of the area recorded as current fallow mentioned
above is due to the subsequent decrease in the cultivated area.
[2] Plague as an epidemic disease first broke out in 1900.

depopulation stopped, but there was also a remarkable re-covery. The population of the district at the end of this decade was found to have increased by 17·1 per cent. This figure has no doubt been swelled by the phenomenal increase of population in the city of Patna. But the statistics show a substantial increase of over 10 per cent in every single revenue thana.[1] In fact, it is remarkable that in the course of a single decade not only has the continuous loss of population since 1891 been made good, but there has also been a net increase of population as compared with the population in 1891. The cultivated area, which had steadily diminished as a result of depopulation, has increased during the decade 1921–31. At the present time, in point of the density of population Patna can compare favourably with the densely populated districts of North Bihar. But it is remarkable that in Patna the percentage of cultivable land is also almost as high as that in the densely populated districts of North Bihar. While about 91 per cent of the total area is cultivable in Saran, Muzaffarpur, and Darbhanga, as much as 88·1 per cent is cultivable in Patna. The extension of cultivation has also been compatible with such a high density of population. Whereas the percentage of the cultivable area which is actually cultivated is 76·9 per cent in Saran, 82·2 in Muzaffar-pur, and 87·6 in Darbhanga, it is as high as 83.4 per cent in Patna. The cultivated area, which had steadily diminished as a result of depopulation, has increased during the decade 1921–31, from 72·9 per cent of the cultivable area to as much as 83·4 per cent.

MONGHYR

The district of Monghyr comes next to Patna in order of the density of population. The mean density was 582 persons to the square mile in 1931. As Mr. P. C. Tallents observed in the *Census Report of 1921*, 'the variation in the population of Monghyr has throughout followed a very similar course to that of the adjoining district of Bhagalpur which it closely

---

[1] It must not be supposed that this figure represents the natural increase of population. Immigration must be regarded as an important factor, and 'Patna and Shahabad owed a substantial part of their gain in actual population to this factor'. (*Census Report, Bihar and Orissa*, 1931, p. 40).

resembles in physical characteristics'. We have seen that in Bhagalpur agricultural development by means of extension of cultivation was arrested as early as the closing decade of the last century, in spite of the fact that there was a large area of cultivable land which could be brought under the plough, and the explanation of such a curious phenomenon is that the natural conditions in the district as a whole have been such as to hamper the extension of cultivation. In Monghyr, also, we observe somewhat the same tendencies, because the physical characteristics are similar to those noted in the case of Bhagalpur. In Monghyr 80·6 per cent of the total area was cultivable in 1921, and only 73·4 per cent of the cultivable area was cultivated. It could by no means be said that the limit to further extension of cultivation had already been reached at an early date. But still the district seemed to be in a decadent state. Between 1881 and 1890 the population increased by 3·3 per cent, between 1891 and 1901 by 1·6 per cent, between 1901 and 1911 by 8·13 per cent, and between 1911 and 1921 it decreased by 4·92 per cent. Thus, the density of population in 1921 was practically the same as it had been in 1891. In Bhagalpur the immigrants outnumbered the emigrants up to 1891, and thereafter the emigrants have outnumbered the immigrants. But in Monghyr the number of immigrants has always been less and the number of emigrants always more than in Bhagalpur. The explanation of such decadent conditions lies not only in the fact that the population has been decimated by epidemic diseases, but also in the fact that the natural conditions in this district have been generally unfavourable to agriculture. More particularly the problem of agriculture in South Monghyr has been the problem of irrigation, and agricultural conditions there in recent times deteriorated owing to the neglect of the sources of irrigation, with the result that the growth of population was seriously checked. But it is interesting to note that the increase of population up to 1911, however small it might be, was accompanied by a good deal of agricultural enterprise in the shape of extension of cultivation. In North Monghyr cultivation extended over large areas in Pharkiya thana. About 1880 the Collector of the district had reported that 'the jungle lands conspicuous in the survey maps of Pharkiya are now very generally studded with fields of corn'. An idea of the agricultural development of this portion of the district may be gathered from the fact that while during the survey of 1845–50 only 35 per cent of the total area was found to have been cultivated, in 1909 as much as 64 per cent was under cultivation and was equal to four-fifths of the cultivable area. The extension of cultivation would have been much more had not this tract been liable to floods, owing to which cultivation was still in the hands of non-resident farmers. In South Monghyr also there had been similar extension of cultivation, although its scope was limited by unfavourable natural conditions. Thus, the construction of the Kharagpur reservoir had resulted in a considerable extension of cultivation in the north-east and in the north-west. All cultivable land there had practically been taken up except that at the foot of the hills. Much of the waste lying in the latter tract had also been cleared within the sixty years after the survey of 1845–50, and it was thought that this process had reached its limits.

Considering the present conditions, we find that during the decade 1921–31, like Patna, Monghyr recovered a good deal of the lost ground. Its population increased by 12·67 per cent during this decade. There was also a corresponding expansion of the cultivated area. The net cropped area was 58·2 per cent of the total area in 1931, as against 50·2 per cent in 1921. In fact, it is reported that fresh land is being constantly brought under cultivation in the Jamui sub-division. At present 80·5 per cent of the total area is regarded as cultivable, while only 72·3 per cent of the cultivable area is cultivated. It might appear that there is much scope for expansion of cultivation. But the unfavourable natural conditions prevailing in South Monghyr, where there is a good deal of cultivable waste, indicate that the scope for agricultural enterprise is really small.

Within the district we observe a close correspondence between the density of population and the extension of cultivation. The river Ganges, flowing through the district from west to east, divides it into two portions. The northern and smaller portion, which covers a little more than one-third of the entire area, is a flat alluvial plain which is highly fertile and grows rich *bhadoi* and *rabi* crops. The eastern portion of this tract is low-lying and swampy and liable to inundation; but a large portion of the land has been reclaimed and has attracted settlers from the southern tract as well as from adjacent localities. The western portion is a continuation of the fertile plain of Tirhut, and is 'almost entirely under cultivation'. Thus, in so far as cultivation has extended very far in the northern tract as a whole, it is natural that it should maintain a high density of population. As a matter of fact, in 1901 the average density in North Monghyr was as high as 966, and in the Begusarai sub-division it was 803. But, as in North Bihar the regions bordering on the Ganges, which have long been centres of dense population, have become decadent in recent times (e.g. the Samastipur sub-division in Durbhanga and the Hajipur sub-division in Muzaffarpur), so also the Begusarai and Teghra thanas in North Monghyr have been losing their population in recent times, because people are migrating to the adjacent regions where rent-rates are lower and agricultural conditions are not unfavourable.[1] The population of these two thanas decreased by more than 10 per cent between 1911 and 1921, and this heavy decrease was attributed in the *Census Report of 1921* to this familiar tendency which we have noted in the case of many other districts of Bihar.[2] The portion of the district south of the Ganges is, to a large extent, alluvial, but the general level is higher, the surface is more uneven and a large area is composed of hills and valleys covered with forest trees or scrub jungle. In this tract cultivation has extended very far in the alluvial tracts along the Ganges which are consequently more thickly populated. Here the density of population varies from 526 to 545 persons to the square mile. Further south there is a good deal of jungle and waste land which can, to a certain extent, be reclaimed. But the lack of

[1] 'For some years past there has been in this sub-division (Begusarai) a steady process of eviction of low-caste tenants by petty *maliks*, and it is probable that a number of these evicted tenants have found their way into Gogri thana in the Sadar sub-division where there has been an extension of cultivation'. (*Census Report*, 1921, p. 41).

[2] *Census Report, Bihar and Orissa*, 1921, p. 41.

facilities of irrigation has hampered the extension of cultivation. In fact the *tanr* lands, which used to grow *kulthi* and other pulses, have relapsed into jungle. Jungles on the banks of the streams can be cleared for the cultivation of rice; but the thin covering of the soil is washed away by rain into the beds of rivers, and the land loses its fertility. Thus, to the south of the alluvial tract running along the Ganges the density is much lower, and it is lowest in the extreme south where there is an abundance of waste land and jungle. It may, however, be noted that the Jamui thana in the extreme south is showing steady development in recent times as a result of extension of cultivation. Thus, the population there increased by 22·17 per cent between 1901 and 1911 (the average increase for the district being 3·13 per cent), and this was attributed to extension of cultivation.[1] The moribund condition of the southern tract as a whole is evidenced by steady migration, which is most active there because the infertility of the soil in a large part of the Jamui sub-division has forced people to seek employment elsewhere, particularly in the tea gardens of Assam.

During the decade 1921–31 the population of the Jamui sub-division increased by 18·10 per cent, as against 9·92 per cent in the Begusarai sub-division situated in North Monghyr. As already noted, there has been a steady extension of cultivation in this sub-division in recent years. Moreover, in the Jamui sub-division 'there is a fairly large proportion of aboriginals and low-caste labourers who would normally have sought employment away from home in mines, mills, docks, tea-gardens and the like, but were restrained from doing so by the industrial depression abroad and the comparatively easy conditions in their own district.'[2]

GAYA

The district of Gaya comes third in order of density amongst the four districts included in South Bihar. Here also the unfavourable natural conditions have hampered the extension

---

[1] *Census Report,* 1921, p. 40.
[2] *Census Report, Bihar and Orissa,* 1931, p. 39.

of cultivation and the consequent growth of population. The average annual rainfall is about 45 inches, no doubt, but owing to the peculiar position of the district it receives a full supply from neither monsoon, and the rainfall is frequently deficient, fitful, or untimely. Besides this, the nature of the soil, as well as the slope of the country, is such as to render the land peculiarly unretentive of moisture. The result is that the district depends for its agriculture on artificial irrigation. Moreover, it largely depends on a single crop of rice, while the other districts of the Middle Ganges Valley can rely to a greater extent on more than one crop. Lastly, the *rabi* crops are not quite of the same high standard as in Patna and other districts of North Bihar. In consequence of these unfavourable natural conditions cultivation has not extended very far. Only 60·1 per cent of the cultivable area has been brought under cultivation, as against 69·8 per cent in North Bihar and 74 per cent in South Bihar as a whole. There is also a large proportion of uncultivable land. Cultivable land amounts to 79·6 per cent of the total area, which is the lowest percentage to be found in the whole of Bihar, if we except Sahabad. All these facts clearly show why, next to Sahabad, Gaya is the most sparsely populated district in the entire Middle Ganges Valley and the density of population there is only 507 persons to the square mile.[1] The agricultural decadence of this district is indicated by the fact that the population has increased very slowly owing to emigration. It is true, no doubt, that the population has been decimated by disease; but the fundamental limiting factor of the growth of population is the unfavourable natural conditions which have hampered the extension of cultivation. In fact, there has been no great extension of cultivation in the last hundred years except in Arwal and Nawada in the north and in certain tracts in the south. Referring to Arwal, Buchanan Hamilton wrote in 1812 that 'a great portion is neglected, and where the soil is poor is chiefly overgrown with thorns of the stunted jungle. Where the waste land is rich, it is overgrown with harsh long grass, which in the dry season loses all vegetation.'

[1] Even as early as 1891 the density of population was 454 persons to the square mile.

The general aspect of this part of the country has been completely changed, as it includes some of the best rice-growing tracts in the district, and the barren waste has now been brought under cultivation. The Daudnagar sub-division (situated in the south) looked equally desolate, and referring to it Hamilton observed that 'this Division has been a good deal neglected and the poorer lands are in general waste. Some of the best land is even neglected, and is chiefly occupied by poor-looking woods of the *Palas*.' But now this sub-division is one of the most prosperous tracts in Gaya. In recent years cultivation has extended in Gaya owing mainly to canal irrigation. The normal cultivated area has increased from 1,728,006 acres in 1876 to 2,000,000 acres in 1921, and this increase has been attributed mainly to the extension of canal irrigation in the western portion of the district.

Within the district we find a close correspondence between density and the extension of cultivation. The district may be divided into two portions—the northern and the southern —with different physical characteristics. The northern portion consists of a flat alluvial plain protected from drought by a wonderful system of indigenous irrigation. Conse-quently it is more densely populated than the southern tract.[1] In fact, the density in the northern tract is twice as high as in the southern tract. The Jahanabad sub-division, situated in the northern tract, is the most highly cultivated and densely populated region in the district.[2] Arwal, one of the two thanas included in this sub-division, was formerly a desolate wilderness, but it has been transformed into the most densely populated area by canal irrigation. It has been attracting immigrants in large numbers, and between 1901 and 1911 its population increased by as much as 14·06 per cent. Similarly the Jahanabad thana added 7·28 per cent to its population between 1901 and 1911. The southern portion of the district is a region of 'broken undulating country merging into long ranges of hills with a wide belt of brush-wood at its base'. Much of this tract is high and barren and

---

[1] The northern tract was in very early times a civilized country, being a part of Magadha, the centre of Buddhism. The southern tract was peopled by the aborigines.

[2] In the Jahanabad thana the density is 786 persons to the square mile.

incapable of cultivation. It is not protected against drought
by irrigation and the soil yields poor and precarious crops.
Consequently the population is sparse and its density does
not rise to more than 300 persons to the square mile.

SAHABAD

The district of Sahabad is the most sparsely populated
district in the Middle Ganges Valley. At the census of 1931
the mean density of population was found to be 456 persons
to the square mile, as against a density of 507 persons to the
square mile in Gaya. In Gaya the percentage of cultivated
area was much lower, viz. 47·9 per cent, as against 59·9 per
cent in Sahabad. But what distinguishes Sahabad from other
districts of Bihar is not the lack of agricultural enterprise in
the way of extension of cultivation, but the very small scope
for such enterprise. In fact, cultivation in this district has
extended over 87·6 per cent of the cultivable area, and this
percentage exceeds even the North Bihar average of 69·8 per
cent. What has been a real hindrance to agricultural development is that the proportion of the cultivable area, which
amounts to 68·4 per cent of the total area, is the smallest to
be found in the entire Middle Ganges Valley. Thus, although
the density of population on total area is barely 456 persons
to the square mile the density calculated on cultivable area
only is as high as 667 persons to the square mile.[1] As a matter
of fact, a very high density has been reached wherever the
supply of cultivable land has been large and the extension of
cultivation has been favoured by the facilities of artificial
irrigation which is the mainstay of agriculture. Thus, there
has been a great extension of cultivation and the consequent
growth of population in the alluvial tract north of the Kaimpur Plateau. Even as late as the Mutiny the country round
Jagadishpur was covered with dense jungle. This jungle
covering an area of over 25,000 acres has been cleared, and

[1] Current fallow in Sahabad is about 3 per cent of the cultivated area which
indicates that the land suffers from over-cropping. Old fallow area is also
comparatively insignificant, and the figures of cultivable jungle do not suggest
that any considerable extension of cultivation is possible. (*Settlement Report,*
1907–16).

the land is now under cultivation and maintains a high density of population. More particularly as a result of the introduction of canal irrigation, arid wastes have been brought under cultivation and have attracted settlers. We can form an idea of the agricultural development of the canal-irrigated tracts by comparing the statistics of cultivation relating to the Piro, Bikramganj and Karghar thanas. In the Piro thana 62 per cent of the total area was cultivated in 1812; in 1909–11, 82·99 per cent of the total area was found to be under cultivation. In Bikramganj the proportion of cultivated area similarly increased from 53·6 per cent in 1812 to 82·54 per cent in 1909–11. In Karghar there was a similar increase from 70·8 to 82·02 per cent. It is interesting to observe that such a great agricultural development has favoured a great increase in the density of population. The population of the district, as a whole, increased by 14 per cent between 1872 and 1881, and by 5·7 per cent between 1881 and 1891. This increase was largely due to the extension of cultivation and the influx of immigrants caused by the opening of the Son canals, so that eventually the density of population has become very high in the northern tract as a whole. In fact, the Arrah thana, which is the most densely populated thana in the district, has a density of 875 persons to the square mile. In the southern tract, which covers the Kaimpur Plateau, the low density of population is due to the unfavourable natural conditions which have hampered the extension of cultivation. The greater part of this tract is unfit for cultivation because it is rocky and covered with forests. There are no facilities of irrigation. Cultivation is confined to lands in the immediate vicinity of the few villages which are scattered over the tableland, and it has extended barely to the well-watered fertile lands lying in the narrow valleys and depressions between the higher ridges. Thus, the southern tract is very sparsely cultivated and also thinly populated. In fact, the Bhabua thana, with a density of only 203 persons to the square mile, is the most sparsely populated tract in the whole of South Bihar.

SUMMARY OF CONCLUSIONS

Certain important conclusions emerge from the foregoing account of the course of agricultural development in the Middle Ganges Valley. The river Ganges, flowing through the middle of this region, divides it into two portions with distinct physical characteristics. It is these physical characteristics which determine the possibilities of extension of cultivation and the consequent growth of population. The northern portion includes the fertile, alluvial plain of Tirhut where the natural conditions are highly favourable to expansion of cultivation. Here the density of population has consequently reached a very high figure, and there is such an extreme pressure of the population upon the soil that barely one acre out of every hundred is given rest in any year, and there is an encroachment even upon the mango groves and the scanty reserve necessary for pasturage. In most of the tracts lying in the plains of Tirhut the growth of population reached its limit by the closing years of the last century. The extreme pressure upon the soil has been relieved by emigration, and it is interesting to observe that the tracts bordering on the Ganges which were the early centres of dense population have become decadent, and the centre of population has shifted to the rice-tracts of the north. It is only in the sub-montane districts of Champaran on the west and Purnea on the east that the density of population has been low, and there is still room for expansion of cultivation. In Champaran agricultural development began in comparatively recent times, and it is far from complete in spite of the fact that it has attracted very large numbers of immigrants from the congested localities lower down in the plains. In fact there is still room for expansion of cultivation and the consequent growth of population in the north-western portion of the district. In Purnea the ravages of the Kosi have hampered agricultural development; but since the beginning of this century the cultivated area has extended because the Kosi has swung westwards across Bhagalpur, and the population of the district has begun to show an upward tendency. On the other hand, in Bhagalpur the agricultural conditions in the northern portion of the district have been rendered extremely unstable by the floods of the rivers; while in the tract south of the Ganges the soil is of inferior fertility; irrigation is insufficient, and there is a large area of uncultivable land. The result has been that cultivation has not extended very far and the density of population has necessarily remained low.

The portion of the country south of the Ganges, which is called South Bihar, has, on the whole, a lower density of population than the northern portion. Here large areas are situated beyond the Gangetic alluvium and are covered with brushwood and jungle. The supply of cultivable land is consequently small. Moreover, agriculture in this region depends mainly on artificial irrigation. The northern tracts bordering on the Ganges are very thickly populated and extensively cultivated, because the land is more fertile and the facilities of irrigation are not lacking. Away from these alluvial tracts not only is the supply of cultivable land small, irrigation is also much more difficult. On the whole, the hindrance to the extension of cultivation and the consequent growth of population in South Bihar is not lack of agricultural enterprise, but the unfavourable physical conditions.

CHAPTER II

DOUBLE-CROPPING AND DENSITY

In this chapter we shall study the significance of the close correspondence between variations in the density of population and variations in the extent of double-cropping. As already said, in the Middle Ganges Valley the large extent of cultivable land and the rapid extension of cultivation have stimulated a remarkable growth of population, and consequently there has been such an extreme pressure of the population upon land that in certain localities barely 1 per cent of the cultivated area is allowed rest in any year. But we must also remember that in this region the physical conditions in respect of temperature and rainfall, which are characteristic of the monsoon regions, are such as to favour the completion of as many as three cycles of plant life in the course of a year, and that it has been found possible to reap two out of the three harvests off the same land in the same season by means of double-cropping. As we shall see presently, double-cropping of this kind contributes as much to agricultural productivity as to agricultural security (which is as much important in a monsoon region like the Middle Ganges Valley), and thus it constitutes one of the essential agricultural factors of the density of population.

It is necessary, first of all, to mark the statistical correspondence between variations in density and variations in the extent of double-cropping. Broadly speaking North Bihar which is more densely populated than South Bihar, has also a larger area which bears more than one crop. Muzaffarpur, the most densely populated district in North Bihar, had also the highest proportion of double-cropped area, viz. 64·8 per cent of the cultivable area; while Purnea, which is the most sparsely populated district, has the lowest percentage of double-cropped area, viz. 9·6 per cent of the cultivable area.

In South Bihar the highest percentage of double-cropped area (27·3 per cent) is found in Patna, which is also the most densely populated district; while the lowest percentage (20·2 per cent) is reached in Sahabad, which is also the most sparsely populated district.

In order to understand the significance of this correspondence between the density of population and double-cropping it is necessary to inquire into the various physical causes which determine the extent of double-cropping. This question has already been fully discussed in a previous chapter, but the main conclusions will bear repetition here. It is obvious that the *kharif* crops, viz. the *bhadoi* and the *aghani* crops in the Middle Ganges Valley, cannot be followed by a second crop of the rabi harvest unless there is sufficient moisture in the soil. Now whether there will be sufficient moisture in the soil depends upon the amount and the distribution of rainfall in a particular tract. In seasons of short rainfall, although double-cropping is possible with the help of artificial irrigation, yet there is always a considerable shrinkage in the double-cropped area. On the other hand, if the rainfall is excessive and the rivers rise and flood the countryside, the soil suffers from water-logging and over-saturation, and a second *rabi* crop after the *bhadoi* or the *aghani* cannot possibly be grown. Secondly, the sufficiency of moisture in the soil after the *kharif* season depends also on artificial irrigation, which is generally indispensable for double-cropping in regions which receive an annual rainfall of less than forty inches. Lastly, whether the land will retain sufficient moisture and will have sufficient plant food depends on the nature of the soil. Thus the *karail* soil has a wonderful power of retaining moisture long after the rainy season. Usually the conformation of the land should be such that it should be neither too high nor too low. If it is too high it will be dry and sandy and otherwise unretentive of moisture; if it is too low it will be water-logged and will be composed of stiff clay unfit to bear a second crop in the same season. Therefore the ordinary light *dhumat* soil which is found in the uplands of the Ganges Valley, and consists of a greater proportion of clay and a smaller proportion of sand, can derive the greatest advantage from a given rainfall and is an ideal soil for double-cropping.

There is, however, one important consideration which must be borne in mind when we examine the problem of double-cropping in the Middle Ganges Valley. The northern portion of this region receives an annual rainfall of more than 40 inches, and the country is inundated in normal years by various streams debouching from Nepal and by the overflow of the Ganges. What is disastrous to agriculture is not generally the deficiency in the total amount of rainfall, but its bad distribution. In fact, the rainfall which this region, as a whole, receives every year is sufficient to leave enough moisture in the soil for double-cropping. The winter rains, beginning from the *Hathiya* asterism in October and continuing at intervals throughout the cold season, are highly beneficial to the *rabi* crops and obviate the necessity of irrigating them by artificial means. It is only in South Bihar where the annual rainfall is less and natural conditions in respect of soil and drainage are unfavourable that artificial irrigation is the mainstay of agriculture, and extensive double-cropping is impossible without it.[1] Consequently, we find in this region a close correspondence between the extent of irrigated area and the extent of the double-cropped area. On the other hand, no such correlation can be traced in the case of North Bihar. Thus in South Bihar only 20·2 per cent of the cultivable area is double-cropped, while as much as 40·9 per cent of the gross cultivated area is irrigated; whereas in North Bihar as much as 80·2 per cent of the cultivable area is double-cropped, while the irrigated area is only 11·7 per cent of the gross cultivated area.

We have seen that if we compare North Bihar with South Bihar the density of population is found to vary directly as the extent of the double-cropped area. We shall now examine the significance of this tendency more thoroughly in the case of the different districts of North and South Bihar, with particular reference to the physical causes which determine the extent of double-cropping. The district of Saran occupies

[1] In fact there are tracts in South Bihar which receive an annual rainfall of less than 40 inches and in which agricultural conditions are similar to those prevailing in the dry regions of the Upper Ganges Valley.

the second place in order of density amongst the different districts of North Bihar, and it is remarkable that it occupies the second place in order of the extent of the double-cropped area, which covers 44·4 per cent of the cultivable area. Extensive double-cropping in this district is due to the presence of a large area of *bhat* land and the alluvial *diara* land. Both the *bhangar* soil, which is composed of stiff clay and bears a single crop of winter rice, and the *bhat* soil are found in regular proportions in the district as a whole. The *bhat* soil, which is the characteristic soil of the uplands situated between the swampy lands and the alluvial diara lands is composed of old alluvium and consists of a light sandy loam remote from the influence of the rivers. As a rule it grows two crops in a year, viz. winter rice which is followed by a spring crop of cereals, pulses, or oil-seeds. Double-cropping is also very common in the diara lands which correspond to *char* lands in Bengal.[1] Some of these lands are very fertile, producing fine *bhadoi* crops before the river rises and good *rabi* crops in winter (e.g. wheat, barley, peas, and mustard). The practice of double-cropping is also universal in what are called *goenr* land, i.e. the highly manured land surrounding the village sites on which maize and *china* are grown in the rainy season and are followed by valuable crops such as opium, wheat, vegetables, and condiments. It is interesting to note that the southern tract which is far more densely populated than the northern tract has also a much larger double-cropped area. For example, in the densely populated Sadar sub-division the average double-cropped area is 46 per cent; in Sonpur and Chapra thanas, which had reached a density of more than 1,000 persons to the square mile in 1891, the double-cropped areas were 57 per cent and 48 per cent respectively. On the other hand, in the Sadar sub-division, which is situated in the northern tract, the double-cropped area was, on the average, only 25 per cent. In Basantpur the small extent of the double-cropped area

[1] 'Some back-water or curve of the river sets up an eddy in the current which becomes sufficiently stationary to deposit a portion of the sand. This sand deposit rises and the water lying stagnant spreads a layer of clay and silt which deepens at every high flood. But if the growth is arrested by the river changing its course so that the formation of land stops at this stage then the land becomes sandy and barren.' *Gazetteer*, Saran.

is due to the fact that the soil is not suitable for the *rabi* crops. In Dirauli the small extent of the double-cropped area is due not only to the existence of extensive rice *chars*, but also to the extensive cultivation of sugar-cane, which requires a fallowing of land preparatory to the crop of a particular season and thus makes it impossible to grow a second crop in the same year.

In Champaran, as in Saran, extensive double-cropping is common on the *bhat* soil of the uplands which grows millets, pulses, cereals, oil-seeds and indigo, on the *bhabni* soil which grows rice and also maize, barley, gram, and other pulses and oil-seeds, and on the *dhobni* soil found in the southern portion of the district which produces spring crops after the autumn harvest. Double-cropped fields are also found in the *char* lands and in the *goenr* lands close to the village sites. Within the district the extent of double-cropping varies directly as the density of population. As already said, the river Sikrana divides Champaran into two well-defined agricultural tracts. The country to the north of this river is more sparsely populated than the country to the south of it, and the extent of the double-cropped area is smaller in the north than in the south. The northern tract is mainly a rice-growing region, and two-thirds of the area under rice is occupied by winter rice which is the only crop of the year except in very favourable seasons, when a catch-crop of coarse pulses ripening in spring may be sown broadcast among the stubble as a second crop. Only one-third of the area under rice is sown with early or *bhadoi* rice, and a second crop of oil-seed or pulse can generally be raised after it has been harvested. In the southern tract, on the other hand, the soil consists of fine light sand and clay which is admirably adapted for double-cropping when the land is neither so low as to get water-logged during the rains nor so high as to be unretentive of moisture. On such land the crops grown in the same season are maize and inferior millets harvested in September, wheat, barley, pulses, oil-seeds, and opium reaped in March and April, and *china* millet reaped in June. Where indigo is an important crop grown in the rainy season a second crop cannot be taken off the land in the same year. The spring crops on the higher lands are, with the exception of *arhar* pulse, generally poor, because the soil is sandy and retains little moisture during the dry season. On the whole, the extent of double-cropping is much greater in the southern tract which naturally maintains a higher density of population. In fact, it is significant that in Adapur, Dhaka and Madhuban where the density of population is more than 800 persons to the square mile the double-cropped areas are 57, 48 and 37 per cent respectively.[1]

Muzaffarpur, the most densely populated district in the whole of the Middle Ganges Valley, has the highest percentage of double-cropped area, viz. 55·3 per cent of the cultivable area. The river Baghmati divides this district into two distinct agricultural tracts. The tract to the north of this river is predominantly a rice-growing region, while in the tract to the south of it land is more fertile, cultivation more intensive, and the density of population higher. In the southern tract double-cropping is extensively practised on the *balsunderi* soil of the uplands. These uplands enjoy an immunity from the early floods, and consequently maize and marua which are very susceptible to excessive moisture constitute the two important crops of the *bhadoi* harvest. These crops (valuable crops themselves) are followed by valuable second crops like barley. In the upland tracts the holdings are smaller, and the reason why the Hajipur sub-division, for example, could maintain a density of 1,251 persons per square mile of cultivated area in 1891 is intensive cultivation in the shape of double-cropping. In the northern tract, on the other hand, the soil is either *bhangar* or *matyari* which is suitable for *aghani* rice. Here the second crops raised consist of cheaper food-grains such as gram and khesari. Linseed is also grown as a second crop after winter rice and is mixed with khesari and other *rabi* crops. In the northern tract holdings are larger and the population is sparse because it is not possible to raise valuable crops by practising intensive cultivation in the form of double-cropping.

The district of Darbhanga maintains a very high density of

[1] It must also be borne in mind that the economic importance of double-cropping is greater in the southern tract as it enables more valuable rabi crops to be raised and thus contributes more to agricultural prosperity. This aspect of the question will be considered in greater detail later on.

population, and the proportion of cultivated area to total area is the highest in the whole of the Middle Ganges Valley. But the remarkable features of agriculture in this district are the relatively small double-cropped area and the preponderance of the *aghani* harvest which covers 63 per cent of the cultivated area, four-fifths of the area under this harvest being occupied by winter rice.[1] In fact, the rice crop occupies a larger gross area and a larger proportion of the net cropped area than in any other district of the Patna division north of the Ganges, and it may be said that, except for a small area in the south Darbhanga, it relies mainly on winter rice. With the exception of the upland tracts of the south the rest of the district consists of a low-lying plain, intersected by numerous streams and marshes, and the lowlands especially in the north are fit for bearing a single crop of rice. The result is that in the district as a whole the extent of double-cropping is relatively small. The southern portion of the district is more densely populated than the northern portion. In the southern portion agricultural conditions are similar to those prevailing in South Muzaffarpur. Here double-cropping is very common on the *balsunderi* soil of the uplands. Owing to the immunity of this tract from early floods, maize and marua, the two valuable *bhadoi* crops are extensively grown, and these are followed by valuable *rabi* crops like wheat and barley. In fact, it is this sort of intensive cultivation which explains why the Samastipur sub-division could maintain as many as 1,000 persons per square mile of cultivated area in 1901. In the northern portion of Darbhanga, on the other hand, apart from the fact that single-cropped rice-lands are found in abundance, double-cropping is of small importance, because the crops grown consist of cheap *rabi* grains, such as khesari, gram, and oil-seeds which are raised as catch-crops on lands devoted to winter rice.

In Bhagalpur the growth of population has been checked, as we explained in the last chapter, by unfavourable natural conditions which have hampered the extension of cultivation so much that the proportion of cultivated area to total

[1] In 1931 the double-cropped area in Darbhanga was only 5·3 per cent of the cultivable area.

cultivable area in this district is the smallest in North Bihar if we leave out the sparsely populated district of Purnea. The same physical causes which have prevented expansion of cultivation have also prevented extensive double-cropping. Hence, with the exception of Purnea, Bhagalpur has the lowest percentage of double-cropped area in the whole of North Bihar. The correspondence between the density of population and the extent of the double-cropped area is also very close, because next to Purnea Bhagalpur is the most sparsely populated district in North Bihar.

The portion of Bhagalpur south of the Ganges is more sparsely populated than the portion north of it. In South Bhagalpur the land is less fertile and natural conditions less favourable for the cultivation of valuable crops by means of double-cropping. In this tract double-cropping is common on lands which are neither too high nor too low and are, therefore, fit for cultivation of winter rice. The soil of these lands is called *kharar* (a blackish soil which is sticky when wet and difficult to plough when dry) which is best suited for the growth of winter rice, and when the rice crop is reaped peas of various sorts, khesari, dal, gram, and linseeds, are sown broadcast in the mud before it dries up and good crops are frequently raised in this way at practically no cost beyond that of the seed. The lowlands subject to inundations are not much cultivated except in winter and spring. The better kinds of uplands in the south yield maize in the rainy season and a second crop of wheat or mustard in winter, while the less fertile ones are sown with millet in autumn and cannot yield second crops. On the whole, double-cropping is confined mostly to lands sown with winter rice, and the second crops consist of cheap catch-crops. In North Bhagalpur, on the other hand, winter rice is not of so much importance, and consequently the second crops grown after the *bhadoi* harvest consist of more valuable crops, so that extensive double-cropping can maintain a high density of population. As a matter of fact, in North Bhagalpur, which is a continuation of the fertile plain of Tirhut, double-cropping has an economic importance which can be compared to that in the densely populated districts of Tirhut. On the other hand, the economic importance of double-cropping in South Bhagalpur is as small as in the sparsely populated tracts of South Bihar, which it resembles in physical features.

The district of Purnea, which is the most sparsely populated district in North Bihar, has the smallest percentage of double-cropped area. Now the total cultivable area includes not only the net cropped area but also the area recorded as current fallow, and the percentage of double-cropped area is small because of the large extent of the area recorded as current fallow. The fact is that over a considerable area the soil is so poor that every few years the fields are left fallow and given rest for a number of years to regain their fertility. That the extent of intensive cultivation in the shape of double-cropping is small is also borne out by the fact that the average size of the holding in Purnea is four-fifths of an acre as against two-fifths of an acre in Muzaffarpur and Durbhanga. As already explained in the last chapter, in the north-western and the southern portions of the district the population has reached a high density in recent times because the ravages of the Kosi have ceased. The extent of the double-cropped area has also reached a high figure in these tracts. Thus, in the Araria sub-division 32 per cent of the cultivated area was recorded as double-cropped during the recent survey and settlement operations. In Forbesgunj and Raniganj the double-cropped area was more than 40 per cent. In the Sadar sub-division, which also contains very densely populated thanas, the average double-cropped area was as high as 38 per cent of the cultivated area. In Damdaha thana, which is now the most densely populated agricultural thana, the proportion was as high as 50 per cent, in Korha it was 40 per cent, in Kasba Amur it was 42 per cent, in Kodwa it was 44 per cent, and in Saifgunj 40 per cent. In some localities in this tract where the lands are very fertile an *aghani* crop and a *bhadoi* jute crop are raised from the same land. In the north-eastern portion of the district, on the other hand, the extent of double-cropping is much smaller, viz. 13 per cent of the cultivated area, and naturally the smaller double-cropped area coexists with a lower density of population.

Let us now turn to the different districts of South Bihar. As already said, South Bihar depends for its agriculture mainly on artificial irrigation, and we find a striking correlation between the extent of irrigated area and the extent of double-cropping in all the districts included in this region, except Monghyr, which receives a heavier rainfall (46·8 inches as against the South Bihar average of 43·5 inches) and in which the natural conditions are similar to those found in North Bihar. The following table will clearly illustrate this correspondence between irrigation and double-cropping in the different districts of South Bihar:

Districts	Mean Density	Double-cropped area (percentage to cultivable area)	Percentage of gross cultivated area irrigated[1]
Patna	898	27·3	51·5
Gaya	507	24·2	48·8
Sahabad . . .	456	20·2	35·6

The district of Patna, which is the most densely populated district in South Bihar, records the highest percentages of double-cropped and irrigated areas. The percentage of double-cropped area may not appear considerable in comparison with what we find in the thickly populated districts of Tirhut; but much of the land is valuable, yielding three or four crops in a year. The upland tract situated between the permanent bank of the Ganges and the low-lying tract to the south is the most densely populated portion of the district. Here particularly the land is very fertile and sometimes bears three or four crops in a year. Practically the whole of the upland tract south of the Ganges near Patna is twice-cropped, with the result that the proportion of double-cropped area to net cultivated area is in Phulwari thana 55 per cent and in Dinapur thana as much as 65 per cent. Moreover, there are rich *diara* lands formed in the bed of the Ganges, which grow *bhadoi* crops before the river rises and the *rabi* crops in winter, both yielding magnificent harvests. In the upland tract wells are most extensively utilized for the cultivation of *rabi* crops,

[1] Gross cultivated area = net cultivated area and double-cropped area.

and thus *do-fasli* irrigation is as important there as in the
Upper Ganges Valley. On the other hand, in the low-lying
tract to the south double-cropping is rendered difficult because
the clay soil does not retain moisture well and the slope from
south to north is such that the rain-water has a tendency to
run into the low *tal* lands when no measures are taken for its
artificial storage. The eastern portion of this tract covering
the Barh sub-division contains *tal* lands subject to annual
inundation from the rivers; but the *rabi* crops constitute the
main harvest and consequently double-cropping is of small
importance. Artificial sources of irrigation, such as reservoirs
and canals, which are meant mainly for the *kharif* crops, no
doubt supply water for the sowing of *rabi* crops; but the
growing *rabi* crops are not, as a rule, irrigated otherwise than
by wells, and it must be remembered that well irrigation is
less important in the lowland tract than in the upland tract
to the north.

The district of Gaya is 'largely a one-cropped district and
for its one crop depends mainly on artificial irrigation'.[1]
Apart from the fact that owing to the peculiar position of the
district the rains are frequently deficient, fitful, and untimely,
the general slope of the country and the nature of the soil
render the land unretentive of moisture as in the lowland
region of Patna. Hence in this district artificial irrigation is the
mainstay of agriculture, and the extent of double-cropping
depends on the facilities of artificial irrigation. The northern
portion of the district consists of an alluvial plain where there
are excellent facilities of artificial irrigation. The density of
population there is twice as high as in the southern tract, and
double-cropping is also much more extensive. For example, in
1918 while 50·6 per cent of the cultivated area was twice-
cropped in Arwal thana, 46·2 per cent in Jahanabad and 30
per cent in Daudnagar, the percentage of double-cropped area
in the southern tract was considerably less. The principal
rice-growing area is situated in the northern part of the
district. It is here also that we find the highest percentage
of double-cropped area, as the double-cropped land consists
mostly of rice-land sown broadcast with *rabi* crops, such as

[1] *Survey and Settlement Report*, E. L. Tanner, I.C.S., 1911–18.

khesari and linseed, before the rice crop is reaped.[1] Of course an exception is found in the case of the thana town Gaya, where extensive double-cropping is due to the presence of a large area of garden land. In the southern tract not only is the soil less fertile and generally unretentive of moisture, but the facilities of artificial irrigation also are smaller. Well irrigation which is so necessary for the growing *rabi* crops is rendered difficult by the rocky soil, and the low percentage of double-cropped area in this tract is due to the fact that irrigation is barely sufficient for the rice crop and cannot provide moisture for a second crop of gram or khesari. The contrast as regards the extent of double-cropping in relation to irrigation will be quite clear if we compare the figures for the Deo and the Tikari estates which typify the agricultural conditions of the southern and the northern tracts respectively. During the recent survey and settlement operations 87 per cent of the cultivated area in the Deo estate was found to be irrigated, while 11 per cent was twice-cropped; whereas in the Tikari estate 44 per cent was found to be irrigated and 81 per cent twice-cropped.

In the district of Sahabad also we find the same correspondence between the density of population and the extent of double-cropping. The country to the north of the Kaimur Plateau is more densely populated because of the greater fertility of the soil and the better facilities of artificial irrigation. With the exception of lands which remain under water for four months and are ploughed up as the water recedes, so that they bear single crops like wheat, barley, pulse, and other food-crops, the rest of the land in this tract grows rice which is followed by second crops in the same year. Double-cropping is common on the *karail* soil which prevails through the whole of the district west of the Arrah–Sasaram Road and north of the Grand Trunk Road; it is fairly retentive of moisture and bears rice as well as *rabi* crops such as wheat, linseed, lentils, and gram. South of the Grand Trunk Road there is a loamy soil called *doras* which is suited to double-cropping and bears rice as well as mustard and linseed. In this tract the facilities of artificial irrigation are better than

---

[1] These are, however, cheap catch-crops.

in the south. The extension of canal irrigation has led to a phenomenal increase in the cultivation of rice and in the extent of double-cropping. In the southern tract, on the other hand, the facilities of artificial irrigation are smaller, and consequently the double-cropped area is also much less extensive.

The district of Monghyr differs from other districts of South Bihar in so far as it receives a heavier rainfall and agricultural conditions prevailing in the northern portion of it are typical of North Bihar. In this district we do not find a correspondence between the extent of the irrigated area and the extent of double-cropping. In North Monghyr population is more dense than in South Monghyr, and the economic importance of double-cropping is also much greater, but only 2·6 per cent of the net cropped area is irrigated as against 41 per cent in South Monghyr. In North Monghyr the average density is 693 to the square mile. The most densely populated tracts are situated in the western uplands formed by the older alluvial deposits of the Ganges and the Burh Gandak. Thus the Begusarai thana supports 693 persons to the square mile. Here we find the same kind of extensive double-cropping as in the uplands of Hajipur and Samastipur in North Bihar. Thirty-six per cent of the net cropped area bears two crops. But the economic importance of double-cropping must be judged not only by the area which is twice-cropped but also by the value of the crops raised as second crops. In Teghra and Begusarai the second crops consist largely of valuable crops such as tobacco, chillies, wheat, and barley grown on highly manured lands which have already yielded a good crop of maize. In the eastern portion of North Monghyr which is liable to inundation and depends mainly on the *aghani* and the *rabi* harvests double-cropping is also extensive.[1] For example, in the Gogri thana 41 per cent of the net cropped area bears two crops. But the second crops grown here consist of cheap catch-crops like khesari, peas and kulthi. South Monghyr, on the other hand, depends mainly on *aghani* rice which is followed by cheap catch-crops. There are extensive areas of dry soil where agriculture depends upon precarious

[1] The marshy lands in this thana, however, produce only a rabi crop.

rainfall, and the available means of artificial irrigation are too scanty to permit of extensive double-cropping.

We shall now consider a very important question bearing on the relation between the density of population and double-cropping. How far may the extent of double-cropping be regarded as an index of agricultural prosperity? Is the economic importance of double-cropping to be judged merely by the extent of the double-cropped area? The obvious answer to this question is that the contribution of double-cropping to agricultural productivity and agricultural security varies in different localities according to the *nature* of the second crops raised, so that the economic importance of double-cropping depends not merely upon the area which bears more than one crop but also upon whether these second crops are valuable or not. In the Middle Ganges Valley the chief *aghani* crops are sown before the *bhadoi* crops are harvested, and similarly the chief *rabi* crops are sown before the *aghani* crops are reaped. Hence it is obvious that an *aghani* crop cannot usually be sown as a second crop after the *bhadoi* harvest. The second crops must necessarily be *rabi* crops grown after either the *bhadoi* or the *aghani* crops. Where *aghani* is the main crop the succeeding second crops consist of cheap catch-crops like khesari, gram, and linseed, because the important *rabi* crops are sown before the *aghani* crop is harvested. Hence it follows that the larger the area under the *aghani* harvest the smaller will be the contribution of double-cropping to agricultural productivity. On the other hand, where the *bhadoi* is an important harvest the second crops raised after it consist of valuable *rabi* crops sown towards the end of September or the beginning of October when the *aghani* crops are still in the fields. Hence we may say that the larger the area under the *bhadoi* crops the greater the contribution of double-cropping to agricultural productivity. Moreover, the second crops raised after a *bhadoi* crop such as rice supply the means of subsistence to the agriculturist when the *bhadoi* harvest is a failure due to early floods. When the *bhadoi* rice crop fails, the valuable second crops, grown with the help of favourable winter rains, enable the cultivators to tide over the economic crisis easily. But where the *aghani* is the main harvest the second crops cannot possibly be a source of relief because, on the one hand, these second crops will consist of cheap catch-crops and, on the other hand, if the *aghani* rice crop has failed for want of rain the succeeding second crops, such as gram and khesari, will be light even if rain falls subsequently. Hence our conclusion is that *the larger the area under the* bhadoi *crops, the greater the contribution of double-cropping to the agricultural security of a particular region.* Thus we can get a fair 'index' of the economic importance of double-cropping if we multiply the double-cropped area by the proportion which the area under the *bhadoi* crops bears to the area under the *aghani* crops.[1] Let us see how far there is a statistical correspondence between such an index and the density of population in some of the representative districts of North and South Bihar.

The district of Muzaffarpur typifies the agricultural conditions prevailing in the densely populated portion of Bihar north of the Ganges. We have seen that the agricultural tract situated to the south of the river Bagmati is more densely populated than that situated to the north of this river. It is interesting to note that the index of the contribution of double-cropping to agricultural productivity is higher in the case of the southern thanas than in the case of the northern thanas.

Southern Thanas	Index	Northern Thanas	Index
Katra	58	Shinar . . .	30
Muzaffarpur . .	44	Sitamarhi . . .	30
Paru	41·5	Pupri . . .	29
Hajipur . . .	54	Belsand . . .	31

In the northern thanas the *aghani* is the main harvest and we find high percentages of rabi and twice-cropped areas. Judged by the area twice-cropped, the economic importance of double-cropping would appear to be considerable; but it is

[1] $\dfrac{\text{Bhadoi area}}{\text{Aghani area}} \times$ double-cropped area will be the required index.

not actually so, because the second crops consist of cheap catch-crops. Double-cropping has a great economic importance in the uplands of the south where the *bhadoi* is the main harvest and the second crops are really valuable.[1]

In Darbhanga also the southern portion is more densely populated than the northern. It will be obvious from the following comparative table that the contribution of double-cropping to agricultural productivity and agricultural security is much greater in the south than in the north:

Northern Sub-Divisions	Index	Southern Sub-Divisions	Index
Madhubani	13[2]	Samastipur . .	28[2]
Sadar	14[2]		

If we were to judge the economic importance of double-cropping merely by the area twice-cropped it would be found to be much greater in the north than in the south. But the northern sub-division, being liable to inundation, depends mainly on *aghani* rice because the early floods are injurious to the *bhadoi* harvest. Consequently the second crops consist of the minor crops of the *rabi* harvest sown as catch-crops on the still-wet rice lands. In the uplands of the south, on the other hand, the *bhadoi* crops are very important, and are followed by valuable crops of the *rabi* harvest. As a matter of fact, the areas under the *bhadoi* and the *aghani* harvests are nearly equal there, and this indicates that double-cropping has a very great economic importance.

The same varying importance of double-cropping from south to north may be observed in the sub-montane district of Champaran. As in Muzaffarpur and Darbhanga, so also

[1] It may be noted that the area recorded as current fallow is larger in the south, because intensive cultivation in the shape of double-cropping which has real economic importance there is accompanied by intelligent methods of agriculture which demand that land should get occasional rest. In the northern tract, on the other hand, the question of leaving rice lands fallow does not arise because such lands deteriorate if left uncultivated and, moreover, because the annual deposit of silt left by inundation prevents the exhaustion of fertility.

[2] In the case of Darbhanga the indices are low in comparison with the indices for other districts of North Bihar. As explained above, this is due to the predominance of aghani rice and the comparatively small importance of the bhadoi harvest.

in Champaran the southern uplands are more densely populated than the rice-growing lowlands of the north, and the
economic importance of double-cropping is much greater in
the south than in the north. The following table will illustrate
this interesting tendency:

Northern Sub-Division	Index	Southern Sub-Divisions	Index
Bettiah . . .	88	Sadar . . .	57
		(Adapur . . .	77)
		(Dhaka . . .	65)

The index for south Champaran is strikingly higher than
the corresponding indices for the southern agricultural tracts
of Muzaffarpur and Darbhanga. But it must be remembered
that in South Champaran the greater part of the *bhadoi* area
is under autumn rice, the second crop after which is an inferior
crop; whereas in the southern portions of Darbhanga and
Muzaffarpur the *bhadoi* crops like maize are followed by
better varieties of *rabi* crops. This limitation does not,
however, affect the relative importance of double-cropping
in the south and in the north. The higher indices in the case
of Dhaka and Adapur clearly indicate that one of the reasons
why these thanas can maintain a density of more than 800
persons to the square mile is the remarkable economic
importance of the system of double-cropping.

Let us now consider the indices in the case of the eastern
sub-montane district of Purnea. As explained above, the
north-western and the southern portions of this district have
reached a higher density of population than the north-eastern
portion. The indices in the following table clearly show the
correspondence between the density of population and the
economic importance of double-cropping:

Sub-Divisions	Index
North-western . .	16
Southern . . .	27
North-eastern . .	7

An important point to be noted in this connection is that in Purnea the extent of the *bhadoi* area does not vary much from one tract to another. It is only the southern subdivision which depends much less on the *aghani* harvest. This means that the variations in these indices are predominantly due to the differences in the extent of double-cropping which, as we have seen, is much greater in the southern and the north-western tracts than in the eastern tract.

The districts of South Bihar may be sharply contrasted with those of North Bihar so far as the economic importance of double-cropping is concerned. What distinguishes South Bihar from North Bihar is the small area under the *bhadoi* crops as well as the small area bearing two crops in a year. Hence in the case of South Bihar the indices of the contribution of double-cropping to agricultural prosperity are low, not only because the twice-cropped areas are small, but also because the second crops of the season consist of cheap catch-crops owing to the comparative insignificance of the *bhadoi* harvest.

In Gaya, which is a typical district of South Bihar, only 6 per cent of the net cultivated area is under *bhadoi* crops, while barely 21 per cent is double-cropped. Consequently the index of the economic importance of double-cropping is very low. But within the district we find the same correspondence between the density of population and the economic importance of double-cropping. The northern portion of the district which consists of an alluvial plain is more densely populated than the southern portion, and it is interesting to note that the economic importance of double-cropping is also greater in the northern tracts than in the arid tracts to the south.

Some Northern Thanas	Index	Southern Thanas	Index
Arwal	6	Nabinagar[1] . .	1·6
Jahanabad . . .	7·8	Barahatti[2] ⎫ Shergatti ⎭ . .	2·3

[1] Situated in the extreme south-west.   [2] Situated in the south.

In the alluvial plain of the north it is possible to obtain cheap catch-crops after winter rice. Moreover, the extent of the double-cropped area is much larger than in the south. In the southern thanas, on the other hand, although the *bhadoi* area is very large yet the extent of double-cropping is very small owing to the deficiency of artificial irrigation, so that the corresponding indices are also very low. It is interesting to note that the index of the economic importance of double-cropping is as high as 33·6 in the case of the thana town Gaya, and this is due to extensive areas of garden land surrounding the city.

In Sahabad, the density of population in the rich and highly cultivated tract to the north is twice as high as in the arid and rocky tracts of the south. It is remarkable that the economic importance of double-cropping is also much greater in the northern than in the southern tract.

Northern Sub-Divisions	Index	Southern Sub-Divisions	Index
Buxar . . .	8·4	Sasaram . . .	6·1
(Dumron Thana .	11·7)	Bhabua . . .	6·3
Sadar . . .	9·0	(Bhabua Thana[2] .	5·0)
(Arrah Thana[1] . .	11·5)		

In the northern sub-divisions the *bhadoi* and the twice-cropped areas are both larger than in the southern sub-divisions. Rice is one of the most important crops of the *bhadoi* harvest and is followed by a valuable *rabi* crop like wheat, which is often sown together with barley or with gram, mustard, or linseed.

[1] The most densely populated thana.
[2] The least densely populated thana.

CHAPTER III

AGRICULTURAL WATER-SUPPLY AND DENSITY

THE Middle Ganges Valley, one of the early centres of dense population in India, constitutes a region of moderate rainfall, an 'intermediate zone', which, according to Brunhes, favours a high density of population. It is a region where the natural vegetation is monsoon forest in which the trees become leafless in hot weather. The rainfall varies from 40 inches in the west to just over 70 inches in the northern part of Purnea, the annual precipitation being less than in the very wet Delta region but more than in the dry Upper Ganges Plain. The climate is warm enough to enable many plants to complete their cycle of growth during the intervals of seasonal rainfall and floods. Numerous rivers and their tributaries flowing from Nepal carry large quantities of soluble substances and alluvium, and serve as sources of irrigation. But the activity of the rivers in relation to agricultural economy is far less important in the Middle Ganges Valley than in the Delta region. It is remarkable that in regard to the density of population this region maintains its intermediate character in the same way as from the meteorological point of view, it stands midway between the dry Upper Ganges Plain and the very wet Delta region. But what is still more significant is the striking correspondence between the variation in the density of population and the variation in the amount and distribution of rainfall within this region as indicated by the comparative table given below:[1]

Sub-Regions	Average total rainfall	Mean density per sq. mile	Average from March 1 to May 31	Average from June 1 to Sept. 30	Average from Oct. 1 to Nov. 30	Average from Dec. 1 to Feb. 28
North Bihar .	51·99	642	4·20	44·33	2·44	1·02
South Bihar .	44·81	502	2·16	38·71	2·49	1·45

[1] The figures are taken from the *Season and Crop Report, Bihar and Orissa,* 1932–3.

The figures given in this table reveal a striking co-variation between the amount of rainfall and the density of population. Let us note the climatic peculiarities of North and South Bihar to realize the full significance of this tendency. On the whole the range of temperature in the Middle Ganges Valley is less wide than in the Upper Ganges Plain; it is 68 degrees in the former as opposed to 75 degrees in the latter. The annual precipitation is also heavier. But within this region the conditions are different in the tracts north and south of the Ganges, South Bihar being subject to a more extreme climate accompanied by a smaller amount of rainfall. But the fact which is important in relation to agriculture is that North Bihar receives much more rainfall than South Bihar between March 1 and September 30, a period which covers not only the monsoon season but also the period of growth of summer crops. In fact the *bhadoi* harvest is of greater importance in North Bihar than in South Bihar, because the success of this harvest depends upon good rainfall in June and July which is essential for the ploughing operations and the preparation of seed-beds. On the whole, in North Bihar the total annual rainfall is distributed in such a way that as many as three cycles of plant-life can be completed in the course of a year. On the other hand, in South Bihar, although the *bhadoi* harvest supplements the other two harvests to a certain extent, yet the area under it is far less than in North Bihar, because South Bihar receives much less rain between June 1 and September 30, the period of growth of the *bhadoi* crops. But as regards the winter rains which are crucial for the *aghani* harvest and necessary also for the *rabi* harvest, North Bihar does not enjoy any natural advantages over South Bihar.

It must be remembered, however, that in North Bihar natural moisture is supplied not only by rainfall but also by the annual floods of the rivers flowing down the valley. In Muzaffarpur and Darbhanga the most marked characteristic of the river-system is that, owing to the deposit of silt carried down from Nepal, the rivers flow on ridges elevated above the surrounding country, and each pair of rivers thus encloses a shallow depression consisting of a series of lowlands leading into one another. These are first filled by local rainfall, and then the surface water passes off from one to another, until its flow is checked by some raised ground. Having no other course to take, it breaks into one of the nearest rivers at a point where the banks are low after the level of the stream has somewhat subsided.[1] It is in this way that the rivers serve as drainage channels although they flow on raised beds. It is obvious that such a river-system ensures a large agricultural water-supply from floods and the overspill of the rivers. In fact Muzaffarpur and Darbhanga do not depend entirely on rainfall and so do not suffer from famine or scarcity even when the deficiency of rainfall might justify one or the other.[2] In times of famine sometimes the flooded land is the only land which bears crops. For example, in years of drought the *diaras* and other lands, which are usually liable to inundation, yield bumper crops of maize which in other years might be swept away or destroyed by floods. In wet years also floods are productive of as much good as harm provided they are not very high and come early in the season, because the farmers get time to re-transplant if the crops are destroyed, while the land is also enriched by the deposit of silt. In the neighbouring districts of Saran and Champaran, on the other hand, agriculture derives much less benefit from the seasonal floods. For a long time Saran was very much liable to destructive floods. But the construction of the Saran embankment, which has protected it from floods, has upset the level of natural drainage and choked up the spill channels. Saran is one of the driest districts in Bihar and the rainfall there is also capricious. In many years irrigation from the spill channels which flow from the north-west to the south-east of the district is not required. But in years of drought when every drop of water in the district is sought to be utilized, the spill channels ought to be valuable sources of irrigation. But the embankment which runs along the right bank of the Gandak has closed the mouths of the spill channels which mostly take their rise from the Gandak. The result has been that the amount of water flowing through

[1] *District Gazetteer*, Muzaffarpur.
[2] See evidence of Mr. L. Hare, Commissioner, Patna Division: *Report of the Indian Irrigation Commission*, 1901–8, Appendix.

them has been much reduced.[1] Thus land has been deprived not only of a part of its supply of irrigation but also of the annual deposit of fertilizing silt. Moreover, the face of the country has been altered by human interference with nature in such a way as to raise difficult problems of drainage. Similarly in the sub-montane district of Champaran agriculture gets little benefit from the spill-water and has to depend entirely on seasonal rainfall in the absence of artificial irrigation. But while the agriculturists of Saran have readily accommodated themselves to the new situation created by the deficiency of flood irrigation by developing the means of artificial irrigation, Champaran has long depended almost entirely on rainfall, and it is this difference which partly explains why Saran has maintained a higher density of population (although it is lower than in Muzaffarpur and Darbhanga) than Champaran.[2] Farther east in North Bhagalpur and Purnea the importance of flood irrigation to agriculture is very great. In North Bhagalpur there is very little high land, and a large part of the country is subject to inundation from the many rivers which traverse the country and from the overflow of the Ganges over its northern bank. The rivers are inter-connected by numerous channels of considerable width and depth called *dhars* and, except in years of drought, serve as supplementary sources of irrigation. Similarly the eastern portion of Purnea, which maintains a high density of population, is drained by the river Mahananda and is intersected by numerous streams and channels, while it also contains a number of large marshes which are never completely dry.[3]

The contrast between North Bihar and South Bihar is conspicuous not only when we compare the rainfall figures, but also when we compare the relative importance of flood irrigation in these two regions. In South Bihar flood irrigation is entirely insignificant except in the tracts bordering

---

[1] Evidence of E. F. Growse, Offg. Additional Commissioner of Patna: *Report of the Indian Irrigation Commission*, 1901–3, Appendix.

[2] Recently, however, the agricultural situation in the northern portion of Champaran has been changed by the construction of the Tribeni Canal, which was completed in 1912. This canal was constructed as a protective work.

[3] *Gazetteers*, Purnea and Bhagalpur.

on the Ganges. For example, the Barh sub-division in Patna depends almost entirely upon the floods from the Ganges and other rivers. Similarly in Sahabad and Monghyr the lowlands along the banks of the Ganges are liable to inundation which obviates the necessity of artificial irrigation. But away from the Ganges a large portion of the cultivated area consists of dry soil not liable to annual inundation. Moreover, the soil, which consists of old alluvium, is unable to absorb or retain moisture, and the somewhat rapid drainage of the country northwards tends to reduce the efficiency of the small amount of rainfall which this region receives in normal years. As we shall see presently, this has raised difficult problems of the storage and distribution of water by artificial means and has increased the difficulties of agriculture.

When we consider the relation of rainfall to agriculture in the Middle Ganges Valley nothing seems more striking than the reactions of ill-distributed rainfall upon the entire agricultural economy. In this region the succession of crops and the timing of agricultural operations peculiar to each harvest are so nicely adjusted to seasonable rainfall which must be adequate for each agricultural operation, that the freaks of the seasons have far-reaching effects upon the fortunes of the cultivator. The total annual rainfall in this region is normally distributed in such a way that three cycles of plant-life can be completed within the entire agricultural year. While this has contributed to the high productivity of agriculture, it has also exposed it to the dangers of ill-distributed rainfall, because the rainfall which is important for the harvests is not one which exceeds or falls short of a given annual total but one which is timely and well-distributed. For both the *bhadoi* and the *aghani* harvests there must be heavy rainfall in June. But for the *aghani* harvest which is the main crop, a specially heavy rainfall in the first part of July is necessary. If a dry period comes too soon the young seedlings get burnt up by the sun and never recover. The August rain must be steady. If there is a failure of rainfall too early in September the rice in the ear cannot form and there would be nothing left but husk. Again, if in the end of September or the beginning of October the crops do not get sun they will not ripen, and if the rain continues they will rot and be useless. In the case of the *bhadoi* crops also there must be good rain in June and July for ploughing up the land and preparing the nurseries, but a dry period is always necessary towards the end of August and the beginning of September to ripen the grain. Another dry period is necessary in the harvesting season about September. Moreover, a good rainfall at the end of the monsoon is also necessary for securing moisture for the crops of the spring harvest which are sown in October and November and, thereafter, light rain at intervals is required to refresh the growing plants. It is obvious that such a nice adjustment of agricultural operations to meteorological conditions is upset in years of drought and excessive rainfall, especially when the deficiency or excess is found to occur at a time when it is disastrous to agriculture. In a monsoon region, however, the danger of drought is more frequent (in fact a dry year comes once in four years) and far more disastrous than the danger of excessive rainfall. Hence it is important for us to study the nature and extent of artificial irrigation in North Bihar and South Bihar and to consider next how far it can counteract the effects of drought upon the harvests.

The extent and sources of artificial irrigation in these two regions are indicated in the comparative table on p. 175.[1]

The nature of artificial irrigation in a region depends essentially upon the characteristic physical conditions governing agriculture. In this respect, as Brunhes says, 'our activity restricted in its modes and in its effects is further subject to the influence of natural conditions on the limits within which it may be exercised'.[2] A study of these limits is important from the point of view of adjustment of population to the economic resources and possibilities, while it warns us both against violent human interference with nature and supine indifference to her vagaries. We have already studied the characteristic climatic and physical conditions prevailing in North Bihar and South Bihar respectively. We shall now interpret the statistics embodied in the following table by

[1] *Report of the Royal Commission on Agriculture in India*, Vol. XIII, p. 289: Replies to the Questionnaire submitted by Mr. A. D. Tuckey, I.C.S., Director of Land Records and Surveys, Bihar and Orissa.

[2] Brunhes, *Human Geography*, p. 533.

reference to the limits imposed upon the human control of natural environment.

PERCENTAGE OF CROPPED AREA IRRIGATED

District	Govt. Canals	Private Canals	Tanks & Ahars	Wells	Other Sources	Total
South Bihar						
Gaya . . .	4·3	16	26·8	6	1·7	54·8
Patna . . .	2·2	21·6	24·3	6·7	4·8	59·6
South Bhagalpur .	—	16·5	5·5	1·2	12·8	36
South Monghyr .	—	7	20	3	12	42
Sahabad . .	22·3	3·8	10·3	4·8	·7	41·9
North Bihar						
Muzaffarpur . .	—	·06	·24	1·2	·41	1·9
Saran . . .	—	1·8	4·2	12·2	1	19·2
Champaran . .	2·9	3·7	·3	·1	1	8
Darbhanga . .	—	·2	2·8	·4	3·1	6·5
North Monghyr .	—	—	·3	·2	2·1	2·6
North Bhagalpur .	—	—	·5	·2	3·8	4·5
Purnea . . .	—	—	—	—	—	1·5

Of the four western districts of North Bihar, Muzaffarpur and Darbhanga maintain the highest density of population to be found in the whole of the Middle Ganges Valley. But there it is the bounty of nature which has favoured such a phenomenal density of population. Both the districts are well-watered and possess a fertile soil retentive of moisture. In Muzaffarpur the irrigated area is small owing to spill irrigation in the northern tracts and the natural moisture of the soil in the southern tracts; while in the central portions of the district there are expanses of swamps and *jhils* in the Doab between the Baghmati and the Gandak. In the north the sources of artificial irrigation are tanks and streams. Cultivators build embankments across the rivers in the dry season and irrigate lands by raising the level of the rivers. *Pains* or artificial channels are common, but the construction of wells is rendered impossible by inundation. It is only in the southern tracts that well irrigation is facilitated by the nature of the soil and the height of the water-level, and 78 per cent of the irrigated area gets its agricultural water-supply from wells. In fact, while 1·9 per cent of the total cropped area in the district is irrigated 1·2 per cent is irrigated from wells, and this shows that artificial irrigation, negligible as it is, has some importance only in the highlands of the south. In Darbhanga, as in Muzaffarpur, the rivers flow on raised beds. Moreover, the country lies on a low level, in places indented with chains of shallow marshes marking the lines of drainage by which surplus water is drained away. These physical peculiarities have favoured spill irrigation. Artificial irrigation which is very common in the north has been found possible by utilizing the small hill-streams by the system of *pains* or artificial channels, while tanks are also used for expediting transplantation or preventing withering during a break in the rains. Out of the total area under irrigated crops which amounts to 6·5 per cent, the area irrigated from tanks and *ahars* constitutes 2·8 per cent, while that irrigated from other sources, such as rivers and streams, constitutes 8·1 per cent. In fact the importance of the latter sources of irrigation can be realized from the fact that the three tracts which escaped during the famine of 1896–7 owed their agricultural security to irrigation from the rivers. The extent of well irrigation is small except in the highlands of the south, and even there it is confined to special crops grown near the wells. The general belief is that irrigation once begun must always be continued, because in the loamy soil generally found in the southern tract irrigation forms a crust below the surface which impairs the fertility of the land unless irrigation is continued. But it must be remembered that the crops grown here do not require artificial irrigation, and the supply of water also is not adequate.

The two other districts situated in the western portion of North Bihar are Saran and Champaran which maintain densities of 927 persons per square mile and 608 persons per square mile respectively. In Saran the *bhangar* or clay soil which is unproductive without irrigation is not confined to one tract as in other districts; it alternates with *bhat* soil which does not depend too much on irrigation and can grow dry crops. But Saran is the driest district in North Bihar in which artificial irrigation is a necessity in normal years as in the dry regions of the Upper Ganges Valley. Moreover, as already said, the erection of the Gandak embankment has rendered spill irrigation impossible, so that the streams which relieve the lowlands of surplus water and also formerly served as spill channels now dry up in summer and their beds are sown with spring crops. Consequently there has been a remarkable development of artificial irrigation in this district. The percentage of cropped area which is irrigated is as high as 19·2—a figure which is far above the corresponding figures for other districts of North Bihar. But it should be noted that 12·2 per cent of the net cropped area (out of a total of 19·2 per cent) is irrigated from wells. In this respect Saran resembles the congested districts of the eastern portion of the Upper Ganges Valley which are situated at or near the rainfall line of 40 inches and in which there has been a phenomenal development of well irrigation. In the greater part of this district well irrigation has been facilitated by the fact that sub-soil water is found very near the surface. Thus wells have become a source of agricultural security so far as the *rabi* harvest is concerned, and it is not unthinkable that the *aghani* harvest can also be rendered safe by the development of well irrigation.[1] In the neighbouring district of Champaran spill irrigation is less important than in Muzaffarpur and Darbhanga. The soil is moist and the rainfall is also heavy, so that in a year of normal rainfall little necessity is felt for artificial irrigation. But the rainfall is extremely capricious. There is no doubt artificial irrigation from streams by channels, and the area thus irrigated, accounts for a little less than half of the total cropped area irrigated. But the sources of many of these streams being in Nepal, they represent unreliable sources of irrigation. Moreover, in the tracts situated at a distance from the rivers the crops depend exclusively on rainfall. From the river Sikrana which flows through the district there is little irrigation in ordinary years, and in abnormal years it is difficult to throw weirs

[1] But as explained in Chapter I this district has been losing its population by migration of farmers to neighbouring tracts where natural conditions are less unfavourable, so that further development of well irrigation, which is always costly, may be regarded as unlikely.

across it and save the crops. In the higher lands of the district, which consist of loamy soil, irrigation is seldom, if ever, practised for reasons explained above. It is only in the northern portion of the district which is liable to suffer from drought that artificial irrigation from canals has long been regarded as a reliable means of resistance against drought. Consequently the opening of the Tribeni canal in 1912 has increased agricultural security and has favoured the growth of population in a tract which was, to a large extent, agriculturally undeveloped.[1] But taking the district as a whole, the facilities of irrigation are inadequate and are not likely to increase so far as to favour a very great increase of population.

The tracts situated in the eastern portion of North Bihar are mainly a continuation of the fertile plain of Tirhut, and we find the same importance of spill irrigation which, combined with sufficient rainfall, obviates the necessity of artificial irrigation on a soil which is quite retentive of moisture. In fact, the natural supply of moisture in this portion of North Bihar is so ample that the extent of the cropped area which is irrigated is the smallest in the entire Middle Ganges Valley. The district of Purnea gets an annual rainfall of 67·9 inches. The soil is mostly very retentive of moisture and the extent of spill irrigation may be realized from the fact that as much as 5 per cent of the total area is under water during the rains.[2] The result is that barely 1·5 per cent of the cropped area is artificially irrigated and the only crops so irrigated are tobacco and other crops, such as garden produce, grown on homestead lands. Such crops are irrigated from temporary wells which can be constructed very cheaply owing to the small depth of the water-level.[3] Tanks are rarely used because they are liable to be silted up. Similarly in North Monghyr and North Bhagalpur the cropped area under artificial irrigation is insignificant. In North Monghyr a small area is irrigated from tanks and *ahars* or artificial channels which are more important than tanks as sources of irrigation.

[1] The Tribeni Canal irrigates 66,566 acres.
[2] The rivers rise early in May owing to the melting of the Himalayan snows. In fact, the district is very liable to destructive floods.
[3] The total number of such wells was 24,701 during the settlement operations, 1901–8.

In fact, the *ahars* constitute the main source of irrigation in Gogri thana and are utilized for irrigating the rice crops.[1] But on the whole the two sources together constitute barely ·3 per cent of the cropped area. The area irrigated from wells is barely ·2 per cent and is mainly confined to one thana where valuable crops such as chillies and tobacco are raised. The largest area is, however, irrigated by lifting water from rivers, lakes, etc. (2·1 per cent).

Let us now consider the nature of artificial irrigation in South Bihar. South Bihar presents a sharp contrast to North Bihar in regard to both annual rainfall and the extent of spill irrigation. Although the system of dry farming in South Bihar has, to a certain extent, counteracted the effects of the deficiency of natural irrigation, yet agriculture there depends precariously upon artificial irrigation. In South Bihar the total amount of annual rainfall is less than in North Bihar; moreover, agriculture gets little benefit from spill irrigation, which is such an important factor in the agricultural economy of North Bihar.[2] Further, the efficiency of rainfall, small in amount that it is, has been reduced by the dry soil and the rapid drainage of the country. In Sahabad, for example, there is an average fall of the level northwards of three feet in the mile, and the soil which consists of old alluvium is unable to absorb or retain moisture. In Patna also the clay soil which is found in the greater part of the district cannot retain moisture well, and the slope of the country is such that rain-water has a tendency to run into the low *tal* lands. Similarly in Gaya the drainage water flows northwards to the Ganges from the high Chotanagpur Plateau through the outlets provided by a series of rivers and hill-streams, and the slope of the country is such that nearly all of these water-courses become dry after the rainy season. Thus the soil which is itself dry has been rendered more unretentive of moisture owing to the rapid drainage of the country. It is obvious that under these natural conditions artificial irrigation which is indispensable for agriculture is possible by storing up the rain-water which would otherwise

[1] Even there only one acre in every ten under rice is irrigated.
[2] It is only the lands bordering on the Ganges which depend on the floods that fertilize the soil for the rabi crop and supply the moisture for its growth.

be drained away very quickly. 'This is effected by means of low embankments thrown up in the depressions lying between the ridges and gentle undulations which break the surface of the country. The long shallow tanks thus formed are called *ahars*. Their utility is further increased in some cases by water-channels (*pynes*), constructed to the nearest stream or water-course, which lead into them the water which would otherwise flow past the fields and thus make them the receptacle of all the water available in the neighbourhood.'[1] Whenever required, 'the water is let out from the *ahar*; and the fields are also bounded by banks which prevent the escape of water until the crops are thoroughly watered'.[2] It may appear that artificial irrigation of this kind is provided best by means of canals as in the western portion of South Bihar, where the Sone canal and its branches have been the most important sources of irrigation. But it must be remembered that 'the rivers of South Bihar are, excepting the Son, generally too small to feed any canal system'.[3] Most of the rivers are non-perennial streams which depend entirely on rainfall and cannot be relied upon for ensuring a regular supply of water. Hence obviously the farmers have mostly to depend on artificial storage of water. We must note in this connexion another important fact which has a direct bearing upon the nature of artificial irrigation in South Bihar. In all the districts of this region rice is the most important crop, and the land requires irrigation from June to the middle of October, a period which covers the rainy season in Bihar. There is a great demand for water in June and July, when it is indispensable for transplanting paddy. There is a further demand during the critical period of *hathiya* asterism, because water is then necessary for maturing the ripening grain, and also because the practice of draining the field in September makes it absolutely necessary to supply artificial irrigation to the rice crop. Such a demand cannot be possibly met by wells

[1] 'A big pyne may irrigate a hundred or two hundred villages or more. Ahars are pre-eminently suited for the higher lands where pynes cannot go, because pynes can only follow the valleys of the streams.' *Report of the Irrigation Commission*, Appendix, p. 208.

[2] *Gazetteer*, Gaya.

[3] *Report of the Royal Commission on Agriculture in India*, Evidence Volume, p. 309.

which are ordinarily suitable for the irrigation of winter crops.[1] Consequently the *ahars* and *pynes* which can command a larger supply of water during the different stages of the growth and maturity of crops constitute the principal source of irrigation in South Bihar. The importance of such artificial irrigation is indicated by the statistics embodied in the above comparative table.[2] In Gaya, Patna, South Monghyr, and South Bhagalpur artificial irrigation is mostly supplied by *ahars* and *pynes*. In South Bhagalpur only 5·5 per cent of the cropped area is irrigated from tanks and *ahars*; while as much as 16·5 per cent of the cropped area is irrigated from private canals.[3] Here the importance of irrigation from canals is due to the fact that embankments are thrown up across the streams that flow northwards from the hilly southernmost part of the district, and a network of distributaries leads the water from field to field. It will be seen that wells constitute an important source of irrigation only in South Bhagalpur and South Monghyr where they are indispensable for the special crops of the *rabi* harvest. In the former the sinking of wells is cheap, and in some villages masonry wells are sunk at the expense of the landlord for the irrigation of the sugar-cane fields, and in the latter there is a tendency to sink every year temporary earthen wells which last for a few seasons and are suited to a sandy soil. In other districts the rocky soil in the south has prevented the development of well irrigation. It is only in the north of these districts that sub-soil water is near the surface; but there irrigation is supplied largely by other sources. Lastly, government canals represent one of the important sources of irrigation in the arid western portion of South Bihar. Such a source of irrigation which, unlike *ahars* and *pynes*, does not depend exclusively on local rainfall is surely a great boon to the farmers, as it increases agricultural security. But as already explained, there is very little scope for the extension of canal irrigation

[1] The average area irrigated by wells is about five acres.
[2] See p. 175.
[3] 'Irrigation from private channels and that from ahars cannot properly be distinguished. The water from ahars is distributed through a channel often and ahars are often filled by water from private channels. The two figures thus must be added to give a true idea of private irrigation.' *Settlement Report*, Gaya, 1911–18, E. L. Tanner, I.C.S.

in South Bihar because the supply of water from the rivers is extremely unreliable. Nature has been hostile to man in this region, and the lack of unfailing sources of irrigation has hampered agricultural development and the consequent increase of the density of population.

This point requires more careful consideration, as it has a direct bearing on the problem of the density of population in South Bihar. This region, as we have seen, depends precariously on artificial irrigation which is supplied mostly by *ahars* and *pynes*. But this indigenous system of irrigation, ingenious as it is, has certain serious drawbacks and has been encountering serious difficulties which, under the present conditions, cannot be overcome. In the first place, the catchment areas of *ahars* are not generally large, and the amount of water which can be stored up depends very largely on local rainfall; consequently the supply of water is not as large as it should be; and, what is more important, is uncertain. In the second place, owing to continual wear and tear the embankments are swept away during heavy rains. Moreover, The number of *pynes* is apt to diminish owing to the want of proper head-work to control the flow as well as to regulate the water-level of the channel at its entrance. Much damage is caused by *pynes* scouring out at the head, and sometimes such deepening results in the channel of the *pyne* becoming ultimately the course of the river. In this way the original bed of the river becomes silted up; the tract of country formerly irrigated from it by other *pynes* taking off lower down are left without means of irrigation, and cultivated lands are converted into waste; while the main stream having adopted the artificial channel of the *pyne* cuts away the adjoining land and floods and depreciates other lands by a deposit of sand.'[1] In the next place, irrigation from *ahars* and *pynes* fails completely when it is most needed in a dry year, i.e. in the beginning or the end of the *kharif* season. Indeed, the general practice of draining the rice-fields in September leads to a very great demand for water when the *hathiya* rain fails, and such a demand cannot be met by the small quantity of water stored up in *ahars*. Lastly, the efficiency

---

[1] *Gazetteer*, Gaya.

of this system of irrigation has been very much reduced by want of organized efforts to control the distribution of water. As Brunhes observes: 'When the output of available water is regularly subject to considerable variation, the cultivator of the arid zones will run very great risks if a definite organization does not control the distribution. He is uncertain of the quantity of water that will be available and the amount of water that his neighbours through arbitrary monopolization will allow to reach his field or garden.[1] Under such geographic conditions men are naturally inclined to escape from this psychological state of uncertainty and anxiety by joining their common interests under fixed laws.'[2] But unfortunately in South Bihar there is no such common organization, voluntary or otherwise, for an authoritative regulation of water-supply and for the maintenance and improvement of the common sources of irrigation. *Ahars* and *pynes* are maintained by landlords who get a return on their investment in the shape of a portion of agricultural produce under the prevailing system of produce rents. Owing to the gradual disintegration of property, the maintenance of *ahars* and *pynes* has been seriously neglected. Consequently agricultural insecurity has increased, while there is considerable bitterness between the landlords and the tenants who generally prefer to commute produce rents into cash rents.[3] Moreover, it is custom which regulates the supply of water, and conflicting claims naturally

[1] The following typical illustration of such monopolization which, though not technically arbitrary, is yet clearly anti-social was given by Babu Arikshan Sinha, General Secretary, Bihar Provincial Kisan Sabha, in the course of his evidence before the Royal Commission on Agriculture: 'Some four years ago there was drought in my locality. By the grace of God the Baya river became full of water up to its highest level. People on both sides of the Baya river tried to irrigate their lands by taking water from that river. But some Zamindars got their zirat lands irrigated but would not allow tenants to take water through their zirat lands. Consequently poor cultivators had to undertake a course of one mile for water to come to their lands and it took at least twenty days for three hundred bighas to be irrigated. But water could not stay for twenty days in the Baya river and only about two-thirds of the lowlands in one block could be watered before the water ran to the Ganges.'

[2] Brunhes, *Human Geography*, p. 534.

[3] Mr. Devaki Prosad Sinha, M.A., M.L.C., rightly pointed out in his evidence before the Royal Commission on Agriculture in India that 'the control of irrigation in the hands of private individuals is often a weapon for the oppression of the poor'. 'Zamindars have neglected irrigation with a view to wreaking vengeance upon refractory tenants': he said that he knew instances bearing out this statement.

lead to agrarian disputes. On the whole, it is sad to reflect how the entire agricultural economy has been rendered precarious and unstable for want of a rational control of the natural sources of irrigation.

It is obvious, however, that no such difficulties as regards the control and distribution of water can arise under the system of canal irrigation. But it must be remembered that canal irrigation has touched barely the fringe of the problem of artificial irrigation. It has been confined to a small area in the west, and, as already explained, there is very little scope for its extension. Moreover, even in the canal-irrigated strips there are large areas outside the canal system. But what is more important to bear in mind is that there is too great pressure on the supply of canal water during the critical period of *hathiya* asterism. No farmer will, in any circumstances, take water till the *hathiya* asterism has set in, and the canal department has to irrigate within ten or fifteen days every acre under lease.[1] Mr. T. H. Toogood, Superintending Engineer, Sone Circle, admitted in his evidence before the Famine Commission of 1901–3 that the Sone canals had a capacity of only 6,850 cusecs by which not more than 360,000 acres under the *kharif* harvest could be irrigated. In fact, the limit to the number of leases which the canal department can accept is determined by the amount of water wanted during the *hathiya* asterism. 'It is of no avail irrigating to their full capacity, say 516,000 acres, during July and August, if they cannot water that area in 14 days in October. Should there be a good rainfall during this period the 516,000 acres may mature. But if the *hathiya* is a dry one, some of the crop will fail to obtain water and must perish.'[2] Thus it is not difficult to imagine the critical situation created by the failure of the *hathiya* rainfall as in 1899 when the canal department had to refuse applications for irrigating 40,000 acres. Again, such a situation has tended to become more desperate as a result of the change in the character of cultivation brought about by the introduction of canal irrigation. It was anticipated that the opening of the canals will be followed by

[1] This is, as already explained, due to the universal practice of running the water off the rice-field in September.

[2] *Report of the Indian Irrigation Commission*, 1901–3, Part II, p. 157.

an increase in the area under the *rabi* crops on the higher lands on both sides of the canals. But contrary to expectations canal water began to be utilized for *kharif* crops (especially rice) which are grown at a lower level in the valley between the ridges. The result has been an enormous increase in the *kharif* area; but the increasing cultivation of wet crops which depend completely upon canal irrigation in dry years has increased agricultural insecurity in the canal-irrigated tracts and exposed them to the danger of famine.

The above survey of the nature and sources of artificial irrigation in North Bihar and South Bihar suggests a sharp contrast between the two regions in respect of facilities of irrigation. The contrast is more clear when we study the effect of drought upon the harvests, and the best approach to this problem will be to study the relative deficiency of rainfall and the relative shrinkage in the gross yield of principal crops in these two regions during 1907–8, a typical year of drought. The relevant facts are given in the following comparative tables:

RAINFALL IN 1907–8 AS COMPARED WITH NORMAL

(In inches)

		North Bihar	South Bihar
March 1 to May 31	Actual . . .	4·72	2·85
	Normal . . .	4·07	2·10
June 1 to Sept. 80 .	Actual . . .	85·51	37·63
	Normal . . .	45·00	38·84
Oct. 1 to Nov. 30 .	Actual . . .	·26	—
	Normal . . .	2·80	2·71
Dec. 1 to Feb. 29 .	Actual . . .	1·67	2·91
	Normal . . .	1·21	1·56
Total . .	Actual . . .	42·16	42·89
	Normal . . .	53·8	45·21

AVERAGE GROSS PRODUCE (1907–8)
(In percentage of normal yield)

	North Bihar	South Bihar
Winter rice	51	45[1]
Autumn	81	52
Wheat	75	49[1]
Indian Corn	92	67[1]
Gram	78	46[1]
Linseed	57	61
Til	86	86
Rape and Mustard . . .	78	47
Sugar-Cane	94	73
Tobacco	77	54

The statistics given above indicate clearly the effects of ill-distributed rainfall upon the harvests and bring into sharp relief the relative agricultural security of North and South Bihar in a year of drought. It will be seen that in North Bihar there was little appreciable deficiency of rainfall in the first and the fourth periods, and almost the entire deficit was confined to the *kharif* season. The result was that both the *bhadoi* and the *aghani* crops were seriously affected by the huge deficiency of rainfall. The *bhadoi* crops suffered from want of moisture in July, while the absence of rain after the beginning of September aggravated the injury. At the same time the failure of the *hathiya* rainfall completed the destruction of the *aghani* crop which had already suffered from want of moisture during the period of transplantation. In South Bihar, as the statistics show, the rainfall between March 1 and May 31 was above normal. The unusually heavy rainfall in March and April (1907) damaged the *rabi* crops when they were ripening and were being harvested.[2] The monsoon rainfall was almost normal, but the abnormally heavy rainfall in August caused floods and injured the crops.

[1] Winter rice, wheat, Indian corn, and gram represent normally about 70 per cent of the total harvest of the year, of which winter rice represents as much as 40 per cent. Autumn rice, which is so important in North Bihar, constitutes a little over 1 per cent of the total harvest in South Bihar.

[2] *Season and Crop Report*, Bengal, 1907–8, p. 1.

What was, however, disastrous to agriculture was the failure of rainfall in September and October owing to premature cessation of the monsoon. This diminished the gross yield of winter rice, which failed totally on the high lands, and also reduced the area as well as the yield of the *rabi* crops harvested in 1908. Thus it is clear that the failure of crops in the entire Middle Ganges Valley was due to ill-distributed rainfall and the premature cessation of the monsoon. As already explained, what vitally affects agriculture in this region is not rainfall which either exceeds or falls short of a given annual total, but rainfall which is ill-distributed and unseasonable. In fact, the decrease in the gross produce of principal crops both in North Bihar and South Bihar was essentially due to the failure of the *hathiya* rainfall and the absence of rain in October and November. It is interesting to note that the deficiency in the total annual rainfall was very much smaller in South Bihar than in North Bihar.[1] Moreover, while the monsoon rainfall was normal in South Bihar, almost the entire annual deficit was confined to the *kharif* season in North Bihar. But in spite of this South Bihar was not better off than North Bihar simply because agriculture in South Bihar depends so precariously on good rainfall during the period of *hathiya* asterism. At the same time it is highly significant that the gross yield of the principal crops, particularly winter rice, wheat, indian corn, and gram which constitute 70 per cent of the total harvests, decreased *much more* in South Bihar than in North Bihar. This merely confirms the fact which we have already explained, viz. that the sources of artificial irrigation in South Bihar are so inelastic and unreliable that they cannot adequately counteract the effects of drought upon the harvests. In this region the natural conditions governing agriculture are unfavourable and the efforts of man to control his environment by developing more reliable sources of artificial irrigation have not been successful. The result has been that low agricultural productivity and agricultural insecurity have combined to check an increase in the density of population.

[1] The deficiency was about 4·5 per cent in South Bihar, while it was more than 10 per cent in North Bihar.

CHAPTER IV

CROPS AND DENSITY

IN this chapter we shall examine the problem of the density of population in the Middle Ganges Valley specifically from the point of view of agricultural productivity. It is obvious that such an inquiry is fundamentally an inquiry into the nature of the climatic and hydrographic conditions which determine the geographical distribution of crops and hence the high or low agricultural productivity of different regions.

The Middle Ganges Valley lies between the dry Upper Ganges Valley and the very wet region of the Deltas. 'We find that its characters are between the two, and its crops are a mixture of those most important in the drier regions and those found in the Deltas region.'[1] It is important for our purpose to observe the nature of this combination of dry and wet crops. Rice, one of the most important staples, requires a mean summer temperature of more than 75 degrees. Moreover, the largest rice regions have an annual rainfall of 50 inches and a rainfall of 5 inches a month during the growing season. It would appear, therefore, that these ideal conditions are found in North Bihar which receives an annual rainfall of 51·7 inches. In South Bihar, which receives an annual rainfall of only 48·8 inches, although the natural environment is not so favourable yet it is sufficiently favourable for the cultivation of rice and, as we shall see presently, the rice crop contributes largely to the agricultural productivity of this region. In fact it is only in regions situated beyond the rainfall line of 40 inches, where the period of high temperatures is longer, that the importance of rice is much smaller, until gradually the climatic limit is definitely reached in the southern portion of Middle Doab and the Central India Plateau which is a neighbouring region. Wheat, another

---

[1] Longman's *Regional Geographies of India: The Indian Empire*, Part I, French and Stamp, p. 134.

important staple, has an altogether different range of environment. The conditions which are favourable to the cultivation of rice are precisely those which are unfavourable to the cultivation of wheat. In the Middle Ganges Valley the climate is so moist that the wheat crop is liable to suffer from rust. Most of the important wheat regions of the world have an annual precipitation of less than 30 inches. But where the rainfall is 45 inches or more rusts and fungus diseases are prevalent. Moreover, a hot and dry climate produces a fine-stemmed plant the grain of which is hard, glassy and rich in nitrogen, while a moist climate produces a coarser-stemmed plant with the grains relatively soft and mealy and poor in nitrogen.[1] Thus it is obvious that in the whole of the Middle Ganges Valley the importance of wheat is very small. It is a more important crop in South Bihar than in North Bihar where the climate is much more moist. Moreover, wheat that is grown in this region is not pure wheat but is mixed with barley and oil-seeds to guard against a total failure of the crop. Barley, another important staple of the *rabi* harvest, has a remarkably wide range of environment. It is the chief *rabi* crop in the moist rice-growing regions where wheat cannot be raised under favourable conditions. Thus it is an important crop of the *rabi* harvest in the Middle Ganges Valley as a whole, particularly in North Bihar. Maize, another important crop in the *kharif* harvest, 'so readily adapts itself to its surroundings that it is successfully grown over wide climatic ranges'.[2] The great corn regions of the world are areas of continental climate characterized by a large range of temperature. Except where irrigation is practised most corn is grown in regions having an annual rainfall of over 20 inches and a summer temperature averaging about 75 degrees. In America most intensive cultivation is practised in the region where mean temperature is from 70 to 80 degrees and the annual precipitation is between 25 and 50 inches. In the Middle Ganges Valley, also, the conditions of rainfall and temperature are not unfavourable to the cultivation of maize. In fact maize constitutes one of the most important crops of

[1] J. Warren Smith, *Agricultural Meteorology*, p. 185.
[2] Ibid.

the *bhadoi* harvest in this region. Sugar-cane, another wet crop of the *kharif* harvest, requires high temperature and constant supply of moisture. Hence it is grown in all parts of the Gangetic Plain, its importance varying with the facilities of irrigation. Gram, another crop in the *rabi* harvest, can be grown successfully on various classes of soil. It can be sown on heavy clay land as well as light sandy soils. Hence the range of environment of this crop is very wide. But the importance of this crop is very small in the Middle Ganges Valley because the land is devoted to better classes of crops, and it is usually sown as a second crop on the rice-lands.[1] Another class of *rabi* crops having a considerable importance in this region consists of oil-seeds which cannot be grown to a large extent in the drier regions of the Upper Ganges Valley, but find the most favourable environment in this region.

It will be seen that of the crops just mentioned there are some, like gram and maize, which have a very wide range of environment. Now the extent to which these crops are grown depends upon the extent to which other more valuable crops can be raised in the same environment. For example, juar can be grown neither on the heavy clay land nor on the lightest soils. Loamy soil and soil composed of light clay are suitable for this crop. In the Middle Ganges Valley the importance of this crop is very small because barley and other more valuable food-grains are grown in preference to juar on these better classes of soil. Thus the importance of a crop depends not only upon its own range of environment, but also upon the range of environment of other valuable crops which may be grown in preference to it.

Let us now study the varying importance of the different wet and dry crops in relation to the agricultural productivity of North Bihar and South Bihar respectively. The relevant facts are given in the following comparative tables which show the relative percentage of different crops to the total harvest of the year:

---

[1] This crop has a considerable importance in the drier regions of the Upper Ganges Valley, where the wheat crop has a small importance.

NORTH BIHAR

PERCENTAGE OF PRINCIPAL CROPS TO THE TOTAL HARVEST

	Winter Rice	Sugar Cane	Autumn Rice	Maize	Wheat	Barley	Gram	Linseed	Til	Rape and Mustard
Muzaffarpur .	29·64	·39	4·91	7·87	3·14	13·35	1·97	1·85	·02	·33
Saran . .	20·91	2·04	3·72	11·94	4·84	14·57	3·28	4·45	·08	·49
Darbhanga .	40·55	·71	3·89	3·65	2·21	7·21	1·51	7·16	·02	1·94
Champaran .	29·47	·55	11·95	6·48	5·64	11·47	1·99	3·42	·29	1·06
Bhagalpur .	39·97	·85	13·55	7·49	6·90	2·14	3·65	3·53	·26	2·60
Purnea . .	38·98	·61	27·51	·29	1·18	·40	1·33	·62	—	7·78
Average—North Bihar .	33·25	·85	10·84	6·19	3·90	8·19	2·29	3·50	·10	2·36

The figures have been taken from *Season and Crop Report, Bihar and Orissa, for 1932–33,* Appendix V.

SOUTH BIHAR

PERCENTAGE OF PRINCIPAL CROPS TO THE TOTAL HARVEST

	Winter Rice	Sugar Cane	Autumn Rice	Maize	Wheat	Barley	Gram	Linseed	Til	Rape and Mustard
Patna . . .	42·80	1·60	1·13	9·06	9·98	5·96	6·12	1·06	·04	·99
Monghyr . .	55·57	1·53	·76	2·79	7·08	8·87	5·19	3·63	·03	·73
Gaya . .	43·15	2·49	2·66	2·08	12·27	8·96	10·91	1·18	·30	·92
Sahabad . .	21·22	·41	1·18	18·48	9·11	7·48	8·20	1·45	·07	1·96
Average—South Bihar .	40·68	1·50	1·43	6·85	9·61	5·19	7·60	1·83	·11	1·15

The Figures have been taken from *Season and Crop Report, Bihar and Orissa, for 1982–33,*
Appendix V.

The most striking fact that is revealed by these statistics is the predominance of rice. Both winter rice and autumn rice constitute 44·09 per cent of the total harvest in North Bihar and 42·11 per cent of the total harvest in South Bihar. We have already explained fully in a previous chapter how the cultivation of rice contributes very greatly to the agricultural productivity of a region in which the increasing pressure of the population upon land is relieved by the development of intensive subsistence farming, and why extensive cultivation of rice coexists everywhere with high density of population, while extensive cultivation of wheat coexists with comparatively low density of population.

But while it is true that in the Middle Ganges Valley the predominance of rice cultivation is thus the important cause of high rural density, we must not overlook the relative importance of winter rice and autumn rice from the point of view of both agricultural security and agricultural productivity. Winter rice is sown broadcast on the seed nurseries after the commencement of the rainy season in June or July. After four or six weeks there is transplantation, after which the plants are allowed to mature. Then the water is drained off and the lands are allowed to dry for ten or fifteen days, at the end of which they are again flooded.[1] Owing to this practice rainfall at this time becomes absolutely essential. In fact, if there is failure of late rains towards the end of September or in the beginning of October, i.e. during the period of *hathiya* asterism, the winter rice does not mature at all and there is an almost total failure of the crop. We have already explained how in this region it is not possible to irrigate the rice-fields by artificial means to any considerable extent in the event of a failure of late rains. In North Bihar schemes of artificial irrigation are bound to be uneconomical for the simple reason that artificial irrigation is not required in normal years. Moreover, the streams of North Bihar are mostly non-perennial streams, so that the supply of water is too unreliable to feed any canal system. Well irrigation is also out of the question, because wells cannot stand owing to inundations and also because *aghani* rice, which is the main

---

[1] This is locally called *ningar*.

crop, cannot be properly irrigated from wells. In South Bihar the capacity of *ahars* is too small for the storage of the immense quantity of water that may be required for the irrigation of rice-fields. Moreover, the *ahars* are apt to dry up in years of drought and thus fail to protect the crops. In South Bihar also most of the streams except the Sone are non-perennial streams which cannot feed any canal system. And it is important to bear in mind that even in those agricultural tracts which have been brought within the Sone canal system the rice crop cannot be rendered safe when there is a failure of *hathiya* rainfall because there is too great pressure on the supply of water during the ten or fifteen days which constitute the critical period.[1] Thus it is clear that in the Middle Ganges Valley as a whole the predominance of winter rice is always accompanied by a high degree of agricultural insecurity. In fact, it is generally true to say that the higher the percentage of net-cropped area under winter rice in a particular tract of this region, the greater the economic distress in the event of a failure of *hathiya* rainfall. The following statistics relating to the famine of 1897 will illustrate this conclusion in a striking manner:

PREDOMINANCE OF WINTER RICE IN RELATION TO FAMINE[2]

District	Percentage of cropped area under winter rice	Highest number of persons relieved on any one day	Percentage of persons relieved to total population affected by the crop failure
Darbhanga . . .	57·33	253,910	10·49
Muzaffarpur . .	42·35	139,355	6·93
Saran	29·11	85,173	5·75

We shall now consider the importance of winter rice from the point of view of agricultural productivity. It is no doubt true that winter rice is itself a heavy-yielding food-crop and is thus a highly productive crop from the economic point of

[1] See Chapter III, pp. 184–185.
[2] J. H. Kerr, *Survey and Settlement Report*, Durbhanga, 1896–1903.

view. But the question of the economic importance of winter rice must be examined in relation to the nature of double-cropping which is associated with the cultivation of winter rice. It has already been explained in a previous chapter how agricultural productivity may be enhanced by the practice of double-cropping and how extensive double-cropping coexists with a high density of population. But it has also been pointed out that the economic importance of double-cropping depends not merely upon the area which bears more than one crop in the same season, but also upon whether valuable crops can be raised as second crops on the land which has already borne a *kharif* crop.[1] Hence we must not consider the high productivity of winter rice by itself; we must consider also the nature of the other *rabi* crops which are grown after winter rice as second crops. As already said, 'In the Middle Ganges Valley the chief *aghani* crops are sown before the *bhadoi* crops are harvested, and similarly the chief *rabi* crops are sown before the *aghani* crops are reaped. Hence it is obvious that an *aghani* crop cannot usually be sown as a second crop after the *bhadoi* harvest. The second crops must necessarily be *rabi* crops grown after either the *bhadoi* or *aghani* crops.'[2] Where *aghani* is the principal crop the succeeding second crops consist of cheap catch-crops like khesari, gram, linseed, and peas, because the more valuable *rabi* crops like wheat and barley will be sown before the *aghani* crop is harvested. 'Hence it follows that the larger the area under the *aghani* harvest the smaller will be the contribution of double-cropping to agricultural productivity.'[3] Moreover, in abnormal years the cheap catch-crops sown as second crops cannot obviously relieve the acute economic distress which is caused by the failure of winter rice. Thus when the productivity of winter rice is taken together with the productivity of the *rabi* crops which are sown as second crops we find that the predominance of winter rice in a certain agricultural tract does not imply that the productivity of agriculture as a whole is high.

On the other hand, when we consider the importance of

---

[1] See Chapter II, pp. 163–164.　　　　　　　　[2] Ibid., p. 163.
　　　　　　　　　　　[3] Ibid., p. 163.

autumn rice and other *bhadoi* crops in relation to agricultural security and agricultural productivity we reach different conclusions. In the first place, the predominance of autumn rice and other *bhadoi* crops means greater agricultural security. *Bhadoi* rice, for example, is reaped in September, so that it is possible for the farmers to get a bumper crop even when the *aghani* rice has failed due to the failure of the *hathiya* rainfall. In fact, a late monsoon which is disastrous to the winter rice crop is sometimes actually an advantage to maize, one of the most valuable *bhadoi* crops. In the agricultural tracts bordering on the Ganges a late monsoon is usually accompanied by a late rise of the Ganges, and the result is that the farmers get a bumper crop of maize. Moreover, an early failure of the monsoon gives an early *rabi* season and, as the farmers depend as much on well irrigation as on rainfall, late rains do not affect very much the yield of the valuable *rabi* crops. Again, when there is a failure of winter rice elsewhere due to the late monsoon, the money value of the early *rabi* crops increases and yields a higher return to the farmers in these agricultural tracts. It must be remembered, however, that the *bhadoi* crops are frequently destroyed by inundation. But even then the plants are pulled out and utilized for feeding the cattle, and when the water recedes the remains of the vegetation are converted into manure and the land reploughed and sown with wheat, barley, peas, and gram, which yield a very good return. On the other hand, when winter rice fails the *rabi* crops yield a very small return not only because they consist of cheap catch-crops, but also because the yield is very poor even when rain falls subsequently. In the second place, the predominance of autumn rice and other *bhadoi* crops also means higher agricultural productivity. With favourable winter showers a good *rabi* crop can be raised on land which was sown with *bhadoi* rice. Other *bhadoi* food-crops like maize and marua can also be followed by valuable *rabi* crops such as wheat, barley, and mustard.

Let us now examine the comparative statistics of crops in relation to the agricultural productivity and the agricultural security of North Bihar and South Bihar. The conclusions regarding the varying importance of principal crops which follow from the statistics given above are summarized below.

NORTH BIHAR

(1) The smaller importance of winter rice.
(2) The greater importance of *bhadoi* crops like rice and maize.
(8) The greater importance of oil-seeds and barley.
(4) The smaller importance of gram and wheat.

SOUTH BIHAR

(1) The greater importance of winter rice.
(2) The smaller importance of *bhadoi* crops.
(8) The smaller importance of oil-seeds and barley.
(4) The greater importance of gram and wheat.

It is clear that the importance of *bhadoi* crops and of the valuable *rabi* crops, such as oil-seeds and barley, which are mostly raised as second crops, is greater in North Bihar than in South Bihar; while winter rice together with inferior *rabi* crops, such as gram and mixed wheat, is more important in South Bihar than in North Bihar. It was anticipated that in South Bihar the introduction of canal irrigation would lead to an increase in the area under the *rabi* crops as in the canal-irrigated areas of the Upper Ganges Valley. But contrary to expectations, there has been an enormous increase in the area under the *kharif* crops, especially winter rice, with the result that agricultural insecurity has increased. It must also be remembered that the contribution of double-cropping to agricultural productivity is greater in North Bihar than in South Bihar, and this is due to the predominance of *bhadoi* crops. Thus, whether we look at the problem of the density of population from the point of view of agricultural productivity, or from the point of view of agricultural security, it becomes easy to explain why North Bihar as a whole should maintain a higher density of population than South Bihar.

It is interesting to note in this connexion that there is another method by which we can grasp the relative agricultural productivity and agricultural security of North Bihar

and South Bihar. As already explained, agricultural prosperity in the Middle Ganges Valley is evidenced by a statistical
correspondence between the twice-cropped and the *bhadoi*
areas. The reason is that where a large area under the
aghani crops is accompanied by a large area under the *rabi*
crops, the figures for *rabi* area are inflated by the inclusion of
large areas under cheap catch-crops like khesari; whereas it is
only on *bhadoi* lands that valuable *rabi* crops can be raised
as second crops. Hence Mr. Stevenson-Moore suggests that
'by adding the *bhadoi* and *rabi* areas and deducting the
aghani area we get a fairly correct measure of agricultural
prosperity.'[1] Now the indices of prosperity worked out on
this basis would be 37 and 31 for North Bihar and South
Bihar respectively. It will be seen that this interesting
statistical result provides a striking verification of the conclusion which was stated in the last paragraph.

The correspondence between agricultural productivity and
density can also be clearly traced when we consider the
variation in density from one agricultural tract to another
within the districts of North and South Bihar. In North
Bihar, for example, the uplands bordering on the Ganges are
more densely populated than the lowlands situated in the
North. The uplands are immune from floods, so that it is
possible there to sow a comparatively large area under the
bhadoi crops. The lowlands, on the other hand, are exposed
to inundation and hence the staple crop is necessarily *aghani*
rice. The area under the *rabi* crops is much larger in the
rice-growing lowland region than in the upland tract. But
as already explained, the figures for the *rabi* area in the rice-
growing region are inflated by the inclusion of large areas
bearing cheap catch-crops rather than valuable *rabi* cereals
which follow the *bhadoi* crops. Consequently the index of
prosperity is lower in the case of the northern lowlands than
in the case of the southern uplands. To illustrate this conclusion let us turn to the crop statistics relating to the northern
and the southern thanas of Muzaffarpur, Durbhanga, and
Champaran and the corresponding indices of agricultural
prosperity.

[1] Stevenson-Moore, *Survey and Settlement Report*, Muzaffarpur, 1892-9.

MUZAFFARPUR (NORTHERN THANAS)
Density Low

	Bhadoi	Aghani	Rabi	Index of Prosperity
Shinar . . .	31	68	74	42
Sitamarhi . . .	31	63	66	34
Pupri	30	65	68	33
Belsand . . .	29	65	77	41

MUZAFFARPUR (SOUTHERN THANAS)
Density High

Katra . . .	48	46	74	61
Muzaffarpur . .	42	39	59	62
Paru	43	31	46	48
Lalgunj . . .	46	39	41	49
Mahua . . .	40	41	43	42
Hajipur . . .	44	29	63	79[1]

DURBHANGA (NORTHERN SUB-DIVISIONS)
Density Low

	Bhadoi	Aghani	Rabi	Index of Prosperity
Madhubani . .	22	71	47	2
Sadar	25	66	47	6

DURBHANGA (SOUTHERN SUB-DIVISION)
Density High

Samastipur . .	41	39	46	48[2]

[1] It is significant that in Hajipur a high index of agricultural prosperity coexists with a remarkably high density of population. In 1891 the density of population here was as high as 1,251 persons to the square mile.

[2] Such a high index explains why this sub-division could maintain as many as 1,000 persons per square mile of cultivated area in 1901.

CHAMPARAN (NORTHERN SUB-DIVISION)
Density Low

	Bhadoi	Aghani	Rabi	Index of Prosperity
Bettiah . . .	42	48	58	52

CHAMPARAN (SOUTHERN PARGANAS)
Density High

	Bhadoi	Aghani	Rabi	Index of Prosperity
Adapur . . .	54	40	64	78[1]
Dhaka . . .	49	86	64	77[1]
Madhubani . .	40	87	60	68[1]
Govindgunj . .	52	84	49	67

In South Bihar the density of population is higher in the northern alluvial tracts bordering on the Ganges than in the arid tracts to the south. In Sahabad, for example, the density of population in the northern tract is twice as high as in the rocky and dry regions of the south. It is interesting to note that in the case of Arrah, which is the most densely populated thana situated in the northern tract, the index of prosperity is 63; whereas in the case of Bhabua, which is the least densely populated thana in Sahabad, the corresponding index is only 47. In the case of Gaya also the indices for Barachatti and Shergatti, the two sparsely populated thanas of the south, are 12·4 and 11·4 respectively. On the other hand, the indices for the northern thanas are higher: the index is 22·7 in the case of Jahanabad, 33·8 in the case of Daudnagar, 27·8 in the case of Nabinagar, 33·7 in the case of Amangabad, and as high as 46·6 in the case of town Gaya. Similarly, the index of prosperity for North Monghyr which maintains a higher density of population than South Monghyr is as high as 80, such a high index being due to the fact that only 29 per cent of the cropped area is under winter rice.[2]

[1] It is significant that density in these thanas is over 800 persons per square mile.

[2] In this region the Teghra and Begusarai thanas maintain a density of more than 800 persons to the square mile. There agricultural productivity is high not only because winter rice is an unimportant crop but also because maize, a valuable *bhadoi* crop, is the staple crop and is followed by valuable *rabi* crops such as tobacco, chillies, barley, and wheat.

PART III

TRENDS OF AGRICULTURE AND POPULATION IN THE GANGES DELTA

INTRODUCTION

In the Delta of the Ganges we come across a natural region which supports a phenomenally high density of population. In common with the Ganges Valley the Ganges Delta falls within an intermediate zone lying between regions characterized by extremes of rainfall. As Brunhes observes, such a zone contains the early centres of dense population in which natural conditions have been favourable to the fullest and best development of humanity.[1] We have seen how throughout the Gangetic Valley there is a striking correspondence between the density of population and the amount of annual precipitation. Density increases from west to east and varies directly as the amount of annual rainfall which is the determining factor in tropical agriculture. We find the same tendency in the Gangetic Delta. But what distinguishes the Ganges Delta from the Gangetic Plain is the unique importance of the changes in the courses of the Ganges and its distributaries in the Delta region and their effects upon drainage, soil fertility, and the configuration of land, with all their concomitant reactions on agriculture, sanitation, and the movements of population. It is, therefore, necessary to study the character of the deltaic rivers which determines the nature of the rural economy of the Delta and is one of the limiting factors of the growth of population.

In a deltaic region when the main river reaches the delta, the force of the current is checked, and owing to the slight slope of the country it cannot carry away its heavy burden of silt which is deposited in the river-bed and on the banks. The level of the latter is thus gradually raised. Another feature of the deltaic river-system is that the main river no longer receives tributaries but discharges its silt-laden water through numerous distributaries. At the height of the rainy season when the river comes down in flood the flood-water

---

[1] Brunhes, *Human Geography*, p. 67.

with its heavy load of silt flows through the distributaries which overflow their banks and cover the adjoining lowlands with a rich layer of silt. Although the silt, which the Ganges deposits annually, has a large proportion of silica, mica, and argillaceous earth yet it contains a good deal of fertilizing properties. This annual deposit of silt maintains the natural fertility of the soil and keeps agricultural productivity at a high level. Hence everywhere in the world a deltaic region is one in which both extensive and intensive cultivation have reached a remarkable phase of development without taxing very much the ingenuity and resources of man. Consequently there is a strong presumption in favour of the theory set forth by La Blache that 'The largest human settlements must have been located in the section of the lower valley where the over-burdened stream succeeded in depositing its load'.[1] It must also be remembered that these deltaic distributaries also serve as natural drainage channels. The flood water pouring through them scours and flushes the countryside and, as soon as the seasonal floods subside, the surplus water is drained away to the sea. The activity of these distributaries in scouring and draining the country and providing natural flushing solves the problem of sanitation in a region which is over-flooded during the rainy season, due to heavy rainfall and high river floods, and in which the slight level of the country otherwise raises a difficult problem of drainage and sanitation. In fact, wherever the distributaries fail to function as drainage channels, the lower land between the high banks of the rivers remains waterlogged long after the rainy season, and becomes a breeding-place of the germs of tropical diseases like malaria and cholera, which have checked the growth of population in vast tracts of Western and Central Bengal. Thus the activity of the rivers and distributaries is the determining factor of both health and subsistence in a deltaic region and controls the movement and growth of population. Let us consider next another aspect of the activity of the deltaic rivers. An important factor in the hydrography of such rivers is the change in the course of the main river regulating the entire river system.

[1] P. Vidal De La Blache, *Principles of Human Geography*, p. 75.

As already said, the heavy load of silt which the main river in the Delta carries during the rainy season is deposited on the banks and in the river bed due to the slight slope of the country. But a considerable quantity of it also finds its way through the distributaries to the wide expanses of lower lands in the surrounding country. Now this is a process by which the level of the country is raised by gradual stages, and the Delta is formed continuously up to the same level. But as soon as lower lands are levelled up completely and the process of land formation is completed, there is bound to be a change in the course of the main river. The silt is increasingly deposited on the banks and in the river bed, and when the main channel is filled up the river seeks another channel in the adjoining lower ground. This tendency is strikingly illustrated by the onward sweep of the Ganges successively through the different tracts of the Delta from west to east. Emerging from the upper levels round the Raj Mahal hills and prevented by their rocky barrier from flowing further to the west, the main waters of the Ganges originally flowed along the general course now indicated by the Bhagirathi. As this channel was gradually filled up and the delta-building function of the Ganges and the system of distributaries connected with it was finished, its activity ceased and it sought a new channel towards the east, where a new tract of the country became the scene of its creative activity, while the larger streams or channels passing through the flat country deserted by the Ganges unavoidably diminished in size, and the quantity and the force of the water they carried were gradually reduced. The oscillations of the Ganges towards the east have, however, been sufficiently slow, with the result that successive stretches of low country have been filled up gradually, and have been raised to the flat high level characteristic of old alluvial formations. But still it is remarkable that in the course of only a few centuries the Ganges has traversed in its eastern march wide tracts of the country and has wandered successively from the rocky western limit of the Delta flat towards the eastern. It left its old channel, the Bhagirathi, apparently in the sixteenth century, and began to find an outlet through other channels farther east,

including the Gorai in Faridpur. Each in turn became the
main channel, the Ganges continuing its march to the east
and leaving the distributaries to the west to dwindle and die.
Finally it swerved more directly to the east across its old
channels and found a course down the Padma, which was
nearly the same as at present except that it turned south
below Goalundo, passed close to Faridpur and flowed past
Madaripur by what is known as the Arial Khan. There is
another important episode in the history of the Ganges which
has had a determining influence on its subsequent career.
The Brahmaputra formerly flowed farther to the east through
Mymensingh and joined the Meghna near Bhairab Bazar.
After 1787, as a result of a change in the course of the river
Tista which, instead of being a tributary of the Ganges,
found its way into the Brahmaputra, the Brahmaputra was
diverted to the west, and following the channel of the Jamuna
joined the Ganges near Goalundo, and the united stream fell
into the Meghna near Chandpur. The accession of the
Brahmaputra prevented the Ganges from finding a new
channel farther east.

Throughout the Ganges Delta we find different stages in
the process of land formation as conditioned by the activity or
otherwise of the Ganges and its distributaries. The deltaic
soil varies from the hard clay of the old alluvial formations
to soft clay of the new alluvial formations rich in mineral
and vegetable substances. The old alluvial formations consist of tracts in which the process of land formation is all
but complete. Here land has been raised to the same flat
level, rivers have diminished in size, and sluggish streams
carry a small quantity of water and swell up only when the
Ganges rises in flood. Sometimes the last stage in the life
of the rivers is reached, the rivers being choked up with silt
and parcelled out into stagnant pools overgrown with weeds.
Practically the whole of Western and Central Bengal with the
exception of the littoral tracts lies in a moribund delta, in
which the activity of the rivers has almost ceased, and decadent conditions of health and subsistence have checked
the growth of population through successive decades. As
contrasted with the moribund delta there is the active delta

covering the greater portion of Eastern Bengal. Here the great rivers are building up land and throwing up new alluvial formations rich in agricultural possibilities, while sometimes there is diluvion of land sufficiently old and supporting a teeming population. But here also the varying stages in the life and activity of the rivers are clearly discernible. The onward march of the delta-building rivers to the east continues to this day. The rivers have become less active in the northern portion of this region than in the south-eastern portion covering the littoral tracts, particularly in the vicinity of the Meghna estuary. It is in these littoral tracts that the healthiest and most fertile regions of the Ganges Delta are situated at the present time, and in these tracts the increase in the number of teeming population knows no bounds.

We are now in a position to characterize generally the trends of the movement and growth of population in the Ganges Delta against the natural background sketched above. The important generalization which can be made regarding the distribution of population in the Ganges Delta is that the density of population has a tendency to increase at a higher rate in the fertile and healthy tracts of the active delta than in the decadent regions of the moribund delta, where both agricultural productivity and public health are at a low level. In Bengal 'during the last seven decades the relative distribution of population between north and south has altered comparatively little. The greatest changes of population distribution have been between east and west. The uninterrupted recession eastwards of the median point conveniently illustrates the proportionately larger growth of population in Eastern than in Western Bengal.'[1] This is a striking statistical generalization of very great import. It shows not only that at a particular point of time the density of population is higher in the active than in the moribund delta, but also that the same dynamic natural factors, all of which are inseparably connected with the activity of the deltaic rivers, are still operating to widen the difference in density through successive decades up to the present time. The moribund delta, *Rarh* as it was called in ancient times,

[1] *Census Report*, 1931, p. 8.

was the scene of activity of the deltaic rivers probably up to
the sixteenth century. Here extensive areas had been brought
under cultivation and land had always supported a high
density of population. But the tide has definitely turned in
comparatively recent times as a result of the shifting of the
course of the Ganges. There has been widespread deterioration of soil owing to the slow death of the rivers; defective
drainage has rendered vast tracts of the country extremely
insanitary and unfit for human habitation; population has
been decimated by diseases like malaria and cholera, and
those who survive as victims of malaria have little vitality
left in them to resist natural calamities like epidemic diseases
and unfavourable natural conditions under which agriculture
has to be practised. The result has been that agricultural
productivity has declined, the death-rate has increased, while
at the same time there has been a steady migration of people
to healthy and fertile regions. In either case there has been
rural depopulation on a large scale throughout the moribund
delta, and land has gone out of cultivation to a considerable
extent.[1]

In the active delta, on the other hand, there has been
a steady growth of population through successive decades.
Here there has been great extension of cultivation due to
clearance of jungles or colonization of new alluvial formations.
Agricultural productivity has always been high owing to
favourable natural conditions. The death-rate has been low
because of the comparative immunity of the people to malaria
and cholera, which are the scourge of the moribund delta.
And it is a striking fact that although there is migration of
people from the north to the littoral tracts in the south and
the fertile lands near the Meghna estuary in the south-east,

---

[1] The following account of agricultural deterioration caused by malaria in
Jessore illustrates how the process of depopulation sets in: 'The agricultural
population stricken by malaria have lost their physical vigour and energy and
are growing more and more lazy and inert every day and are incapable of hard
work in the field or at home. The result is that their fields remain half
ploughed and cattle are not properly attended to, and the yield of crops is in
consequence very poor. Under normal conditions the country could produce
double as much crops as it now produces. There is dearth of labour everywhere
during the harvest season and the lands do not get proper treatment. A lot
of land lies fallow and those that are cultivated do not yield full crops.' *Survey
and Settlement Report*, Jessore, 1920–24.

yet the increase of population in this region as a whole is due principally to a very great natural increase of population.

The above summary of broad facts concerning the relative growth of population in the moribund and in the active delta raises an interesting question of economics, as well as of vital statistics, a very brief examination of which will not be out of place here. The contrast between the two regions, as we have noticed, manifests itself in favourable or unfavourable conditions of health and subsistence, and both these dynamic factors of population growth are governed by the hydrographical character of the deltaic rivers. It is true, no doubt, that as a matter of fact unfavourable conditions of health coexist with unfavourable economic conditions, because both are effects of the same cause. But is there any causal connexion between conditions of health and economic conditions? What is the bearing of either set of conditions on the growth of population? The relation between conditions of health and the growth of population is quite clear from the vital statistics. For example, as a result of a systematic inquiry made between 1911 and 1916 Dr. C. A. Bentley, Director of Public Health, was able to trace a very close correlation between the changes of population in the decade 1901–11 and the prevalence of malaria as indicated by the spleen index and the malaria fever index. In the census report of 1931 also a close correlation was traced between the changes of population in 1911–21 and the changes in 1901–11.[1] A study of vital statistics shows clearly that in Eastern Bengal the natural increase of population is faster not only because the death-rate is lower, but also because the birth-rate is higher. In Western and Central Bengal, on the other hand, the natural increase of population is kept down by a high death-rate associated with a low birth-rate.[2] But the relation between

[1] The author of the report pointed out that, 'in the case of certain districts which have proved exceptions to the rule of correlation it is known that there have been changes in the prevalence of malaria in recent years and that, but for these, the correlation would have been closer than it is'. *Census Report*, 1921, p. 87.

[2] The figures for relative birth-rates are 188 for Eastern Bengal, 160 for Central Bengal, and 146 for Western Bengal. *Census Report*, 1931, p. 199.

The common generalization that high death-rates and high birth-rates go together does not apply to Western Bengal. It is likely that malaria has reduced fecundity, for it is sigificant that there is a somewhat close negative

the growth of population and the economic resources and possibilities of different tracts is not clear on the face of it. The fact, however, seems to be that diseases must be regarded as instruments of adjustment of population to economic resources. Physiological immunity and power of resistance to disease depend essentially on vitality, which again depends on economic conditions. Thus economic conditions react powerfully on conditions of health, and although vital statistics very often obscure the effect of economic conditions on the movement and growth of population over short periods, yet when we study long-run tendencies we realize fully the overwhelming importance of economic factors. In fact, it is true to say, as Dr. Bentley holds, that malaria manifests itself in Bengal as the instrument of the adjustment of the growth of population to economic conditions, and that it is not the root cause of depopulation but appears in localities which suffer adverse economic conditions.

correlation between the incidence of malaria and the birth-rate. Indeed, in estimating the true loss of population due to malaria in the districts of Hughli the superintendent of census operations in 1881 took account of the fact that 'apart from actual mortality the fever reduced the vitality of the survivors, thus diminishing the birth-rate'. A similar view was taken in the *Census Report* of 1891 in which it was said of Hughli that 'there is reason to fear that fever is still very prevalent and if not as fatal as of old it indirectly reacts on the reproductive and recuperative powers of the population'. (*Census Report*, p. 99). Another fact which must be taken into account is that the birth-rate in Eastern Bengal is higher because the Moslem population who predominate in numbers increase much faster than the Hindus.

CHAPTER I

EXTENSION OF CULTIVATION AND DENSITY

IN a predominantly agricultural region the problem of the adjustment of population to economic resources can best be studied by explaining the variations in the density of population in terms of agricultural possibilities. A convenient method of approach to this problem is, as we have already demonstrated, to observe the process and stages of agricultural development as determined by the extension of cultivation. In fact, the extent to which cultivation has expanded or contracted, or has a tendency to expand or contract, is a clear indication of the agricultural possibilities of a particular tract, and of its capacity to maintain a given density of population. As Samuel Van Valkenberg has pointed out, in the case of a country like India, cropped land 'reflects the complex of physical factors relief, climate and soil—particularly—so dominantly that other elements in the environment can almost be considered negligible.'[1] Whenever these physical factors are favourable to agricultural development, cultivation has a tendency to extend to its final limit, and there is a progressive increase in the density of population. On the other hand, wherever natural conditions have become adverse there is a shrinkage of the cultivated area, general agricultural decadence, and rural depopulation. The contrast between the active and the moribund delta from the point of view of population density and agricultural development in relation to extension of cultivation is illustrated by the following comparative table (see p. 212).

The figures given on p. 212 clearly show how the density of population varies with agricultural development and enterprise as indicated by extension of cultivation. It is obvious that in examining the possibilities of agricultural development

[1] 'Agricultural Regions of Asia, Pt. IV, India'; *Economic Geography*, April 1933, p. 112.

in a particular tract we must consider not only the scope for such development, but also the extent of agricultural enterprise. The percentage of cultivated area to total area is an index of both. But it is important for our purpose to have an idea of either separately. Our task is easy if we interpret the statistics in the fourth and the fifth columns a little carefully. The percentage of cultivable to total area is a clear index of the scope for agricultural development by means of extension of cultivation. It is apparent that such scope is very much restricted in Central Bengal, while Eastern and Western Bengal are almost on a par so far as the scope for expansion of cultivation is concerned.[1]

Natural Division	Mean Density	Percentage of cultivated area to total area	Percentage of cultivable area to total area	Percentage of cultivated area to cultivable area
Central Bengal .	566	81·6	56·7	55·7
West Bengal .	618	47·5	78·3	60·7
East Bengal .	985	71·1	79·6	89·3

The real contrast, however, is clearly seen when we consider the percentage of cultivated area to cultivable area, which is an index of agricultural enterprise so far as it relates to extension of cultivation. The statistics show that agricultural enterprise increases with the density of population; it is greatest in Eastern Bengal, in which as much as 89·3 per cent of the cultivable area is cultivated, and is least in Central Bengal, in which unfavourable conditions of health and subsistence have led to a shrinkage of cultivated area, and only 55·7 per cent of the cultivable area is cultivated. Thus on the whole it appears that in Central Bengal the percentage of cultivated area to total area is lowest not only because the scope for expansion of cultivation is limited most, but also because agricultural enterprise is least. The percentage of cultivated area to total area is lower in Western Bengal than in Eastern Bengal not so much because the scope for the

[1] It must be noted that the real cultivable area is probably less in Western and Central Bengal because the statistics include old fallow, which in the moribund delta is very often uncultivable.

extension of cultivation is more restricted in Western Bengal, as because unfavourable natural conditions have discouraged agricultural enterprise in Western Bengal.[1]

We shall now study in greater detail the course of agricultural development as determined by the extension of cultivation in the different tracts of the moribund and the active delta. Amongst the natural divisions of the Ganges Delta, Central Bengal, which is situated in the moribund delta, maintains the lowest density of population, viz. 566 persons to the square mile, and only 31·6 per cent of its total area is cultivated. Between 1872 and 1931 population has increased in this tract by 36·4 per cent as against 90·1 per cent in Eastern Bengal. But it must be remembered that the increase of population in Central Bengal is, to a large extent, due to the extension of cultivation in the Sunderbans and the growth of population in Calcutta and in the industrially developed neighbouring area. The average for Central Bengal has been pushed up by very large percentage increases in the case of 24 Parganas and Khulna. The population of 24 Parganas has increased by as much as 81·8 per cent between 1872 and 1931. This increase is mainly due to the growth of population in Calcutta and the neighbouring industrial areas, and the extension of cultivation in the Sunderbans. In Khulna also the population has increased by 54·1 per cent in the same period. There also the increase has been mainly due to the extension of cultivation in the Sunderbans. On the other hand, in Nadia and Jessore, which are the typical districts of the moribund delta, the population has increased in the same period by only 2·0 and 0·2 per cent respectively.[2]

[1] In this connexion it is interesting to compare the tracts in the Ganges delta with those in the Middle Ganges Valley. In the Middle Ganges Valley North Bihar is more densely populated than South Bihar. The percentage of cultivated area is higher in North Bihar than in South Bihar. But South Bihar is not lacking in agricultural enterprise in so far as the percentage of cultivated area to cultivable area is almost the same as in North Bihar. What has been an obstacle to agricultural enterprise there is the limited area of cultivable land. Thus South Bihar resembles Western Bengal so far as the scope for expansion of cultivation is concerned, but differs entirely from Central Bengal in respect of both agricultural enterprise and scope for expansion of cultivation.

[2] It was pointed out in the *Census Report* of 1921 that 'Central Bengal has gained nothing since 1872 except through industrial development in the neighbourhood of Calcutta and the extension of cultivation into the Sunderbans and in the south of 24 Parganas and Khulna'; *Census Report*, 1921, p. 27.

Murshidabad is the most densely populated district in Central Bengal, maintaining a density of 656 persons to the square mile. In this district the percentage of cultivated area to total area is as high as 52·1 per cent, as against an average of only 31·6 per cent for the whole of Central Bengal, while 68·3 per cent of the cultivable area is cultivated, as against an average of 55·7 per cent for the whole of Central Bengal. But the district seems to be decadent from the point of view of the growth of population. Between 1872 and 1931 the increase of population has been only 14·1 per cent as against the average of 36·4 per cent for the whole of Central Bengal. The river Bhagirathi divides this district from north to south into two well-defined tracts. To the west of the Bhagirathi the land is formed of hard clay and nodular limestone, generally well raised and well drained. It is interspersed with numerous swamps and beds of old rivers. The rivers have their sources in hill torrents and receive sudden floods. But the floods are not sufficiently high to inundate the land for a long time. Hence the land does not receive the annual deposit of silt, and is not so fertile as alluvial land in the active delta.[1] Moreover, this tract has to depend on artificial irrigation, and relies to a great extent on the winter rice crop, which is liable to fail in years of drought.[2] But agriculture in this tract does not suffer from water-logging and defective drainage which are so common in the moribund delta. For example, the Hijal tract, situated in the southwest of the district, is widely inundated during the rains, but becomes perfectly dry in the cold weather. Hence the incidence of malaria is very low in this tract, and it attracts a steady stream of immigrants from the malarious areas in the neighbouring districts. Even as early as 1891 it was reported that Murshidabad 'receives a large number of immigrants from the fever-stricken districts of Burdwan and Nadia'.[3] During the next decade, while the increase of population was only 3 per cent in the low-lying tracts to the

[1] The most densely populated thanas lie in the alluvial tracts along the course of the Bhagirathi. The density there is over 1,000 persons to the square mile.

[2] Artificial irrigation is indispensable owing to the physical configuration of the country and the quality of the soil.

[3] *Census Report*, 1891, p. 91.

east, it was 18 per cent on the average in the highland tract. This progressive increase of population has been possible through extension of cultivation. In fact, this tract is in a state of high cultivation. Except for *bils* and marshes and a few patches of jungle there is comparatively little waste land. Even the beds and banks of the *nullahs* and *bils* as they dry up are almost exclusively devoted to the production of rice. There is even terraced cultivation on the slope of the undulating lands. The tract to the east of the Bhagirathi covers the alluvial lowlands of a deltaic region. Here land has been very fertile, and has always supported a much higher density of population than land in the western tract. But in recent times the slow death of the Bhagirathi and its distributaries has been reacting unfavourably on the agriculture and sanitation of this tract. Moreover, it was pointed out as early as 1911 that 'the action of nature has been interfered with by the marginal embankment along the left bank of the Bhagirathi, which prevents the inundation which would otherwise occur.'[1] It is not unlikely that the disastrous effects of the slow death of the Bhagirathi have been aggravated by human interference with nature.

Jessore, a typical district of the moribund delta, comes next to Murshidabad in order of the density of population. In this district 39·1 per cent of the total area is cultivated, as against an average of 31·6 per cent for the whole of Central Bengal, while 60·5 per cent of the cultivable area is cultivated, as against an average of 55·7 per cent for the whole of Central Bengal. But what is remarkable is that the population of this district was found to be almost the same in 1931 as in 1872, the increase of population between 1872 and 1931 being only 0·2 per cent. The explanation of this phenomenon is extensive rural depopulation, which is the effect of deterioration of the soil, water-logging, defective drainage, and high incidence of malaria, the usual chain of causes which bring about economic retrogression in the moribund delta. In this district the density of population is higher in the southern and south-eastern portions than in the western and the north-western portions. The district as a whole is an alluvial tract

[1] *Census Report*, 1911, p. 95.

intersected by numerous rivers which are connected by cross
channels. Formerly the rivers and channels in the north
and the west drew their supply of water from the Padma, the
parent stream, either directly or through its spill channels.
But gradually the land was raised above the flood-level by
periodical inundations. The result has been that the rivers
in this tract have lost their connexion with the parent stream
and are beyond the reach of tides, and except during the
rainy season, remain within the limits of their high banks.
Hence these rivers have silted up and have become more and
more shallow, while the channels have also deteriorated and
are full of weeds. Thus the land which used to receive
fertilizing silt has lost its high fertility, and the drainage of
the depressions, which is always difficult in a deltaic country,
has become almost impossible owing to the silting up of the
mouths of the rivers and drainage channels. The result of
these changes has been that land has gone out of cultivation
to a very large extent and the incidence of malaria has increased.[1] There is evidence to show that these disastrous
changes have taken place in comparatively recent times.
An estimate made in 1876 by Lord Macdonell in his report
on the Food Grain Supply of Behar and Bengal shows that
the area under cultivation in the Jhenida and the Magura
sub-divisions was 75 per cent of the gross area. As regards the
Bangaon sub-division, the Sub-Divisional Officer's estimate
was that five-eighths of the total area was under cultivation,
but Lord Macdonell considered this as an underestimate,
and came to the conclusion that the proportion of cultivated
land there was not less than in the other two sub-divisions.[2]
But while 75 per cent of the total area was cultivated in 1876,
only 39·2 per cent is under cultivation at the present time.[3]
The Jhenida sub-division has suffered much from the stag-
nation of its rivers, and much land has gone out of cultivation.

[1] The effect of defective drainage is that stagnant pools are formed and the
homesteads are covered with jungle, while good drinking water becomes
scarce.

[2] *Gazetteer*, Jessore.

[3] In the Western tract 'the river banks all bristle with depopulated towns
and villages which were once populous and flourishing. . . . Vast tracts of
cultivable land are lying fallow in the Jhenida and Bangaon sub-divisions,
where, on account of decreasing demand for land its value is gradually
diminishing.' *Survey and Settlement Report*, Jessore, 1920–24.

There is also evidence to show that the mortality from malaria is also heaviest in the western and the north-western tract. In fact 'the fever outbreak commenced in the Jhenida sub-division, chiefly in the villages on the banks of the rivers Nabaganga, Kapotakshi, Bhairab, and Chitra'.[1] The tract to the south and the south-east which supports a higher density of population borders on the swamps of the lower delta. It does not depend for its agricultural water supply on the Ganges flood, but is intersected by numerous tidal rivers which flow backwards and forwards. Owing to these rivers, which still have a flowing current, land has maintained its productivity, so that this is naturally the most prosperous tract in the district. Agricultural development by means of extension of cultivation has no doubt been hampered in this tract by the existence of *bils*, which do not dry up at any time, but most of them are silting up and many have been reclaimed and brought under cultivation.[2]

The district of Nadia, with a density of 531 persons to the square mile, comes third in order of density amongst the districts of Central Bengal. Nadia is also one of the typical decadent districts of the moribund delta. 75 per cent of the total area of this district is cultivable, but only 27·8 per cent of the total area is cultivated, as against the average of 31·6 per cent for the whole of Central Bengal. While in Murshidabad and Jessore more than 60 per cent, and in Central Bengal as a whole 55·7 per cent of the cultivable area is cultivated, in Nadia barely 37 per cent of the cultivable area is under cultivation. The figures show that although there is much scope for expansion of cultivation, yet unfavourable natural conditions have seriously hindered the development of agriculture by means of extension of cultivation. As in Jessore so also in Nadia there has been rural depopulation on a large scale owing to the same essential causes connected with the cessation of the activity of the delta-building rivers, so that the population of this district has increased by only

[1] *Census Report*, 1891, p. 76.
[2] 'The bils and morasses are still undergoing a process of land formation and what were vast sheets of water twenty years back are now in places paddy-fields growing aman crop in abundance.' *Survey and Settlement Report*, Jessore, 1920–24.

2 per cent between 1872 and 1931. The whole district is a flat alluvial formation intersected by numerous backwaters, minor streams and swamps. The main rivers have been silting up for more than two centuries, and the country has been raised to such a level that the soil may agriculturally be classed as highland.[1] The soil, which varies but little all over the district, is a light sandy loam possessing but little fertility and incapable of retaining moisture. It has become barren, as it is no longer enriched by the fertilizing silt which was deposited by river floods when the rivers were active. The very light manuring which is applied to land is insufficient to compensate for the loss of fertility due to continuous cropping. The result is that land is becoming less and less capable of yielding a good economic return. This is clearly indicated by the statistics of cultivation, which show a steady diminution of the net cultivated area. Such a tendency implies that 'it is more and more necessary to allow the land to lie fallow for longer periods between croppings,' and that 'the soil in Nadia is not sufficiently fertile to enable the same percentage of population to depend upon agriculture as in other districts.'[2] The same cause which has reduced the fertility of the soil is also responsible for the spread and virulence of malaria. The Epidemic Commission appointed by Government in 1881 to enquire into the causes of the malaria epidemic ascribed it to 'obstructed drainage and water-logging of the soil, which had been intensified by a gradual filling up of the *bils* by the deposit brought in from the rivers: this again had been supplemented by a gradual but continuous rise in the level of the river beds, thus causing . . . a general derangement of levels so serious as to affect the natural drainage of the country.'[3]

[1] It appears that as early as the beginning of the last century the Bhagirathi swerved eastwards by a sudden change of course and left the town of Nadia and a considerable strip of land north and south of that city on its right bank.

[2] Report of the District Collector quoted in the *Census Report* of 1901, p. 94.

[3] *Census Report*, 1901, p. 93. The silting up of the rivers has also been responsible for destructive floods. When there are simultaneous freshets in the Ganges and the Brahmaputra, the waters of the former, banked up at Goalundo by the latter, are forced to find egress to the sea by the rivers of Nadia which have been silted up and are inadequate to carry such a large volume of water to the Ganges, with the result that there is widespread flood. (*Census Report*, 1891, p. 89.)

The district of 24 Parganas, with a density of 516 persons to the square mile, stands fourth in order of density amongst the districts of Central Bengal. It also comes fourth in order of the percentage of cultivable area to total area. Only 45·6 per cent of the total area in this district is cultivable, as against the average of 56·7 per cent for Central Bengal. The large area of uncultivable land is accounted for by extensive water-logged depressions in the north and the Sundarban area in the south, which covers one-third of the total area of the district. But we must not conclude from these facts that the scope for agricultural development by means of extension of cultivation and the consequent possibilities of an increase of population are rigidly limited. Most of the area which is regarded as uncultivable is fit for cultivation, and natural conditions are not so unfavourable to agricultural enterprise as in other districts of the moribund delta. That agricultural enterprise has not been lacking in this district is indicated by the fact that as much as 52·2 per cent of the cultivable area is cultivated, as against the average of 55·7 per cent for the whole of Central Bengal. In fact, as already said, the increase of population in this district during the last few decades has to some extent been due to the extension of cultivation into the Sundarban area. The district contains two natural divisions, viz. the northern inland tract and the low-lying Sundarbans towards the seaboard on the south. The northern tract is situated in the moribund delta. Here the rivers are stagnant and their beds are out of reach of the tidal action of the main river. The banks have been raised by the deposit of silt, and the rivers, being confined during the rainy season to the high banks, cannot carry silt to the lower lands. The result has been that soil has deteriorated, while the depressions, which cannot be raised by the deposit of silt, have become stagnant and can never be completely dry. Large areas in this tract are occupied by *bils*. Some of them are natural drainage basins and can never be dry, while others are connected by spill channels with the rivers. Formerly the spill channels carried silt during the floods and also carried away the surplus water. But now, the rivers having silted up, the spill channels no longer perform these functions. The whole of the northern tract is in a state of high cultivation, the density of population there is also high, and cultivation has recently extended by the draining and reclamation of swamps. But the unfavourable natural conditions characteristic of the moribund delta have checked the growth of population in this tract. Several of the central and northern thanas have become decadent, and, as already said, but for the increase of population in the industrially developed areas near Calcutta the population would have remained as stationary as in other parts of the old delta. The southern tract, on the other hand, is situated in a region which exhibits the process of land formation in an unfinished state. The portion of the Sundarban area on the sea face no doubt contains swamps and morasses covered with low forest and scrubwood jungle, and is not fit for habitation and cultivation. But the northern inland portion has been reclaimed by means of embankments, which prevent the onrush of saline water. The southern tract as a whole is very sparsely populated. In some thanas bordering on the Sundarbans the density is only 100 persons to the square mile, as against the high density of about 1,000 persons to the square mile in some of the northern tracts. The progress of reclamation in the Sundarbans has, however, been attracting settlers. 'But the population in the Sundarban tracts is not at all equal to what the amount of land under cultivation would lead one to expect.'[1] In the first place, the high fertility of land makes it easy for a cultivator to keep large areas under cultivation. Secondly, the cultivating seasons being later than those in the north, land is cultivated by migratory non-resident farmers. Moreover, 'many of the cultivators besides having a holding near their own houses have also another eight or ten miles away, which they visit only occasionally when they have no work to do.'[2] But still the fact remains that the whole of this area, which is a new deltaic region, offers immense possibilities for agricultural development by means of extension of cultivation and the consequent growth of population.

The district of Khulna, with a mean density of 347 persons to the square mile, occupies the last place in order of density

---

[1] *Gazetteer*, 24 Parganas.   [2] Ibid.

amongst the districts of Central Bengal.[1] It resembles the district of 24 Parganas in important respects. It appears from the statistics that only 43·2 per cent of the total area of the district is cultivable, as against 45·6 per cent in 24 Parganas and the average of 56·7 per cent for Central Bengal. But in Khulna, as in 24 Parganas, the small percentage of cultivable area is due to the existence of jungle tracts in the Sundarban areas and numerous marshes in the north of the district. Most of this so-called uncultivable area is not really uncultivable. It is highly fertile, and it awaits the axe and the plough. The district is a flat deltaic country, in which the banks of the rivers are higher than the surrounding country, so that the land sloping away from them on either side is broken up into a series of depressions, and numerous marshes have been formed. In the northern portion of the district land is high, and ordinarily lies above the flood level, while the southern portion lies in a delta still in the process of formation. In the northern portion, which is in a state of high cultivation, population is fairly dense, the density of population being much higher there than in the less extensively cultivated areas in the south. In the northern tract density increases from west to east. To the north-west, particularly in the northern portion of the Satkhira subdivision, where the country is comparatively high, the crops are not exposed to salt water inundation, the curse of the agriculturists in this district. Here we find the old settled villages surrounded by land which had been in a state of high cultivation. As early as 1891 the district magistrate reported that 'all the land in the Kalaroa thana has already been cultivated. While the southern thanas import labourers, Kalaroa, like the neighbouring thanas of Jessore, exports them.'[2] Population had also reached a high density, and the Satkhira sub-division had in the past always supported a higher density than other sub-divisions. But in recent times

[1] 'Compared with the rivers of Nadia and to a less extent with those of Jessore the rivers of Khulna still carry large volumes of water which periodically flush the land. Hence her population is still on the upward grade, but in nature's good time she will have to suffer the travail of the emergence of upland from the embryo deltaic stage and it is unlikely that this period will be long delayed.' *Survey and Settlement Report*, 1920–26, p. 44.

[2] People have emigrated from Kalaroa to the clearances in the Sunderbans.

this sub-division has become decadent owing to the usual
causes of decadence to be found in the old delta, while the
eastern tracts, including the Sadar and the Bagherhat sub-
divisions, have become progressive. In 1926 current fallow
amounted to 79,000 acres in the Satkhira sub-division,
against 10,000 acres in the Sadar sub-division and 9,000 acres
in the Bagherhat sub-division. Such a large area under current
fallow in Satkhira, which implies a corresponding reduction
of the cultivated area, is nothing but 'the beginning of the
economic results of the death of the western rivers'.[1] The
north-eastern tract, on the other hand, is a low-lying tract
intersected with numerous marshes. Here the only places
suitable for dwellings are the highlands along the banks of
the rivers. The percentage of cultivated area is low owing
to large areas of *bil* land, which consist of large flat tracts on
which hardly a tree will grow. Sometimes the marsh lands
can easily be brought under cultivation, for the creeks bring
down rich river silt and also drain away the surplus water.
But in many cases the *khals* have ceased to be proper drainage
channels. The result is that cultivators have to wait till the
fields dry up, and in years of heavy rainfall dry cultivation
becomes impossible. But the curse of agriculture in this
tract is the salt water that comes up from the sea through
the channels in the Sunderbans and makes the water of the
rivers brackish.[2] Here successful agriculture is possible only
when strong embankments are built to shut out the salt
water, and when rainfall is heavy enough to sweeten the
rivers at the end of June.[3] The unfavourable natural conditions just described have checked the growth of population
in this tract, and at the present time it is only by extensive

[1] In the western thanas where the rivers are dying the increase of population
since 1872 has been much smaller than in the eastern thanas where the rivers
are still active. The present density of population thus increases from west to
east, and there is also a rough correspondence between the variation in density
and the variation in the percentage of cultivated to cultivable area.

[2] The old rivers Betna, Kobadak, Bhadra, etc., having lost their connection
with the Ganges, 'serve rather as conduit pipes by which the salt water is
carried upwards than as channels for distributing sweet water.' *Survey and
Settlement Report*, Khulna, p. 15.

[3] But it must be remembered that 'the embanking of the saline rivers with
high and strong embankments with a view to keeping out salt water from
the crops has had the natural effect of confining the salt tide and so forcing it
higher and higher up the rivers'. *Survey and Settlement Report*, p. 15.

reclamation of marsh land that it can support a higher density of population.[1] In the Sunderban area to the south population is still very sparse. But the jungle is being steadily pushed back and highly fertile virgin land is being brought under cultivation. In Khulna, as in 24 Perganas, a good deal of the work of reclamation is carried out by non-resident farmers. But the number of regular settlers is gradually increasing.

We shall study next the course of agricultural development as determined by the extension of cultivation in Western Bengal, which stands second in order of density amongst the natural divisions of the Ganges Delta. In this region as a whole the general tendency is for the density of population to increase from west to east. The eastern portion lying to the west of the Bhagirathi consists of districts whose civilization is as old as the Aryan occupation of the country. When the Bhagirathi was a mighty stream the country to the east of it (covering the districts of Central Bengal) was the active delta. But still the country to the west of the Bhagirathi had not grown into a moribund delta; the rivers there were still active, the productivity of land was high and the country was inhabited by a teeming population. But in recent times the whole of this tract has become a moribund delta, due to the eastward march of the Ganges. The main rivers have silted up, not only because the natural process of delta formation is almost complete, but also because the natural drainage of the country has been obstructed by the construction of a network of embankments and dams for the purpose of irrigation and prevention of floods. The result has been deterioration of soil and waterlogging. Thus not only has there been agricultural deterioration on a large scale, but this

---

[1] 'The process of reclamation of saline swamps is still going on. Advantage is taken of the fact that salt water plants will grow only within access of the salt water. As it is practically impossible to eradicate them without excluding the salt water, the land to be reclaimed is completely enclosed by an embankment thrown round it. It is then drained of the salt water. The jungle inside is then cleared and the land prepared for sowing or planting.' Sarat Chandra Mukherjee, *Survey Settlement of the Dihi Dhandra Estate in the Khulna District*, 1905–9. It may be noted that the growth of population as a result of extension of cultivation into the marsh lands is not a recent event. In the *Census Report* of 1891 we find that 'the growth of population in Mullahat was explained by large reclamations of swamp land making room for new residents. A similar cause was at work in Khulna thana.' *Census Report*, 1891, p. 77.

tract has also become notorious for the high incidence of
malaria and other epidemic diseases. In fact, during the
decade 1911–21, which was characterized by the great influenza epidemic, the decrease of population was found to be
greatest 'over a strip of country running from north to south
in Western Bengal, and lying just east of the line marking
the transition from the new alluvial soil of the delta to the undulating laterite formation to the west of it'.[1] On the whole,
but for the increase of population in the industrially developed
areas along the Bhagirathi, the population of this tract has
shown a tendency to remain stationary through successive
decades. As distinguished from the eastern portion there is
the western portion, which is a lateritic formation much less
fertile than the alluvial eastern portion. Here the extent of
the cultivated area is small owing to extensive areas of uncultivable land, and population is much less sparse than in
the eastern portion. Thus in Western Bengal, taken as a
whole, the growth of population seems to have been restricted
by agricultural deterioration and disease in the alluvial tracts
and the small scope for extension of cultivation in the barren
uplands of the west.

The district of Howrah, with a density of 2,105 persons to
the square mile, is the most densely populated district in
Western Bengal. But it must be remembered that of all the
districts in Bengal Howrah is least dependent on agriculture.
There is a large industrial population in the riparian areas.
Even in the interior villages are tending to be semi-urban in
character and contribute largely to the artisan class. Every
thana supports more than 1,200 persons to the square mile.
Agricultural conditions, however, are not unfavourable to
the growth of population. Agricultural development has no
doubt been hampered by the existence of numerous swamps
in the north and the liability of the lowlands in the south to
destructive floods. But elsewhere the land consists of rich
alluvial soil, which receives annual deposits of fertilizing silt
from the Damodar and the Rupnarain, with the result that

---

[1] *Census Report*, 1921, p. 27. The high mortality from influenza in this region was obviously due to the fact that the vitality of the people had already
been sapped by malaria and agricultural deterioration acting and reacting on
each other.

'practically all the land at present cultivable has been brought under the plough, and very little is left fallow'.[1] In this district also there has been extension of cultivation by the reclamation of swamps. For example, it was pointed out in the census report of 1891 that in the Jagatballabhpur thana 'a large area of land has been brought under cultivation and is now fully populated, while the reclamation of swamps in Amta is said to explain the increase of population'.[2] Thus it appears that the only way in which the area under cultivation can increase and population can grow in the rural areas of this district is to reclaim some of the existing swamps, or to protect the part of the country liable to inundation.

The district of Hughly, with a density of 938 persons to the square mile, comes second in order of density amongst the districts of Western Bengal. But in Hughly, as in Howrah, the high density of population has been largely due to the growth of population in the industrially developed tracts along the river Hughli. The population of the district has, however, reached a stationary state. Like Jessore, Hughly contained in 1931 almost the same number of inhabitants as in 1872, the actual increase between 1872 and 1931 being only 0·5 per cent. This fact is remarkable, especially when we find that the industrial areas of the district attract a large number of immigrants. But the explanation of this fact is quite simple when we consider the natural disabilities from which the people of this district suffer. The district contains large areas of waste and uncultivable land, and the pressure of the population on the cultivated portion is, therefore, intense. The river Damodar, which passes through the district, divides it into two distinct classes of soil. The tract lying to the west is subject to the fluvial action of this river, as well as of the Rupnarain. The Damodar, flowing on a bed too narrow for the passage of its flood water and restricted on the east by a high embankment, spills over its right bank during the rains. The villages, particularly on the southern side, are protected against floods by innumerable embankments, otherwise cultivation becomes precarious. Moreover, the smaller streams, which come down in flood, change their

[1] *Gazetteer*, Howrah.   [2] *Census Report*, 1891, pp. 94–5.

courses in the lower levels in the most unexpected way and increase the uncertainty of crops. In this area we come across extensive areas of waste land, and the density of population is low. In the country to the east of the Damodar, which is protected against floods by the high embankment along the bank, the crops are secure, the land is in a state of high cultivation and the density of population is high. On the whole, the agricultural possibilities of Hughly are limited by the control of river floods and the reclamation of marsh lands.[1]

The district of Burdwan, with a density of 583 persons to the square mile, comes next in order of the density of population. The statistics of cultivation and population show a remarkable resemblance between Burdwan and Howrah. In both districts more than 80 per cent of the total area is cultivable, but only about 40 per cent of the cultivable area is cultivated. Moreover, so far as the trend of the growth of population is concerned, both of them have reached a stationary state. In Hughly the population has remained almost completely stationary. In Burdwan the increase between 1872 and 1931 has been only 6·3 per cent, which is the lowest percentage to be found in the whole of the Ganges Delta except Hughly. The district may be divided into two distinct natural divisions. The eastern portion, comprising the Burdwan, Kalna, and Katwa sub-divisions, is a wide alluvial plain watered and built up by the Ajoy, the Bhagirathi, and the Damodar. The southern edge of this tract borders on the seaboard and is a recent formation. The Ganges, in the course of its eastward march, has left long loops of disused channels all along its western banks, and the soil here is waterlogged and swampy. The whole of the eastern tract is extensively cultivated, there are no large uncultivated pastures here, and the density of the population is high. But the development of agriculture and the growth of population in this alluvial tract have been hampered by the derangement of drainage levels, caused by the embankments constructed

[1] At the census of 1901 the greatest increase of population was found in the Serampur sub-division, and this was partly due to the reclamation of marshy swamps. Recently a good deal of land has been reclaimed as a result of the Dankuni and Rajpur schemes and has been available for cultivation.

either for the purpose of preventing floods or for the purpose of irrigation. The main rivers in this tract receive numerous smaller tributaries, which are merely drainage channels for carrying off the surplus water collected in the rice fields. But these channels are very often embanked for purposes of irrigation, and the embankments offer a great obstruction to the natural drainage of the district. The result is that land is liable to floods, while waterlogging leads to outbreaks of malaria. The Damodar embankment, on the other hand, has obstructed the flow of silt-bearing flood water, so that the level of the river bed has risen owing to the increasing deposit of silt, and floods have become more frequent and destructive. The western tract of Burdwan beyond Galsi is a high undulating country, in which the soil is composed of laterite and is dry and porous. Here extensive areas are covered with *sal* forests, and it is chiefly in the depressions and along the edges of the numerous drainage channels that rice is cultivated in terraces banked up on the slopes of the undulating country. The percentage of cultivated area here is, therefore, low and the population is also sparse. In fact, the lowest density in Burdwan is found in the Kaksa and Ausgram thanas, where the laterite soil gradually merges into the alluvial silt. But it must be remembered that there has been considerable extension of cultivation in this tract, which was a wilderness of *sal* forest about a century ago.

The district of Birbhum, with a density of 558 persons to the square mile, comes next in order of density. In this district the process of denudation by the clearing of jungles has reacted unfavourably on the entire agricultural economy. In the *Brahmanda* section of *Bhabishyat Puran*, a work composed in the fifteenth or the sixteenth century, it is stated that three-fourths of this district consisted of jungle and only one-fourth was under cultivation. The process of extension of cultivation by the clearing of forests has continued for several centuries. But there is no doubt that the unrestricted clearing of jungles has had the direct effect of reducing the amount of annual rainfall and rendering large areas absolutely barren. Moreover, successive rains have washed away the soil of the uplands and have left only a bed of hard *kankar*, on which nothing will grow. It is only in the valleys, in which paddy fields have been surrounded by ridges for keeping in the water supply, that the soil cannot be washed away into the rivers. Thus large tracts in the undulating country to the west have become sterile and unfit for cultivation. At the present time the district contains two distinct natural divisions, viz. the alluvial tract to the east covering the Rampurhat sub-division, and the laterite undulating country to the west covering the Suri sub-division. The eastern tract is a low-lying, alluvial formation. Here the land is often enriched by the deposit of silt from the rivers. But, as a rule, the rivers when in flood only deposit sand. Consequently embankments have been built in many cases to protect the cultivated area from the drifts of sand. But, on the whole, the soil in this tract is fertile and the proportion of cultivable land is highest. The result has been such a great extension of cultivation that grazing grounds have become scarce, and practically the only pasture lands are small plots of common land near the villages which yield poor and scanty grass. Thus the favourable natural conditions in this tract have stimulated the growth of population, and the average density of population is about 600 persons to the square mile. The fertility of the soil in the eastern tract has been for a long time attracting immigrants from the barren uplands of the west. As early as 1891 it was noticed that 'migration of population is the chief cause of the variation of thana population. The attraction of the more fertile soils in the north and east has withdrawn the cultivating class from the less productive laterite areas in the south and west.'[1] Again in the Census Report of 1911 we find the Rampurhat sub-division characterized as 'one of the most progressive tracts in West Bengal'. It was 'more populous by 29 per cent than it was in 1881, whereas the population of the Sadar sub-division had increased by only 11 per cent'.[2] The western tract, on the other hand, is an undulating upland in which, as already pointed out, extensive areas have become barren, and successful cultivation is possible in the depressions and the slopes only by artificial

---

[1] *Census Report*, 1891, pp. 98–9.   [2] Ibid., 1911, pp. 84–5.

devices for storing rain-water. In this tract, therefore, cultivation is less extensive and population sparse.

Midnapur, which comes next in order of density, has a mean density of 534 persons to the square mile. In Midnapur, as in Birbhum, the eastern half of the district, which is an alluvial formation, is more densely populated than the western portion where there is a laterite soil, covered here and there with jungles and inhabited mostly by aboriginal tribes. The percentage of cultivated area also increases from west to east. While 45 per cent of the total area is cultivated in Sadar West, 78 per cent in Sadar East and 77 per cent in Ghatal, as much as 82 per cent is cultivated in Contai and 85 per cent in Tamluk, in which the density of population is more than 1,000 persons to the square mile. Again, 52 per cent of the cultivable area is cultivated in Sadar West, 80 per cent in Sadar East, 85 per cent in Ghatal, 90 per cent in Contai and 93 per cent in Tamluk.[1] The figures show clearly that the higher density of population in the east is due to greater agricultural enterprise, as indicated by the extension of cultivation. At the present time there is very little scope for further extension of cultivation in the alluvial tract. Only a few patches of waste land are met with here and there, and the lands under cultivation are not allowed to lie fallow for any long period. Let us consider the significance of the figures given above against the background of physical conditions. The eastern portion of Midnapur is an alluvial formation similar to the deltaic region of the Ganges Valley. Here the rainfall is much higher than in the uplands of the west and the soil also is highly fertile. But human interference with the natural drainage of the country has seriously affected both agriculture and public health.[2] In the first

[1] It must, however, be remembered that the pressure of the population on the soil is not so great as the figures would indicate because most of the land grows only one crop in the year.

[2] In 1878 in the course of a letter on the subject of Burdwan fever the District Collector quoted the following extract from a letter from the Civil Surgeon: 'The Government embankments no doubt control the floods, and their utility as far as I know has never been questioned; but there can be very little doubt that they also obstruct the drainage of the country and that to a very large extent. The sluicing arrangements are lamentably deficient and only allow surface water to flow off. They are much too few in number and are, moreover, faulty in construction, their floors are in many instances above

place along the sea coast and in the low-lying country intersected by tidal rivers and creeks it has been found necessary
to raise embankments called *bheris* to keep out salt water.
In the second place, embankments have been constructed
round considerable areas of cultivated land to protect it from
the floods of the rivers, which not only cause damage to the
standing crops but also destroy the fertility of the soil by
deposits of sand. Lastly, cross-dams are also constructed in
the beds of most of the non-tidal rivers to divert the water
to the cultivated land in summer months. Thus the entire
alluvial tract is covered with a network of embankments and
cross-dams. The result has been that the action of the tides
is restricted, the mouths of the rivers are silted up and the
entire country has a tendency to remain waterlogged. All
these effects have become the fruitful causes of malaria,
agricultural deterioration and rural depopulation, particularly
in the Ghatal sub-division, which lies in an ill-drained depression situated between the lowlands along the sea-coast
and along the estuary of the Hughly and the uplands of the
west. Formerly the Ghatal sub-division was the most
prosperous tract in Midnapur. But its population has been
steadily diminishing in comparatively recent times, and
considerable areas formerly cultivated are now covered with
thorn jungle.[1] An idea of agricultural deterioration that has
long set in in this sub-division is derived from an estimate of
the outturn of rice per bigha made in 1875, according to which
the outturn had diminished by 11 per cent in 30 years. Under
these conditions it is natural that there should be steady
emigration of cultivators from this sub-division to the healthier
and more fertile tracts to the west and the east. The tendency
to the westward migration of population was clearly noticed
in the census report of 1891, in which it was pointed out in

the level of the country, so that their utility for drainage purposes may well
be questioned.' The Collector added that: 'It was this system of embanking
which has deprived the country of its natural increment of deposit and kept
it permanently depressed, while its drainage channels have gradually become
irrigation channels, its waterways choked up and the whole area water-
logged.' *Settlement Report*, Midnapur, A. K. Jameson, I.C.S.

[1] 'Large tracts in Ghatal, Daspur, Bhagabanpur and Pataspur thanas are
steadily getting worse, and unless some steps are taken in the near future they
will in time go out of cultivation.' *Midnapur Settlement Report*, A. K. Jameson,
I.C.S.

no uncertain terms that 'the internal movement of the people from the centre to the west of the district is an indubitable fact'.[1] But at the same time there is also another stream of emigration from the densely populated and ill-drained tracts in the north-east and the centre of the district to the reclaimed Jalpai lands along the sea-coast and the tidal rivers. These lands had been reserved for the manufacure of salt in Mohammedan times. After the salt manufacture was stopped the land was cleared and surrounded with embankments to keep out salt water. Now they yield abundant crops and are an attraction to cultivators in distant parts of the district. The western portion of Midnapur is an undulating country with a laterite soil and contains extensive areas of uncultivable land covered with *sal* forest. In this tract cultivation was confined, up till recent times, to the hollows between successive ridges, because those hollows form catchment basins retaining moisture and also because the soil of the hollows is enriched by detritus washed down from the slopes. But recently cultivation has extended at the expense of the forest and there is terraced cultivation on the slopes of the ridges, so that the density of population has increased. There are still large areas of uncultivated land, but most of it is either barren waste with no soil, or jungle, the clearing of which is neither desirable nor profitable. Hence in this tract there is little room for further growth of population through extension of cultivation.

The district of Bankura, with a mean density of only 424 persons to the square mile, is the least densely populated district in Western Bengal. Barely 44·8 per cent of the total area of this district is cultivated, and only 69·8 per cent of the total area is cultivable. This district has been described as the connecting link between the plains of Bengal on the east and the Chota Nagpur Plateau on the west. The eastern portion is a low-lying alluvial tract, extensively cultivated and densely populated. The western portion is an undulating country, interspersed with rocky hillocks and broken up into low ridges and valleys. Here cultivation is less extensive and population sparse. The eastern portion covering the Vishnupur

[1] *Census Report*, 1891, p. 95.

sub-division is almost entirely under cultivation. The thanas of Indas and Kotalpur and the north of the Sonamukhi thana are the continuation of the alluvial plains of Burdwan and Hughly, and the soil is composed of rich recent alluvium. Here the density varies from 600 to 700 persons to the square mile. The western portion of Bankura, on the other hand, constitutes a barren country covered in many places by low scrub jungle. In the *Brahmanda* section of *Bhabishyat Puran* Bankura was described as a 'country overspread with impenetrable forests of *sal* and other trees.' But at the present time except in the west and the south, where large trees abound, the whole of the western tract is covered with stunted jungle and presents a desolate appearance. The explanation of this curious phenomenon is, however, simple. In Bankura, as in Birbhum, the surface of the soil has been denuded by indiscriminate clearing of forests. The larger trees were felled long ago by the woodman or the charcoal burner. Now even the roots and stumps have been dug up and burnt down for charcoal kilns. The consequence is that the surface soil, being deprived of the protection afforded by nature, is washed away by every fall of rain, leaving large areas of hard compact *kankar* on which nothing will grow. Sometimes, no doubt, the cultivation of rice has increased by the reclamation of extensive jungle tracts especially round the Sonthal villages.[1] But the barren soil and difficulties of irrigation have restricted the expansion of cultivation and the consequent growth of population. The western tract is healthier than the alluvial tract to the east and is inhabited by aborigines who are extremely prolific. But still the density of population in this tract is less than 400 persons to the square mile. The explanation of such a low density is that there is very little scope for extension of cultivation, and that agriculturists have been migrating from the uplands to seek their livelihood elsewhere. In fact, such a tendency was noticed in the Census Report of 1901, and the slow growth of population in the western tract was explained 'by movements of hardy aborigines who migrate to

[1] The process of reclamation is that at first full powers of the soil are developed by the cultivation of inferior crops so that the land is fit for the cultivation of superior crops later on.

coal-fields or Assam rather than earn their living from the unwilling soil of their native uplands'.

We shall now study the course of agricultural development and the growth of population in relation to extension of cultivation in the Active Delta, which covers the inland districts of Dacca, Faridpur, and Tipperah and the littoral districts of Bakarganj and Noakhali.[1] There has been very great scope for agricultural enterprise in the shape of extension of cultivation in the whole of the Active Delta. The proportion of cultivable area to total area varies from 72·3 per cent in Tipperah to as much as 89·3 per cent in Bakarganj, and full advantage has been taken of the high fertility of the soil by extending cultivation to an almost 'extreme limit. Thus the proportion of cultivated area to cultivable area varies from 89·9 per cent in Bakarganj, to as much as 95·6 per cent in Tipperah. In fact, in the purely alluvial tracts of the Active Delta the great pressure of the population on the soil and the high floods alike prevent the growth of woods or jungle, and the whole country is an unbroken expanse of cultivated land. The consequence has been that land has been supporting a teeming population which is still multiplying at an amazing rate. The whole of the Active Delta may be divided into two zones, the northern or inland and the southern or littoral. The northern zone is the 'seat of an old civilization, Buddhistic, Brahmanical and Mussalman, occupied for centuries by a teeming population.'[2] Here the land consists of comparatively old alluvium. As an early centre of dense population it has almost reached the limit of agricultural development by means of extension of cultivation. The southern zone, on the other hand, is a more recent alluvial formation, hardly mentioned in Hindu times. Here the rivers are still active, and there has been great extension of cultivation by clearing jungles and colonizing the new

[1] It may be noted that the western boundary of Eastern Bengal has been shifting with the eastward march of the Ganges. 'Before the Padma channel of the Ganges was formed South-eastern Bengal must have extended up to the Bhagirathi, but it has since then receded, century by century, the district of Nadia being first withdrawn. Eastern Jessore is still a fluvial tract, but the time is not far distant when the Madhumati or Gorai on its eastern edge will be the boundary of Eastern Bengal, and the whole of Jessore will cease to be a part of the true delta.' *Census Report*, 1891, pp. 39–40.

[2] *Census Report*, 1891, p. 40.

alluvial formations. But there is still room for extension of cultivation, and people have, in recent times, been migrating from the overcrowded tracts in the northern zone to the highly fertile, but sparsely populated, littoral tract in the southern zone.[1]

In the northern zone the district of Dacca has the highest density of population, viz. 1,265 persons to the square mile. In this district 84·9 per cent of the total area is cultivated. This is a low figure, as compared with the corresponding figures for other neighbouring districts, but the reason why the percentage of cultivated area is small is that a considerable portion of the district is occupied by a high and undulating table-land towards the north called the Madhupur jungle. The extreme pressure of the population on the soil is, however, indicated by the fact that as much as 94·8 per cent of the cultivable area is cultivated.[2] In fact, outside the Madhupur jungle there is hardly any cultivable land left, and in recent decades the population has increased mainly as a result of the extension of cultivation into the Madhupur jungle, in spite of the fact that a general dearth of water in this tract has been a serious hindrance to the extension of cultivation. At the Census of 1891 it was noticed that the remarkable increase of population in Kapasia in the Sadar sub-division, and in Rupganj and Raipur in the Narainganj sub-division, had been due to the extension of cultivation into the Madhupur jungle which was facilitated by the development of the jute trade.[3] At the census of 1901 also it was observed that population had increased by 22 per cent in the Kapasia thana, and the explanation given was that large numbers of immigrants had been pouring in to open up the jungles of Bhowal. During the next decade, too, cultivation extended still farther in the jungles of Bhowal and the population of Kapasia increased by 26 per cent, that of Raipura

[1] See p. 207.

[2] Only 1 acre in 25 acres of land capable of bearing crops is left fallow every year, compared with 1 acre in 10 in Bakarganj. 'This implies that a period of 156 years is required until every acre has been relieved of its burden of bearing its one or two annual crops.' *Survey and Settlement Report*, Ascoli, p. 40.

[3] In Raipura and Rupganj the greater part of the jungle area has recently been brought under cultivation and the population has increased between 1872 and 1911 at the rate of 3 per cent per annum.

by 19 per cent and that of Keraniganj by 17 per cent. It appears that people have been migrating to the north both from the overcrowded tracts in the south, and from the Manickganj sub-division which has been subject to diluvion and in which much land has gone out of cultivation or grows very poor crops.[1]

The district of Tipperah, with a mean density of 1,197 persons to the square mile, stands second in order of density amongst the inland districts of the northern zone. In this district 72·3 per cent of the total area is cultivable and 95·6 per cent of the cultivable area is actually cultivated. 'Except in the undeveloped part of Bengal the land which is culturable but not cultivated is usually high land, especially that of which the soil is inclined to be porous. When it is not required for a homestead, and does not get and retain enough water to ensure a satisfactory rice crop, it is not considered worth cultivating. In Tipperah and on the Noakhali mainland, with their heavy rainfall coming early and late, there is little area that will not produce a crop and repay cultivation.'[2] That the uncultivable area in Tipperah is greater than in other districts is due to the existence of so many tanks. The percentage of cultivated to cultivable area, which is highest in the whole of the Ganges Delta, shows how intensely the land is utilized to support a highly dense population. In fact, the growth of population in recent decades has been rendered possible by a great extension of cultivation into the forest areas of the south-western part of the district and the new alluvial formations along the Meghna. At the present time the highest density of population is to be found in the thanas bordering on the Meghna from Nabinagar to Chandpur, the average density being 1,187 persons to the square mile in 1911. In 1881 the Chandpur sub-division had a density of only 490 persons to the square mile. By 1891 the density rose to 641 persons to the square mile. Reviewing the causes

[1] The effect of river-action on the changes in the density of population is clearly seen in the Manickganj sub-division. Here the Padma has raised considerable tracts of land to such a high level that the internal water-system has been destroyed. Census statistics show that the check to the increase of population commenced in the area farthest up the alluvial bed of the river Padma.

[2] W. H. Thompson, I.C.S., *Settlement Report*, Tipperah, 1915–19.

of the remarkable growth of population in this district between 1881 and 1891 the District Magistrate observed that 'the largest increase appears along the banks of the Meghna and its main distributaries, vast areas of *char* land, formerly the habitation of pigs, being now under cultivation. The increase is most marked in tracts which formerly comprised a large extent of waste lands or where the subsidence of rivers has opened out new lands for cultivation.'[1] Since the Revenue Survey the cultivated area in the district has increased by 4 per cent of the total area. Most of this increase has been due to extension of cultivation into jungles which constituted 6·3 per cent of the total area, and which were situated mostly in the south-western part of the district.[2] Moreover, the addition of new alluvial *chars* to the mainland has also made it possible for the tracts along the Meghna to support a very high density of population. But it must be remembered that in recent times agricultural enterprise in the shape of extension of cultivation has reached its limits in the densely populated riparian areas along the Meghna estuary. During settlement operations in certain riparian areas in 1909–15 it was noticed that as much as 82 per cent of the total area was under cultivation, only 5 per cent of the cultivable area was not cultivated, while 2 per cent covered with reeds was nearly all in the new accretions which were about to be brought under cultivation.[3]

The district of Faridpur, with a density of 1,003 persons to the square mile, stands third in order of density amongst the districts of the northern zone. From the agricultural point of view the district may be regarded as consisting of two portions, viz. the southern portion which is an alluvial formation characteristic of the Active Delta, and the northern portion which resembles the old alluvium of the moribund delta. The agricultural contrasts of the Ganges Delta are seen to best advantage in Faridpur. The northern portion

[1] *Census Report*, 1891, p. 75.
[2] Internal migration of population from north to south was observed in the *Census Report* of 1891 (see p. 75).
[3] 'Reeds are deliberately grown to increase the deposit of silt and raise the level of the char, so that it may be brought under cultivation.' B. C. Prance, I.C.S., *Survey and Settlement of Riparian Areas of the District of Tipperah*, 1909–15.

(covering the Goalundo sub-division and the northern part of the Sadar sub-division) may be described as 'an infinite series of flat sandy plains broken by a large number of old water-courses'.[1] It lies on a moribund delta in which the activity of the rivers has ceased. The land has been raised to such a level and the rivers have silted up to such an extent that in ordinary years there is no general distribution of river-borne silt.[2] It is only the lower lands in the depressions that receive a top dressing of fertilizing silt during the season of the floods. Thus the fertility of the soil has decreased, malaria has made its appearance, and rural depopulation has followed. In 1891 the District Magistrate explained 'the decrease of population in thana Bhusna as due partly to the silting up of the river Barasia,' and he added that it 'is comparatively thickly wooded and covered with jungle, a large number of cultivators having been obliged to shift their residence to the neighbouring thana of Balia Kandi'.[3] In recent years in Balia Kandi and Bhusna and in the contiguous part of Faridpur and Goalundo a large part of the country has relapsed into jungle. The decadence of this tract is indicated by the statistics of population. For example, between 1881 and 1911, while population increased by 50 per cent in the south-eastern tract and by 40 per cent in the south-western tract, it increased by only 7 per cent in the northern portion of the district. The southern tract (covering the Madaripur sub-division and the southern portion of the Sadar sub-division) is a typical deltaic country in which the process of land forma-tion is still going on. It is full of rivers 'which are broad and deep, heavy in the flood season with constructive silt, yet sufficiently active to work their will upon a land of plastic mud'.[4] Here the process of land formation is haphazard, the rivers eating away banks and sweeping the old country, while raising fresh flats of mud to take their place a few years later. In the aggregate, however, the area of land is always increasing and the level of the country is gradually rising. The whole

---

[1] *Gazetteer*, Faridpur.
[2] The Garai and the Madhumati still carry a large volume of water from the Ganges, but the silt-laden water cannot be distributed because the dis-tributaries have been silted up at their mouths.
[3] *Census Report*, 1891, p. 72.   [4] J. C. Jack, *Settlement Report*.

of this alluvial tract, which is subject to the fluvial action of
the rivers, consists of land of very great fertility and supports
a very dense population. While the Goalundo sub-division
supports a density of less than 800 persons to the square mile,
in the alluvial tract the density varies from about 900 to
1,400 persons to the square mile. This high density of
population is due to great extension of cultivation. There is
little cultivable land that is left uncultivated. The greater
part of the uncultivated area is occupied by homesteads and
domestic crops, such as bamboo and thatching grass. Marshes
are ploughed up as soon as they silt up sufficiently to permit
of cultivation, while *chars* or alluvial formations are occupied
as soon as they show signs of rising above the level of the
rivers. In fact, the great increase of population in the thanas
of Madaripur, Sibchar, and Palong during recent decades
has been possible through the colonization of rich alluvial
formations. In the densely populated marsh lands of the
south-west, on which cultivation is possible only when the
water dries up, there is such an intense utilization of land
that even the uncultivated parts of the country yield an
additional income to the peasants, because fishes are available in abundant quantities and the reeds are also cut and
sold.

We shall now study the remarkable growth of population
as a result of extension of cultivation in the southern zone,
a littoral tract which is the scene of activity of the great rivers
as they discharge their waters into the sea. Here the delta-
building process is witnessed over a wide area and there are
unforeseen changes in the configuration of land.[1] The fertile
soil of this tract rich in vegetable matter has stimulated a
phenomenal growth of population. There has been great
extension of cultivation through the clearing of forests and
colonization of new alluvial formations, and people have long

[1] As Mr. W. H. Thompson says, 'In the deltas of the Nile and the Mississippi
growth goes on at the point where the main waters of the river meet the
salt water and the silt is precipitated. Except that the annual floods mark
periods of activity and quiescence the growth is steady and local; but in the
case of the Ganges the action of the tides moves the silt over such a wide
area, and, interacting with the forces of the river, produces such apparently
haphazard changes in the configuration of the lands that the existence of any
steady growth is obscured.' *Survey and Settlement Report*, Noakhali.

been migrating to this tract from the over-populated tracts of the northern zone.

Of the two districts included in the southern zone, Noakhali, with a density of 1,124 persons to the square mile, has a higher density of population. On the mainland the density is as high as in Dacca and considerably higher than in any district in Eastern Bengal. It is more than double the density in any rural area in Western Bengal and distinctly higher than the density of the most thickly populated parts of the Middle Ganges Valley. The cultivated area is very uniformly about 80 per cent of the total area. The area which is cultivable but not cultivated is very small, when we consider that nearly half of it is reserved for growing thatching grass and reeds. As already explained, in the moribund delta the land which is cultivable but not cultivated consists of old fallow hardly fit for cultivation. But in Noakhali, with its heavy rainfall and with its soil impregnated with vegetable matter, almost all lands which are not cultivated can be converted into gardens of betel and coconut palms. The comparatively large extent of uncultivable area in Noakali (as also in Tipperah) must be accounted for by the existence of numerous tanks which are the only sources of water supply.[1] In fact, in Noakhali cultivation has extended as far as possible with the gradual growth of population. On the mainland 68 per cent of the total area was cultivated, or was fit for cultivation, in 1863–5, as against 71 per cent in 1914–16. At the present time it may be said that every inch of land that is fit for cultivation and is not required for human occupation is brought under cultivation or grows fruit-bearing trees. 'Public grazing grounds on the mainland are non-existent. Every pathway or cattle track is pared down by the cultivators whose fields are on either side until it barely leaves room for two persons to pass one another on foot. The banks of tanks and the slopes of the embankments of public roads are the only grazing grounds.'[2] There is a striking similarity between Noakhali and Tipperah so far as the relative growth of population in different tracts is concerned. In Tipperah the densely populated northern tracts have become decadent

[1] See p. 235. [2] W. H. Thompson, *Settlement Report*, Noakhali, 1914–19.

in recent times, and there has been a remarkable growth of
population directly as a result of extension of cultivation in
the tracts lying along the Meghna estuary to the south and
the west. We find the same tendency in Noakhali. In 1881 the
eastern part of the district was rather more densely populated
than the western part bordering on the Meghna estuary.
Chagalnaia and Ramganj were the old centres of dense
population in which there had been a remarkable growth of
population. In fact, it was observed in the Census Report
of 1891 that in Chagalnaia the density had reached 'the
extraordinary figure for a rural tract in Bengal proper of
947·6 to the square mile'.[1] In recent times, however, the
western part of Noakhali has caught up the eastern and
passed it, and the increase in the density of population has
been rendered possible by the extension of cultivation into
the fertile lands along the Meghna estuary, particularly in
the islands of Hatia and Sandwip, the two new alluvial
islands lying at the mouth of the Meghna. During the present
century the great rivers of the delta have been steadily
building up land on the bight which divides the mainland
from Chittagong, so that by the end of this century the eastern
part of the Meghna estuary will develop into a more or less
solid block of land. It is likely that the population of Noakhali and Bakarganj will go on increasing as a result of the
extension of cultivation into the alluvial formations that are
bound to come into existence in the near future.

The district of Bakarganj, with a mean density of 834
persons to the square mile, is the most thinly populated
district in the Active Delta. The whole of this district is a
recent formation. The rivers which played a great part in
the formation of Bakarganj have no doubt moved eastward
leaving the mainland high and dry.[2] But during the process
of land formation there has been a remarkable increase in
the cultivated area and a consequent increase of population.
Since the Revenue Survey of 1859–65 the rivers have made
additions to the land area to the extent of 180 square miles

---

[1] *Census Report*, 1891, p. 80. In recent times the extraordinary growth of
population has been checked. The extreme pressure on the soil has led to
emigration of peasants to Hill Tipperah.
[2] *Gazetteer*, Bakarganj, 1918.

or at the rate of 4 square miles a year. Moreover, cultivation has expanded also by the reclamation of waste land. During Major Rennel's Survey of 1770-8 the unoccupied waste was 1,125 square miles. At the time of the Permanent Settlement in 1793 it was found to be 925 square miles. During the Revenue Survey of 1859-65 the area was 526 square miles, while during the District Survey of 1901-5 it was found to be only 194 square miles. Assuming that the land area increased by alluvion at the same rate before the Revenue Survey as after it, viz. 4 square miles a year, it appears that the total occupied area has increased, as a result of both alluvion and reclamation of waste land, at the rate of 12 square miles a year. The remarkable extension of cultivation has been accompanied by a great increase of population throughout the nineteenth century. In fact, it has been surmised that the population of this district has doubled itself in the course of the last century. In the present century the pressure of the population on the soil has become intense. It appears from recent statistics that about 10 per cent of the cultivable area is not cultivated, and that new fallow represents usually only 1 per cent of the real area available for cultivation. But still population has been growing fast wherever there are opportunities for the extension of cultivation by the reclamation of jungles and marshes or by colonization of alluvial formations. Thus the large increase of population in Gournadi, Jhalakati, Swarupkati and Bhandaria has been due to the reclamation of *bils*. In Galachipa and Dakshin Shabazpur sub-divisions colonization of alluvial formations has been the cause of the large increase of population, while in Amtali and Matbaria the abnormal increase of population has been due to extension of cultivation as a result of the reclamation of forests.[1] In fact, the waste lands in the south of Bakarganj have long been attracting settlers from the over-populated tracts of the north.[2] This tendency was noticed in the *Census*

[1] Between 1888 and 1918 the population increased by 50 per cent in Dakhin Shabazpur sub-division. During the same period the increase in Amtali and Galachipa was as much as 56 per cent.

[2] The over-populated thanas in the north have become distinctly decadent Thus in the Jhalakati thana which had a density of 1,213 persons to the square mile the population decreased by 4 per cent between 1888 and 1918. In Nilchati and Bakarganj which had a density of about 1,000 persons to the

Report of 1891, and it was said: 'The one governing cause of movement of population in this district is the flow of the surplus population of the northern thanas to the waste lands in the south and east.'[1]

square mile there was an increase of only 6 per cent during the same period. 'It is well known that the increasing population of the southern thanas is recruited from the central thanas of the district, Jhalakati and Firozpur supplying Matbaria, Patua Khali and Bauphal supplying Galachipa, Bhola supplying Barahnuddin.' *Survey and Settlement Report.*

[1] *Census Report*, 1891, p. 78. The following observations of the Superintendent of census operations in 1931 show how population has increased in Bakarganj during the decade 1921–31 as a result of extension of cultivation: 'In Patuakhali sub-division the most important cause of increase is immigration from Noakhali, Faridpur and Tipperah due to the extreme fertility of the soil which has steadily improved since 1921, and to the increasing colonization of the Sundarbans area, particularly in Amtali which has shown an increase of 24·2 per cent in this decade. In Galachipa and Bantal new char areas have become available, and in Mirzapur and Barguna as in Amtali, what was formerly Sundarbans land has been reclaimed and colonized during the decade. In the Pirozpur sub-division also increasing cultivation of jungle areas and marsh land has resulted in increases of population ranging from 9·6 to 21·8 per cent. The whole of the Bhola sub-division compared with the rest of the district is fairly sparsely populated, and its area is increasing owing to the recession of the bay in the south. It therefore offers land for an increasing number of immigrants, and hence its population has increased by 16·9 per cent.'

CHAPTER II

DOUBLE-CROPPING AND DENSITY

IN the Ganges Delta we observe the same correspondence between variations in the density of population and variations in the extent of double-cropping as in the Gangetic Plain. We have shown in the last chapter how throughout the Ganges Delta the trend of changes in the density of population is determined by the varying agricultural possibilities of the different tracts. We have discussed the nature of the relative agricultural possibilities in the moribund and in the active delta. The contrast between these two regions is the result of the complex chain of causes associated with the activity of the delta-building rivers, and the relative agricultural possibilities are determined by these causes. Now when we talk of agricultural possibilities we have to consider not only the scope for agricultural development by means of extension of cultivation, and agricultural enterprise by which cultivation is extended by a rapidly increasing population, but also the opportunity for getting the most out of land by means of double-cropping. But the extent of double-cropping also depends on favourable natural conditions relating to rainfall, river-floods, soil and physical configuration of land, factors which are closely connected with the activity of the deltaic rivers and distributaries. Thus as regards the extent of double-cropping also we find the same contrast between the moribund and the active delta. The extent of the double-cropped area increases from west to east, and double-cropping contributes to agricultural productivity to a greater extent in the active than in the moribund delta and is an important agricultural factor by reference to which we can explain the variations in the density of population in the different parts of the Ganges Delta.

First of all let us observe the statistical correspondence between the density of population and the percentage of double-cropped area. In the moribund delta as a whole the double-cropped area occupies about 18 per cent of the net cropped area, while it is about 34 per cent of the net cropped area in the more densely populated active delta. In Western Bengal the double-cropped area varies from 9 per cent to 14 per cent in the densely populated districts of Burdwan, Howrah, and Hughly, while it varies from 3 to 5 per cent in the sparsely populated districts of Birbhum, Bankura, and Midnapur. In Central Bengal the percentage of double-cropped area to net cultivated area varies from 17 to 64 per cent in the more densely populated districts of Murshidabad, Jessore, and Nadia, while it is 10 per cent in 24 Parganas and 11 per cent in Khulna. In the active delta the double-cropped area varies from 35 to 50 per cent in the densely populated districts of Dacca, Tipperah and Noakhali, while it is 33 per cent in Faridpur and 13 per cent in Bakarganj. It must be remembered, however, that the economic importance of double-cropping cannot be judged entirely by the extent of the double-cropped area because, as we shall see later on, this depends, to a great extent, on the combination of crops preferred under given natural conditions and the nature of the second crops. But so far as the extent of the double-cropped area is an index of intense utilization of land, the correspondence between variations in the extent of double-cropping and variations in the density of population has a very great significance.

In order to understand the significance of the above tendency it is important to study the nature of the physical causes which determine the extent of double-cropping. It is obvious that double-cropping depends on the sufficiency of moisture retained by the soil after the *kharif* harvest. If the rainfall is insufficient then, in the absence of artificial irrigation, double-cropping would be an impossibility. Moreover, if the rainfall is excessive the soil suffers from over-saturation and water-logging, and a second crop of *rabi* cannot be grown after the *kharif* harvest. Throughout the Gangetic Plain extensive double-cropping depends both on rainfall and irrigation. In the moribund delta there are extensive tracts particularly in the west where the extent of double-cropping is restricted by the small amount of annual rainfall and the absence of the facilities of irrigation. There the unfavourable physical conditions are similar to those found in South Bihar, and double-cropping becomes as difficult as in the dry zones of the Gangetic Plain. But the Ganges Delta, as a whole, receives a very large amount of rainfall which is more or less evenly distributed throughout the agricultural season. Rainfall, both early and late, is so ample that three cycles of plant life can be completed in the course of a year, and the growth and maturity of plants are so fast that two, and sometimes even three, crops can be taken off the same land in the same year. Moreover, the river floods which not only supply moisture to the soil but also deposit a highly fertile silt over it, play a far more important part in the agricultural economy of the Delta than rainfall. And the configuration of land, at any rate, in the Active Delta is such that flood water is drained away after the rainy season, so that the soil does not suffer from over-saturation due to defective drainage, as it commonly does in the Gangetic Plain, and is fit to bear a dry crop in the cold weather after the wet crop has been harvested. The following table shows the close correspondence between the extent of double-cropping and the amount of annual rainfall:

	Percentage of double-cropped area	Annual rainfall in inches
Moribund Delta .	18	59·5
Active Delta .	84	87

The soil and configuration of land are also important physical factors which determine the extent of double-cropping. The land most suitable for bearing second crops must be one which is neither too high nor too low. 'If it is too high it will be dry and sandy and otherwise unretentive of moisture; if it is too low it will be waterlogged and consist of stiff clay unfit to bear a second crop.'[1] Thus in Western

[1] See p. 151.

Bengal double-cropping is common on *sali* lands and *suna* lands, the elevation of which is neither too high nor too low. In parts of both active and moribund delta double-cropping is impossible on low-lying lands which consist of stiff clay soil and are unfit for bearing cold-weather crops. In the active delta, although most of the land is low-lying and below the level of the river floods, yet the floods subside quickly after the rainy season leaving the land not only dry but also rich in silt, so that the soil is fit to bear a second crop, the growth and maturity of which is further aided by rainfall in September and October.

Next we shall study the distribution of the double-cropped area in the Ganges Delta particularly with reference to the physical factors which determine the extent of double-cropping. 'The valuable crops in Bengal are the summer crops, which are taken up about August, and the winter rice crop, which is taken up at the end of the year. Spring crops grown in the cold weather and taken up at the end of it are much less valuable. In order that a summer crop and a winter crop may be taken off the same land, the land must, first of all, be of a suitable level. It must not go under water more than a foot or so in September or the winter rice cannot be transplanted. Both crops will be good ones only if the former gets a good start and can be taken up early and the latter does not get weather too dry for it after it has been transplanted. What is requisite, therefore, is not only a good rainfall in the middle of the rainy season, but also sufficient rain both early and late in the year. It is the rain coming in March, April and May and again in September and October that determines whether a summer crop and a winter crop can be taken off the same land. Whether a spring crop will also be taken depends upon whether the cultivator finds it worth while to put one down. Unless the winter rice has been taken up very late one could be grown almost everywhere in Eastern Bengal.'[1] The close relation between the amount of rainfall in the critical months and the extent of double-cropping is illustrated in the following comparative table:

[1] *Census Report*, Bengal, 1921, pp. 13–14.

	Moribund Delta	Active Delta
Normal Rainfall in March, April and May	9·63	17·92
Normal Rainfall in September and October	12·97	17·56
Total . .	22·60	35·48
Percentage of double-cropped area .	18	34

We must remember that the distribution of the *bhadoi*, the *aghani* and the *rabi* harvests varies according to the total amount of rainfall during the critical months. In the moribund delta the total amount of rainfall during the critical months is much smaller than in the active delta. Moreover, the soil does not get sufficient moisture and silt from the seasonal floods. Hence the cultivators have to choose between summer and winter crops, and a summer crop cannot be followed by a second winter crop. Where the *bhadoi* is the main harvest it cannot be followed by a winter crop, not only because the rainfall in September and October is insufficient, but also because there are no river floods which leave the soil moist after the rainy season. Where the *aghani* is the main harvest the cultivator cannot possibly allow experiments with summer crops to interfere with its chances. Consequently, the second crops are usually *rabi* crops grown after either the *bhadoi* or the *aghani* harvest. But the cultivation of *rabi* crops is hampered by uncertain winter rains and lack of the facilities of artificial irrigation. Thus it appears that unfavourable natural conditions have been responsible for the small extent of double-cropped area in the moribund delta. In the active delta, on the other hand, rainfall in March, April, and May, and again in September and October, is so ample and certain, and the floods of the rivers in June, July, and August rise and fall with such unfailing regularity that both summer and winter crops can be grown on the same land and in the same season. Indeed, if the cultivator likes he can also grow a *rabi* crop on land sown with winter rice, provided that the winter rice crop has not been harvested late, because if it is harvested late there is not sufficient time for wheat or barley to ripen before the rain in March and April which would spoil it.

We shall now study the nature and extent of double-cropping in the different tracts of the moribund and the active delta with particular reference to the variations in the density of population. As already said, the double-cropped area in Western Bengal varies from 9 to 14 per cent in the densely populated districts of Burdwan, Howrah, and Hughly, and from 3 to 5 per cent in the sparsely populated districts of Midnapur, Birbhum, and Bankura. In the densely populated eastern portion of Burdwan the low-lying tracts separating the village sites, which constitute the larger part of the cultivated area, are devoted almost entirely to winter rice.[1] It is only the higher land surrounding the village sites that are suitable for growing a variety of crops, and double-cropping is very common on these lands. *Aus* rice is grown on these high lands and is followed by spring crops like pulses and oil-seeds. In the rainy season these lands are manured by washings of the villages, but the practice is to manure the *aus* lands before rice is sown and to let the following crop benefit by what is left after the rice crop has taken its share. Where artificial irrigation is possible sometimes three crops are grown, viz. *aus* rice, potatoes, and onions. In the sparsely populated western portion of Burdwan double-cropping is rendered impossible by a dry and porous soil unretentive of moisture and the absence of the facilities of irrigation. In Hughly and Howrah also extensive double cropping is found on higher lands of the densely populated tracts on which jute or rice is followed by oil-seeds, or pulses like *mung*, peas, *khesari*, and *musuri*. Otherwise the lower lands which are inundated during the rainy season are almost exclusively devoted to winter rice. In Birbhum the porous soil and rapid drainage constitute the two serious hindrances to successful agriculture. In fact, in this district artificial irrigation is necessary in years of scanty rainfall, and the small extent of

---

[1] Sometimes potatoes are grown as a second crop after winter rice, particularly when there are facilities of artificial irrigation.

the double-cropped area is due to a scanty agricultural water-supply. In the densely populated eastern portion of the district, however, double-cropping is practised on the *do* lands and the *sali* lands. First-class *do* land is sown with *aus* rice which is cut in September or October. It is then manured and ploughed, and cold weather crops such as gram, wheat, *musuri*, linseed, *khesari*, peas, and mustard are sown broadcast. When the cold weather crops have been reaped the land is again manured and ploughed and is sown with *til*. First-class *sali* lands which consist of a moist muddy soil, bear three crops in a year, viz. a crop of aman rice, a crop of *khesari* and a crop of *kesta til*. *Aman* is sown in March and April and is reaped in November and December. *Khesari* is sown among the rice as it begins to ripen and is cut in February and March. *Til* is sown about the middle of March and ripens early in May. In Bankura also the small extent of double-cropping is due to the same unfavourable natural conditions which we find in Birbhum. The soil is porous, and the rapid drainage and percolation reduce the efficiency of a given rainfall. In the sparsely populated upland tracts the soil is too poor to bear two successive crops in a season, and the deficiency of moisture is so great that double-cropping is out of the question. In the more densely populated alluvial tracts to the east, how-ever, double-cropping is practised on what are locally known as *suna* lands. In the *nij suna* lands the main crop is *aus* or *aman* rice which is followed by a winter crop of pulses or oil-seeds. There are also *suna do karpa* lands which grow two superior crops in a year. In fact, the *suna* lands are so inten-isvely cultivated that they are never permitted to remain fallow. In Midnapur there is great pressure of the population on the soil in the eastern two-thirds of the district. 'But the intensity of cultivation is not really so great as in other districts for the reason that most of the land grows only one crop in the year.'[1] In the sparsely populated laterite tracts to the west, double-cropping is impossible owing to the shallow-ness of the soil and the sloping nature of the land. Practically speaking, double-cropping is confined to the *kala* lands, which are situated round the densely populated village sites in the

[1] *Survey and Settlement Report.*

alluvial tracts. These lands are more or less sandy and are either above the ordinary flood level or dry up in time to be sown with *rabi* crops. On these lands a second crop of pulses or oil-seeds is raised after the *aus* or the *aman* rice has been harvested. But *kala* lands form only 8 per cent of the gross cropped area. 'Occasionally one sees a thin crop of *kalai* on paddy land after the winter rice has been cut and a certain amount of jute is grown in Daspur and Panskura thanas followed by winter rice.'[1]

In Central Bengal the proportion of double-cropped area varies from 17 to 64 per cent in the densely populated districts of Murshidabad, Jessore, and Nadia, while it is 10 per cent in 24 Parganas and 11 per cent in Khulna. In Murshidabad the density of population is higher in the Bagri tract to the east of the Bhagirathi than in the Rarh tract to the west of this river. The soil of the Bagri tract is very fertile. It is liable to inundation, but the inundation is shallow enough and the land dries up in the cold weather. The principal crops are *aus* rice and jute, and when they are harvested abundant cold weather crops are raised as second crops. But in the thinly populated lowlands to the south-east over the tract known as Kalantar practically the only crop grown is *aman* rice. In the Rarh tract also the main staple grown on the hard clay soil is winter rice, and the cold weather crops are few. In fact, the nature of the soil and the conformation of land are such as to render artificial irrigation absolutely necessary, but the sources of irrigation are barely sufficient for a crop of winter rice. In Jessore the soil has deteriorated considerably owing to the silting up of the rivers and distributaries. The result has been that the area classified as new fallow is more than four times that in Faridpur. The major portion of this area is composed of lands of poor fertility which require rest in alternate years. Hence it appears that natural conditions in Jessore are unfavourable to double-cropping. But still double-cropping is very common on the high *matial* soil, chiefly found in Bangaon, Jhenida, and Sadar sub-divisions where gram and pulses are raised as second crops on *aus* and jute lands. The extent of the double-cropped area varies

[1] *Survey and Settlement Report.*

from 17 to 24 per cent in these sub-divisions. In Narail and Magura, which are the more densely populated eastern sub-divisions of Jessore, the proportions are 15 and 29 per cent respectively. But it must be remembered that Eastern Jessore closely resembles Bakarganj and Faridpur. Although the low-lying lands remain waterlogged for nearly four months and do not generally yield a second winter crop, yet the heavy yield of *aman* rice more than compensates for the small extent of the double-cropped area. In the district of Nadia the deterioration of the soil has been a serious hindrance to agriculture. 'The soil which varies but little all over the district is a light sandy loam possessing but little fertility and incapable of retaining moisture. It has become barren as it is no longer enriched by the fertilizing silt which was deposited by river floods when the rivers were active. The very light manuring which is applied to land is insufficient to compensate for the loss of fertility due to continuous cropping.'[1] But in spite of the deterioration of the soil there is very extensive double-cropping in this district. In the eastern portion of the district, which is more densely populated than the western portion, the main staple is *aus* rice which is followed by cold weather crops on the same land. In fact, the large extent of double-cropped area in the district, as a whole, is explained by the predominance of *aus* rice, the area under which is more than double that in any other district in the Ganges Delta. In the sparsely populated western portion of Nadia, particularly in the tract known as Kalantar, land is low-lying and is fit to bear only one crop in the year, viz. winter rice. In the district of 24 Parganas the proportion of double-cropped area is only 10 per cent. The lowlands that constitute the greater portion of the cultivated area in the more densely populated northern tracts are mainly under winter rice and jute. They are rarely followed by *rabi* crops. In fact, *rabi* crops occupy barely 4 per cent of the net cropped area, and are mainly confined to the higher lands in the densely populated riparian tracts to the north of the district. It is only on these higher lands that autumn crops are followed by winter crops on the same land. In the southern tract bordering on the Sunderbans

[1] See p. 218, Ch. I.

land is devoted exclusively to a single crop of winter rice.
In Khulna also double-cropping is confined to the densely
populated highlands particularly to the north-west of the
district. In fact, the only areas which have a considerable
quantity of twice-cropped land are the northern police
stations of Kalaroa, Tala, Sathira, Terakhada and Mollahat.
Throughout the rest of the district the *aman* paddy is prac-
cally the only crop grown in the year. In this district the
policy of raising embankments for the purpose of reclamation
of land has rendered double-cropping impossible. The
prematurely embanked land is fit to bear a single crop of
winter rice, because the extremely clayey soil, when deprived
of a top dressing of river silt, bakes like brick as soon as the
rice crop is harvested and cannot grow any other crop till
the next monsoon.

In the active delta most extensive double-cropping is
found in the densely populated districts of Dacca, Tipperah,
and Noakhali. In Dacca no less than 85 per cent of the net
cropped area is made to bear two or more crops in a year.
In this district sometimes *aus* and *aman* are grown together
and *aus* is also succeeded by *aman*. Less often *til* is mixed
with both *aman* and *aus* in order to make a triple harvest.
But commonly the second crop grown on *aus* or *aman* lands
consists of cheaper varieties of *rabi* grains. For example,
khesari pulse which is grown in the lowlands of the district
generally succeeds *aus* or *aman* paddy, while on the high
lands of the north, black mustard is generally grown on the
fields from which a crop of jute or *aus* paddy has already been
taken. In fact, the *rabi* crops in Dacca have not the same
importance as they have in the upper or the middle portion
of the Ganges Valley. Except in the north of the district they
are raised exclusively on twice-cropped lands as ordinary
catch crops. Thus the high percentage of the double-cropped
area, 91 per cent of which is devoted to *rabi* crops grown
after *aus* or *aman* crop, has not the same economic importance
as when *aus* is followed by *aman* or when jute is the important
crop in the *bhadoi* harvest. Hence in the densely populated
tracts of Dacca double-cropping, although smaller in extent,
has a great economic importance because *aus* is sometimes

followed by *aman*, and jute is a more important crop in the *bhadoi* harvest. On the other hand, in the decadent thanas of Manickganj the percentage of double-cropped area is much higher, but the contribution of double-cropping to agricultural productivity is much smaller than in the progressive tracts of Dacca.[1] In Tipperah the natural conditions are highly favourable for extensive double-cropping. The rainfall in March, April, and May is 20·82 inches, as against 10·91 inches in Central Bengal and 8·85 inches in West Bengal. The rainfall in September and October is also fairly high. It is 16·84 inches, as against 13·55 inches in Central Bengal and 12·89 inches in West Bengal. Moreover, the variations in the distribution of rainfall over the months of the rainy season, June to August, have no importance, for the rivers rise and supply the necessary moisture to the soil. Under such favourable conditions the cultivators naturally resort to double-cropping to get the most out of the fertile soil, and it is not surprising that as much as 88 per cent of the net cropped area should bear two ·or more crops. In Noakhali, the natural conditions are most favourable for double-cropping. The rainfall in September and October which is so necessary to refresh the winter crops when the floods are subsiding, is as much as 25·18 inches, the highest figure to be found in the whole of the Ganges Delta. The extent of double-cropping which is 50 per cent of the net cropped area is also the highest in this region. On the Noakhali mainland, which supports the highest density to be found in any rural area in the Ganges Delta, double-cropping usually means sowing of *aman* paddy after *aus* or jute. 'While the seedlings are in the nursery they take up very little space, and the fields can be occupied with another crop while they are growing. The ground is always wet at the time, and it takes only a few days after the summer crop has been removed to plough and make ready the fields for transplanting. The extreme hardiness of the seeds is remarkable.' As Mr. Thompson observes: 'No doubt they could be grown much more extensively but the cultivator does very well without them. The value of the crop is not tempting enough to a man who can

---

[1] This aspect of the question is discussed below.

get such rice and jute crops with so little labour. He does not feel inclined to plough his land two or three times when it is caked to its hardest for the sake of the few rupees that such crops as pulses, linseed, gingelly and mustard will bring in.'[1] On the Noakhali islands, however, land is mostly devoted to winter rice, the proportion of *bhadoi* crops being very small. Hence not only is the double-cropped area small, but its economic importance is also not as high as in the densely populated tracts on the mainland. In Faridpur the proportion of double-cropped area is as high as 33 per cent of the net cropped area. In this district also the second crops are *rabi* crops grown after *aus* rice or jute. In the comparatively high lands in the north and centre of the district rice or jute, which is harvested in July or August, is followed by oil-seeds, pulses, wheat or barley which is harvested in February. A similar rotation of crops is practised in the recently reclaimed alluvial lands. Within the district the distribution of double-cropping corresponds with the distribution of density. The Madaripur sub-division which is the most densely populated sub-division has also the largest extent of double-cropped area, viz. 48 per cent. In the sparsely populated Goalundo and Sadar subdivisions the double-cropped areas are 30 per cent and 37 per cent respectively. In the Gopalganj sub-division the doublecropped area is only 12 per cent because the marsh lands are devoted exclusively to winter rice. The reason why there is so extensive double-cropping in the Madarapur sub-division is that there is so much of *char* land on which *rabi* crops are largely grown after jute is reaped. In fact, in Sibchar as much as 67 per cent of the net cropped area bears more than one crop. In the district of Bakarganj the double-cropped area is barely 13 per cent of the net cropped area. Being a recent alluvial formation, which is so low that it is submerged during the period of seasonal floods, it is pre-eminently a rice district. The staple crop is winter rice which depends for its growth and maturity on river floods, and it is only in small areas that the soil is fit for other crops. Hence the extent of the doublecropped area is naturally small. The second crops grown in Bakarganj are pulses and oil-seeds, which are sown when the

[1] W. H. Thompson, *Settlement Report*, Noakhali.

aman paddy is reaped and the field is still soft, although the water has dried up. But they are regarded as catch crops and little labour and attention is given to them. It appears that under the present conditions the agricultural security which the cultivators enjoy, in spite of having to depend on a single crop, and the heavy yield of *aman* paddy, make it unnecessary for them to resort to extensive double-cropping. But as the density of population continues to increase, it is very likely that the double-cropped area will also increase in the future.

We shall now discuss an interesting question which has an important bearing on the relation between the density of population and double-cropping, viz., How far may the extent of double-cropping be regarded as an index of agricultural prosperity? Should the contribution of double-cropping to agricultural productivity be measured merely by the double-cropped area? The answer to this question is that the economic importance of double-cropping depends not only on the area twice-cropped but also on the nature of the second crops. We have noticed that in the Upper Ganges Valley either the *kharif* or the *rabi* is the main harvest and double-cropping consists in growing cheap *rabi* crops to supplement the *kharif* harvest. In the Middle Ganges Valley, where the annual rainfall is higher, the *bhadoi*, the *aghani*, and the *rabi* are the three harvests. The timing of agricultural operations, as determined by the distribution of rainfall, is such that the chief *aghani* crops are sown before the chief *bhadoi* crops are reaped. The result is that the *bhadoi* crops can never be followed by the *aghani* on the same field, and the second crops must necessarily be cold weather crops grown after either the *bhadoi* or the *aghani*. Moreover, it is only the *rabi* crops grown after the *bhadoi* harvest that are really valuable, while those grown after the *aghani* consist of cheap catch crops. In the Ganges Delta we find striking contrasts. Where the soil is dry and porous and the rainfall insufficient the *aghani* rice is the main crop. *Rabi* crops are raised to a certain extent, but the area under *rabi* crops grown after the *aghani* is insignificant. Where conditions are not so unfavourable a greater proportion of the *rabi* crops are grown as second crops after either the *bhadoi* or the *aghani* harvest. On the other hand, in the active delta, where natural conditions are still more favourable, valuable *bhadoi* crops are succeeded by a valuable second crop of *aghani* rice on the same land in the same season.

Now so far as the contribution of double-cropping to agricultural prosperity is determined by the value of second crops, the striking contrast between the active and the moribund delta is indicated by the statistics of cultivation. In the Ganges Delta the two important crops in the *bhadoi* harvest are *aus* paddy and jute, while the only crop in the *aghani* harvest is *aman* paddy which, when transplanted, has a remarkably high yield. The *rabi* crops do not possess the same importance in the Ganges Delta as in the comparatively arid regions of the Upper and the Middle Ganges Valley. Hence it is obvious that the contribution of double-cropping to agricultural productivity varies directly as the extent to which the *bhadoi* crops are succeeded by *aghani* rice on the same land and in the same season. From a statistical point of view the index of the contribution of double-cropping to agricultural productivity is found out *by deducting the percentage of the net cropped area under rabi crops from the percentage of the net cropped area which is twice-cropped.* If the percentage of the double-cropped area exceeds the percentage of the total area under *rabi* crops, we may conclude that the *bhadoi* crops are followed by *aghani* crops on the same land and in the same season to the extent of this difference. On the other hand, if the difference is a negative quantity, i.e. if the percentage of *rabi* area exceeds the percentage of double-cropped area, the difference indicates the extent to which *rabi* crops are grown independently and shows that the *bhadoi* crops are not followed by the *aghani* crops on the same land and in the same season. The figures given in the table on p. 257 show the contrast between the active and the moribund delta in a striking manner.

It is clear from this table that in the old delta, except in 24 Parganas, Murshidabad, and Khulna, the second crops are invariably *rabi* crops grown after either the *bhadoi* or the *aghani* harvest. The second crop is never *aghani* rice grown

Districts	Percentage of the *rabi* area to net cropped area	Percentage of double-cropped area to net cropped area	Index of contribution of double-cropping to agricultural productivity
	(1)	(2)	(3)
Burdwan . . .	14	14	0
Birbhum . . .	3	3	0
Bankura . . .	10	5	− 5
Midnapur . . .	18	4	−14
Hughly . . .	11	9	− 2
Howrah . . .	14	12	− 2
Average for West Bengal . . .	16·6	8	− 3·83
24 Parganas . .	4	10	+6
Nadia	56	64	+8
Murshidabad . .	40	33	−7
Jessore . . .	21	17	−4
Khulna . .	7	11	+4
Average for Central Bengal . . .	25·6	27	+1·4
Dacca	23	35	+12
Faridpur . . .	24	33	+ 9
Backerganj . . .	7	13	+ 6
Tipperah . . .	18	38	+20
Noakhali . . .	14	50	+36
Average for Active Delta . . .	17·4	33·8	+17·2

after the *bhadoi* rice or jute. Moreover, the excess of the percentage of the *rabi* area over the percentage of twice-cropped area shows that a certain area grows *rabi* crops independently. In Murshidabad, 24 Parganas, and Khulna a certain area bears both *aghani* rice and jute and *aus* rice in the same season. Hence double-cropping has a greater economic importance in these districts. But its importance is much less there than in the active delta, in which on an average as much as 17·2 per cent of the net cropped area bears both *aghani* rice and jute or *aus* rice in the same year.

There is another important fact which is revealed by the figures given above. It will be noticed that the percentage of double-cropped area and the percentage of the area under rabi crops are equally high in the case of Dacca, Faridpur, Murshidabad, and Nadia. But double-cropping in these districts has not that economic importance which is suggested by the high percentage of double-cropped area, because the *rabi* crops grown as second crops are not half as valuable as winter rice. Moreover, it must be remembered that in *jute-growing areas extensive cultivation of* rabi *crops and extensive double-cropping in the absence of jute is a sure indication of agricultural depression.* Jute being a valuable crop has always been grown in preference to *rabi* crops.[1] But the cost of cultivation of jute is much higher than the cost of cultivation of *rabi* crops. Hence wherever *rabi* crops predominate at the expense of jute we find backward agricultural conditions. This conclusion is borne out by the following statistics relating to the backward and the progressive thanas in the district of Dacca.[2]

Thanas	Percentage of twice-cropped area	Percentage of *rabi* area	Percentage of area under jute
Backward Thanas			
Harirampur	49	45	8
Sealo	54	46	15
Manikganj	63	58	11
Progressive Thanas			
Munshiganj	30	30	34
Narayanganj	35	30	30
Rupganj	37	28	29

[1] For example, in Faridpur at the time of the Revenue Survey, a very small area was under jute. 'Now the cultivator in three-quarters of the district may be said to depend on jute. Spring crops which were important formerly are now regarded merely as catch crops.' *Survey and Settlement Report,* Faridpur.

[2] The statistics are taken from the table given in the *Survey and Settlement Report of Dacca,* by F. D. Ascoli, I.C.S.

CHAPTER III

AGRICULTURAL WATER-SUPPLY AND DENSITY

In the last two chapters we have discussed how the density of population varies throughout the Ganges Delta according to the possibilities of both extensive and intensive agriculture which are determined by natural factors, such as soil, level, rainfall, and river floods. In this chapter we shall study, in greater detail, the background of natural environment against which the inter-relations between agricultural possibilities and the movement and distribution of population appear to be really significant.

In agricultural economy the two obviously uncontrollable factors of natural environment are soil and rainfall. It has already been discussed in a previous chapter how the efficiency of rainfall depends upon the texture of the soil, while the efficiency of the soil also in respect of the physical and chemical conditions and the supply of plant food is determined by rainfall and temperature. There is no sharp line of distinction between the physical and chemical conditions of the soil and the meteorological conditions in spite of the fact that the distinction is clearly marked. In fact, these two sets of conditions constitute what we understand by environment.[1] But, on the whole, in a monsoon region like the Gangetic Plain, the differences in the nature and distribution of soils in the different natural regions are far less important than the differences in the amount and distribution of rainfall.[2] In fact, the natural regions of the Gangetic Plain are essentially rainfall tracts in which the distribution of crops is determined essentially by the amount and distribution of rainfall. In the Ganges Delta agricultural water-supply has a unique importance. The entire balance of agricultural economy depends not only upon heavy rainfall, but also upon the deltaic river-system which is an important source of irrigation.

[1] See pp. 59–62, Pt. I.   [2] See p. 87, Ch. IV, Pt. I.

But we must also remember that the delta-building rivers also work out their destiny on the plastic mud, and it is their life and movement that determine the nature of the deltaic soil. Thus where the deltaic rivers and their distributaries are still active they not only supply moisture to the soil, but also build new land and renew the productive powers of the old soil by depositing rich layers of silt. On the other hand, where the deltaic rivers are inactive land becomes high and dry, loses its high fertility and, at the same time, cannot derive moisture from the seasonal floods, or, if it has not already been raised above the flood level, it suffers from water-logging and over-saturation. Hence the only factors of the natural environment which really count in the Gangetic Delta are rainfall and river floods, the two important sources of agricultural water-supply. Before we estimate the relative importance of these two factors it is necessary to study the variations in the amount and distribution of rainfall in relation to variations in the density of population in the moribund and the active delta.

AVERAGE RAINFALL IN INCHES (NORMAL)

	Moribund Delta	Active Delta
March to May . .	9·63	17·92
June to August . .	34·71	49·44
Sept. and October .	12·97	17·56
Nov. to Feb. . .	2·44	3·02
Rainfall in critical months . .	22·60	35·48
Total Rainfall . .	59·75	87·94
Mean Density . .	592	1,084

In the above table we find a striking correspondence between the density of population and the total amount of annual rainfall. But the significance of this tendency becomes clear when we study the relative distribution of rainfall over the entire agricultural season, and its effects upon crops. In a monsoon region the timing of agricultural operations, and the succession of crops depending upon it, are such that it is the seasonable distribution of rainfall rather than its total amount which is of primary importance. The main crops in a monsoon region like the Ganges Delta are wet crops included in the *bhadoi* or the *aghani* harvest. A comparatively small area is under dry crops of the *rabi* harvest, because either the heavy annual precipitation prevents the cultivators from sowing a large area under these crops, or they are regarded as cheap catch-crops which they do not think worth while raising if they have already obtained a good outturn in the *bhadoi* and the *aghani* harvest. Now the success of both the *bhadoi* and the *aghani* crops, either as alternative crops on different lands or as successive crops on twice-cropped lands, depends entirely on sufficient and well-distributed rainfall. For the *bhadoi* crops showers in March and the ante-monsoon showers in April are absolutely necessary for the preparation of the land. From April onwards rainfall is required at frequent intervals, but it should not be heavy or continuous. *Bhadoi* rice is generally sown in May or earlier, and consequently heavy rainfall at this time and in the following months is injurious to the sowing and successful germination of this crop. Scattered showers with intervals of sunshine are, on the other hand, very beneficial. But the total amount of rainfall in March, April, and May is also an important factor of agricultural productivity. If the season opens with good rainfall the natural conditions become favourable for preparatory tillage and early sowings, and if the *bhadoi* crop thus gets a good start it can be harvested early with the help of sufficient monsoon rainfall, so that the same land is fit to receive the transplanted seedlings of *aman* paddy. Now it appears from the comparative table given above that, while the rainfall in March, April, and May is 9·63 inches in the moribund delta, it is 17·92 inches in the active delta. It is obvious that from the point of view of agricultural productivity natural conditions are far less favourable in the former than in the latter region. The only crop in the *aghani* harvest is winter rice, whose fate depends upon sufficient and well-distributed rainfall. For winter rice the most favourable rainfall is the premonitory shower in May or early in June.

The rainfall in the latter half of June and July should be heavy, otherwise transplantation will be hampered, and there should be an interval of comparatively fine weather so as to permit of weeding operations being successfully carried on. Rainfall in September should also be heavy and it must shade off into fine weather with showers in October. The most important factor in the growth of transplanted paddy is rainfall in October, on which the outturn of this crop entirely depends. Now so far as the cultivation of winter rice is concerned, natural conditions are also much more favourable in the active than in the moribund delta. The total amount of rainfall in the monsoon season as well as in September and October is much greater in the former than in the latter region. Moreover, the rise of the rivers in the active delta during the monsoon months makes it almost independent of the vagaries of weather, while agriculture in the moribund delta depends entirely on the amount and distribution of rainfall. As regards winter rainfall, on which the growth and maturity of *rabi* crops essentially depend, the cultivators in the active delta also enjoy a slight advantage. But, as already pointed out, the *rabi* crops have an economic importance only in the dry tracts of the moribund delta where unfavourable natural conditions prevent the cultivators from raising heavy-yielding crops of the *bhadoi* and the *aghani* harvests.

The brief survey of the relation of crops to meteorological conditions shows very clearly the danger to which the agricultural economy in the Ganges Delta is exposed in abnormal years. Normally the total amount of rainfall in a monsoon region is so ample that, given a normal distribution, three harvests can be taken off the land in the course of the year. But although high rainfall is thus a cause of high agricultural productivity, yet agricultural operations being so nicely adjusted to meteorological conditions, there is great agricultural insecurity whenever there is insufficient or ill-distributed rainfall. It is therefore important for us to study in greater detail the sources of agricultural water-supply in the moribund and the active delta, particularly from the point of view of agricultural security in years of drought or ill-distributed rainfall.

In West Bengal the configuration of land varies distinctly from east to west. The eastern portion of this region constitutes a comparatively recent deltaic formation, a flat alluvial plain raised only a few feet above the sea-level, while the western portion is an undulating laterite formation. The alluvial portion is more densely populated than the laterite portion. We also find the same contrast when we consider the nature and sources of agricultural water-supply. In the alluvial tract the main difficulty of agriculture is not lack of water-supply but an excess of it due to inundation of land during the rainy season. The land which is only a few feet above the sea-level is badly drained, and such drainage as there is is very much obstructed by dams or weirs constructed across the rivers and drainage channels for the purpose of irrigating land which has too slight a slope. Sometimes embankments have to be built around fields for the purpose of retaining water on them. For example, in the eastern alluvial tract of Midnapur, 'there are slight differences of level sufficient to determine the flow of the rivers and to make it necessary for the cultivators to build small embankments known as *ails* round individual fields to retain the water on them. As the south-east is reached, even the slight differences of level practically disappear and instead of *ails* round individual fields, there are slightly larger embankments round entire villages of five or six square miles in area within which there is not a difference of a couple of inches between one field and another, and they have simply to keep the water from flowing into the artificial depressions of the drainage channels.'[1]

The result of such interference with natural drainage has been disastrous. An excess of rainfall is sufficient to flood the smaller rivers whose channels are too small and have too slight a slope to carry off much water owing to the slight slope of the country, and flood water bursts through the artificial barriers erected for purposes of irrigation. Moreover, the embankments running along the larger rivers have increased the violence and frequency of floods whenever there are sudden

---

[1] *Survey and Settlement Report*, Midnapur. It must be noted that this system of private irrigation is liable to abuse. For example, in years of heavy rainfall the cultivators very often cut the *ails* to let the water out into their neighbours' fields in order to utilize a golden opportunity of catching fish.

freshets. For example, in Burdwan the tracts lying to the south of the Damodar are liable to floods as a result of obstructed drainage. In Midnapur the construction of a network of circuit and cross-dams has obstructed the drainage of the country by restricting the action of the tides. The mouths of the rivers have silted up, so that they cannot carry off the surplus water especially after heavy rainfall. The beds of the larger rivers being raised above the level of cultivated land by a continuous deposition of silt, there is widespread inundation whenever there are sudden freshets. In Hughly also heavy and continuous rainfall for several days on the Chotanagpur Plateau causes floods in the Damodar and its branches which seriously injure the crops on its western banks. Similarly a heavy local rainfall swells the silted-up drainage channels in the Sadar and the Serampur sub-divisions, and as they have no outlet into the main rivers the water overflows on either side and causes damage to crops. In the laterite portion of West Bengal the problem of agricultural water-supply is entirely different. The soil is dry and porous and the drainage rapid. Consequently the whole system of cultivation depends on the practice of storing rain-water. In fact, 'terrace cultivation' in the laterite portion of West Bengal is the result of attempts to store up rain-water. Here 'the hillsides are converted into tiers of rice-fields, often of the smallest size conceivable which are embanked along their lower edges. The rain-water in its downward course is thus arrested and, instead of being allowed to pass down the hillside in a torrent, is made to irrigate the fields one after another each retaining its first share and no more.'[1] There is another method of artificial storage of water which we find in the district of Howrah. Water is taken in from the Hughly at spring tides and is held up by means of lock-gates in the drainage channels. Some of the smaller creeks are also dammed up, to raise the water-level for impounding a supply of water for dry months.

In Central Bengal also cultivation suffers from water-logging due to defective drainage which is the curse of the

[1] *Gazetteer*, Burdwan. But it must be noted that these private embank-ments are very often inadequate and are not kept in good repair, so that sometimes there are breaches and crops are submerged and washed off.

moribund delta. In 24 Parganas large areas in the low-lying tracts, which constitute the greater portion of the cultivated area, are occupied by *bils* which may be either water-logged swamps or freshwater lakes. Some are natural drainage basins that never dry up and cannot be drained owing to their flat level. Others are connected with the rivers by drainage channels which bring river silt and carry off the surplus water. But in many cases these channels have silted up, so that cultivators have to wait till the swamps dry up, and if there is heavy rainfall they find it impossible to attempt tillage. In Nadia the tract known as Kalantar which stretches through the district in a south-easterly direction is too water-logged to bear any autumn crop. The soil here is unsuitable for regular winter crops, except the *aman* rice crop, which is liable to be swept away by destructive floods in years of heavy rain-fall or wither away for want of moisture in years of drought. In the higher lands no irrigation can be practised for the simple reason that the surface is so uniformly level as to afford little or no scope for a canal system. In Murshidabad artificial irrigation is practised only in the Rarh tract owing to the peculiar conformation of the country. But in the alluvial tract the rainfall and the annual inundations of the rivers are sufficient to supply the necessary moisture. In Khulna in the older alluvial sections of the district cultivation suffers from water-logging due to defective drainage.[1] In the newer alluvial portions where the rivers and the distributaries are still active, the raising of embankments to keep out salt water has resulted in a serious interference with the natural process of land formation and is bound to have serious reactions on agricultural economy. As Mr. Fawcus has pointed out, 'the result of the embanking of the rivers has been to cut off the spill area which silt-carrying rivers need and has in some cases literally choked their beds with the silt which should have gone to building up the land in nature's good time'.[2] In Jessore also while marshes in the eastern portion of the district

---

[1] 'In Khulna district the courses of the majority of the rivers are compara-tively stable, but deltaic action or land-building is still going on; hence almost throughout the district we find water-logged saucers or pockets lying behind the high banks which fringe the river courses': *Survey and Settlement Report*.
[2] *Survey and Settlement Report*.

are silting up owing to river action and are being reclaimed, those in the western portion have remained water-logged owing to the death of the rivers.

The above description of the nature and sources of agricultural water-supply in the moribund delta suggests certain important conclusions. In the alluvial tracts of Western and Central Bengal the problem of drainage which is always difficult owing to the flat level of the country, has been further complicated by embankments constructed for the purpose of irrigation or prevention of floods. Here extensive areas of land suffer from water-logging and peasants have sometimes to depend upon a single crop of winter rice which is liable to suffer from destructive floods in years of heavy rainfall. In the laterite portions of Western Bengal artificial irrigation is absolutely essential even in normal years, and is barely sufficient for a single crop of rice. In Western and Central Bengal artificial irrigation is supplied by connecting private canals with the big rivers, by storing rain-water, and by constructing dams, cross-dams or weirs, on the drainage channels which intersect the alluvial tracts, while a certain area of land is irrigated also from tanks and wells. But it must be remembered that the total irrigated area in Western and Central Bengal forms only a small percentage of the net cropped area. Nor is there much scope for the development of canal irrigation. In the laterite portion of Western Bengal, where artificial irrigation is the mainstay of agriculture, the surface of the country is broken up by low ridges, valleys and hills which make any system of canal irrigation impracticable. Moreover, the catchment areas of many streams is so small that in a season of drought the supply of water would either fail altogether or would be so small as to be of very little use. On the other hand, in the alluvial tracts it is extremely difficult to work a system of canals and distributaries owing to the flat level of the country. Moreover, a canal system cannot be commercially successful when the area covered by it, which is sufficiently flat and low-lying, can produce excellent crops by relying simply on rainfall in normal years. No doubt, as Mr. Jameson has pointed out, although canal irrigation is not a necessity in the alluvial tracts, yet agriculture is benefited by the fertilizing silt deposit in the canal-irrigated areas. In fact, 'crop-cutting experiments show that irrigated land will produce on an average 3 or 4 mds. more per acre than non-irrigated land'. But it is obviously difficult to popularize the habitual use of canal water amongst peasants when they find that they can obtain excellent crops in normal years by depending simply on rainfall. Thus it appears that artificial irrigation in the moribund delta as a whole does not possess the same importance as it has in the more arid regions of the Gangetic Plain. In normal years rainfall is sufficient and well-distributed and supplies ample moisture to the soil. But in abnormal years a considerable proportion of the cultivated area has no protection against the failure or mal-distribution of rainfall. For example, in 1927–8 owing to weak monsoon and the failure of rainfall in October, there was partial failure of the winter rice crop and considerable distress in parts of Burdwan, Murshidabad, Birbhum, and Bankura. But still it is clear from the following table that the proportion of the cultivated area which was irrigated from different sources in Western and Central Bengal was small.

Districts	Percentage of irrigated area to cultivated area
Murshidabad . .	28
Burdwan . . .	42
Birbhum . . .	46
Bankura . . .	34
Midnapur . . .	4·4
Hughly . . .	44

In the active delta the most important source of agricultural water-supply is the river floods. Indeed, it is no exaggeration to say that the entire system of farming and agricultural security in this region depend upon what may be called river economy. In this region rainfall is no doubt more heavy and better distributed than in the moribund delta, but the growth and maturity of crops do not depend entirely on rainfall. Rainfall is indeed necessary at certain periods of the agricultural

season. For example, it is necessary in February for ripening
the cold weather crops and in March for sowing the rice crop.[1]
It is also necessary in September to refresh the plants at
intervals as the flood goes down. In fact, the winter rice
crop and the orchards need rain at the right time, although
delay is not ruinous to crops. But the main work of supplying
moisture to the soil is done by the floods from the great rivers,
the function of local rains being simply to swell the floods
and moisten the higher lands which are more or less beyond
the reach of floods.

The floods of the Ganges and the Brahmaputra are not
synchronous. The floods of the Brahmaputra, which come
down in the month of July, depend at first upon the melting
of the snow in the Himalayas and later upon rainfall in the
catchment area, when the monsoon breaks against the spurs
of the Himalayas. The top of the Brahmaputra flood is
reached in August, when the Ganges begins to rise and keeps
the level of all the rivers high for another month. In the
upper and western portion of the active delta the floods of
the Ganges are as much important as those of the Brahmaputra. But the Ganges does not bring so great a quantity of
silt to the lower and eastern section of the delta and the
height of the flood there is also apparently declining, so that
the agricultural productivity of this tract depends also upon
the large volume of silt-laden water that is carried by the
Meghna from Sylhet during the monsoon season.

The most important function of river floods, as already
pointed out, is not only to supply moisture to the soil but also
to build new land and deposit a fertilizing layer of silt all over
the flooded countryside during the rainy season. The deltaic
rivers have a sufficiently slight fall to have a depositing rather
than an excavating tendency. So long as the current is fairly
swift the silt has a tendency to be borne along towards the
sea, but it is rapidly deposited in the slack water on the banks
where it is caught by high grass or other vegetable growth.[2]

[1] It is obvious that where the percentages of the cropped area under the
bhadoi and the rabi harvests are small, as in Bakarganj, agriculture becomes
independent of the vicissitudes of the seasons.
[2] Sometimes reeds are deliberately grown to help the formation of fertile
soil on sand-banks.

It is in this way that river floods build up highly fertile land all along the courses of the deltaic rivers.[1] In the interior portions of the country, also, the flood water rises so gradually that it has a depositing rather than an excavating tendency, and in the south-eastern portion of the active delta, which borders on the sea-board, the deposition of silt over extensive areas of the country is facilitated by the action of the tides interacting with the force of the silt-laden river stream.

In a deltaic country the fertility of land, which depends entirely on the activity of the rivers, varies from one tract to another according to the nature of the river-action and the character of the silt deposited by the rivers. In the moribund portion of the Ganges Delta the soil which is not annually fertilized by the deposition of silt suffers from a deficiency of organic matter and nitrogen and of chemical substances, such as lime and phosphoric acid. Thus the nature of the soil is such that it is fit for bearing only a limited number of crops. In the active delta, on the other hand, the soil which is subject to annual inundation is rich in organic matter and nitrogen.[2] But its fertility depends upon the nature of river action and the character of the silt carried by the rivers. The silt deposited by the Padma has a large proportion of silica, mica and argillaceous earth and a small proportion of organic matter. Moreover, the fast current of this river has a tendency to carry all the silt to the sea unless it is caught by vegetable growth in the slack water on the banks. Again, the Padma has always a tendency to deposit the lighter particles of sand held in suspension before the heavier clayey matter held in solution is deposited. Now so far as clayey matter constitutes a more fertile deposit the new formations farther downstream are more fertile than formations situated farther upstream.

[1] It must be noted that the rivers have also a destructive tendency. 'So long as the general level of the land remains lower than the pitch of an ordinary flood the rivers in the fury of the flood season continue to eat away banks; to sweep the old country through which their currents carry them and to raise fresh flats of mud to take its place a few years later. The course of a river is not a straight line but a series of oscillations which must always shift if not confined between banks of rocks.' Jack, *Settlement Report*, Faridpur.

[2] It must also be noted that flood irrigation supplies oxygen to the roots of the rice plant. As the roots must have a constant supply of oxygen and as oxygen is in solution in water the floods help the growth of rice plants by making possible a slow movement of aerated water through the upper layers of mud.

On the other hand, the river Meghna carries a large amount of vegetable matter, rich in nitrogen, from the swamps of Sylhet and its current also is straight and slow. The result is that land is heavily laden with silt, is of sufficient consistency as soon as it rises above the water, and is more fertile from a chemical point of view. Thus it appears that the regions which are situated near the lower reaches of the Padma, and are subject to inundation from the Meghna, have a more fertile soil than new formations in the upper and western portion of the active delta. Moreover, it must be remembered that the lower and eastern portion of the active delta owes its exceptional fertility to the action of the tides which spreads the large volume of silt, carried by the Ganges, the Brahmaputra, and the Meghna, over extensive areas of the country. In the deltas of the Nile and the Mississipi formation of land goes on at the point where the main waters of the river meet the salt water and the silt is precipitated. But in the Ganges Delta the action of the tides interacting with the force of the rivers distributes the silt over a very large area. Thus in the lower reaches of the delta, while on the one hand the formation of land is haphazard, on the other hand the distribution of silt over extensive areas maintains the remarkable fertility of the soil. This process is clearly seen in the district of Bakarganj where we observe a striking correlation between density, agricultural productivity, and distribution of river silt.

COMPARATIVE DISTRIBUTION OF SILT AS INDICATED BY THE AREA COVERED BY SMALL STREAMS TO LAND AREA[1]

Sub-Divisions	Proportion of area covered by small streams to land area
Sadar Sub-Division . . .	3·3
Pirozpur Sub-Division . .	4·1
Patuakhali Sub-Division . .	6·7

[1] The table is taken from the *Survey and Settlement Report of Bakarganj* 1900–08, by J. C. Jack, I.C.S.

All the rivers in Bakarganj are tidal; but water comes down these rivers at all times of the year. The country between them is covered with a network of smaller streams which carry silt and deposit it on land. In the north of the district (Sadar sub-division) the level of the country has become so high that these water-courses are dry in summer, but still they fill up in the rainy season and at spring tides. In the Patuakhali sub-division, on the other hand, they always carry water even at low tide. In the northern portion of Bakarganj the water-courses which join two big rivers have a tendency to be silted up in the middle because the tide flows in from both ends, with the result that the rivers are fast drying up and cannot get the annual supply of silt. The table given above shows the extent to which the northern tract has dried up as compared with the southern tract. And it is natural to expect that the higher fertility of land in the south should attract immigrants from the overcrowded tracts in the north in which the activity of the rivers in relation to the distribution of silt has gradually diminished as the process of land formation has been completed.

We have said that the function of river floods in the active delta is not only to deposit silt and build new land but also to supply moisture to the soil. Now when we consider the latter function of river floods nothing seems to be more important than the height of river floods in relation to the level of land. In the moribund delta water-logging due to annual inundation and the destructive activity of river floods have become a menace to agriculture in extensive tracts of the country. As already said, this has been due to the slight slope of the country combined with obstructed drainage. In the active delta the rivers work out their will on plastic mud with such a characteristic thoroughness that drainage levels are adapted to different stages in the process of land formation. So long as the process of land formation continues on land lying below the level of the floods, its slope is such that both the ingress and the egress of flood water are slow and gradual, otherwise the rivers would have an excavating rather than a depositing tendency. When the process of land formation is completed and the land rises to a sufficiently high level it no longer receives a large amount of silt from the annual floods and depends for its productivity more and more on rainfall. But as it has been raised higher and higher by a natural process it does not suffer from obstructed drainage and water-logging. Thus normally the height of flood water on cultivated land depends upon the level of the land as determined by the stage of land formation. It is higher on low-lying lands constituting a comparatively recent alluvial formation than on lands situated on an older alluvial deposit. But we must also remember that the height of the floods depends also upon the volume of water carried by the rivers. In abnormal years there is a danger that the combined waters of the Ganges and the Brahmaputra may rise to an abnormal level causing widespread inundation. And this is possible when the Brahmaputra flood is late and that of the Ganges early. But what is the importance of the height of river floods in the rural economy of the active delta? In the first place, the distribution of harvests depends upon the normal height of the floods in relation to the level of land. Where the land lies at a very low level, and the flood is very deep, it cannot grow even long-stemmed rice, and only *boro* or spring rice can be grown before the water rises. The land which is so high as to be above the level of the floods grows dry crops of the summer and the winter harvests and has to depend entirely on rainfall. On the other hand, the land situated at an intermediate level can grow both the *bhadoi* and the *aghani* crops, and the relative importance of these two harvests again depends upon the level of the land in relation to the height of the floods. In the second place the success or failure of the harvests depends upon the height of the floods. 'If the water is too deep the rice plant is liable to be drowned outright or to be swept away, or the vital force of the plant is exhausted in growing a stem long enough to keep its head above the water, and there is not sufficient vitality left to form good grain in the ear.'[1] Moreover, high floods scour away the earth instead of depositing silt on it. On the other hand, if the floods are low they fail to fertilize and irrigate the higher lands.

Another important factor, on which the success or failure

---

[1] *Gazetteer*, Dacca.

of crops depends to a very large extent, is the duration of the flood. To be beneficial to crops flood water must begin to cover the land in June, should rise gradually until September and then should subside as gradually. When the floods are too early the sowing of both *aus* and *aman* paddy and jute are delayed, while the *aus* crop, which has been sown late, is destroyed by floods just before it is harvested. Sudden rises when either the autumn or the winter rice is young are also very disastrous. But a sudden rise of the flood water is not very common, and if it is followed quickly by a fall it is felt severely only near the Meghna. The floods in the active delta are very rarely late, but sometimes subside too early. When this is so the *aman* crop withers in the higher lands for lack of moisture. Even in the lower lands when the floods drain off too rapidly the stalk of the rice plant collapses from want of proper support and the ears are injured by falling in the water.

The above survey of the nature and sources of agricultural water-supply in the active and in the moribund delta indicates clearly the relative position of the two regions in the scale of agricultural productivity and security. In the active delta heavy and well-distributed rainfall combined with river floods have made the soil more fertile and better adapted to a variety of harvests. Except in the marsh areas the cultivators are not dependent on any single crop. The crops are distributed between different seasons in such a way that their success is independent of the vagaries of weather. Thus the fortunes of the agriculturists are not bound up with the character of the rainfall in a particular season. Secondly, normal rainfall is well-distributed and particularly the rainfall in the critical months of the agricultural season is so ample and certain that crops seldom fail for want of moisture. Thirdly, the river-floods in June, July and August not only renew the productive powers of the soil, but also make agriculture practically independent of the monsoon rainfall. Lastly, as pointed out in the last chapter, rainfall both early and late is so ample and certain that double-cropping can really contribute to agricultural productivity. In the moribund delta, on the other hand, the soil particularly in the old alluvium, can grow only a limited number of crops, and the cultivators have to choose between the *bhadoi* and the *aghani* crops. Both the *bhadoi* and the *aghani* harvests depend largely on the amount and distribution of rainfall in the absence of a complete system of irrigation works. Thus the prospects of the *aus* rice crop are seriously prejudiced by scanty rainfall at the beginning of the monsoon season, while its premature termination is injurious to the *aghani* rice crop. If the rice crop fails people have little to subsist on except maize and inferior millets until the harvesting of the *rabi* crops in the latter part of March. But the *rabi* crops are grown over a comparatively small area, and in a year of short rainfall they are deficient both in yield and area owing to want of moisture at the time of sowing. Thus the failure of the rice crop causes economic distress which very often amounts to famine.

The contrast between the active and the moribund delta from the point of view of agricultural security is clearly seen when we study the effect of drought upon the harvests. The relative deficiency of rainfall and the relative shrinkage in the gross yield of winter and autumn rice in these two regions are illustrated in the following tables by means of the agricultural statistics for the season 1927–8 in which rainfall was not only deficient but also badly distributed.

AVERAGE RAINFALL IN 1927–28

As compared with normal (in inches)

		Moribund Delta	Active Delta
March, April and	Actual . .	7·38	23·49
May . . .	Normal . .	9·63	17·92
June, July and	Actual . .	28·50	34·41
August .	Normal . .	34·71	49·44
September and	Actual . .	9·05	14·50
October . .	Normal . .	12·97	17·56

AVERAGE GROSS PRODUCE IN PERCENTAGE OF THE
NORMAL YIELD OF THE REGION (100)

	Moribund Delta	Active Delta
Winter Rice	40·5	83·4
Autumn Rice	41·4	69·4

It is interesting to note how the character of the season affected the outturn of crops in the active and the moribund delta. When we compare the statistics of rainfall the first thing that strikes us is that while there was a deficiency of rainfall between March and May in the moribund delta the rainfall was much in excess of the normal in the active delta. The result was that the germination and growth of early sown crops were good over the greater part of East Bengal, whereas dry weather somewhat hindered sowings in West Bengal.[1] Secondly, it appears from the statistics that the monsoon rainfall was much more deficient in the active than in the moribund delta, while there was an equal deficiency of rainfall in September and October. Let us see how the deficiency of rainfall in the monsoon season and in the critical months of September and October affected the crops in these two regions. It is obvious that a weak monsoon was bound to affect seriously the transplanting operations in the case of winter rice. In fact, these operations were greatly hampered, particularly in some of the districts of West Bengal. 'Over considerable tracts in these districts the total rainfall was so deficient that transplanting never took place at all. This barren area would have been larger than it was had not favourable rainfall in early September facilitated further transplantation.'

But it seems that while in the active delta good early rainfall combined with river floods counteracted the effects of a considerable deficiency of monsoon rainfall, in the moribund delta the deficiency of early rainfall hampered preparatory operations, and the deficiency of monsoon rainfall hampered the transplantation of winter rice and the maturity of

[1] *Season and Crop Report of Bengal*, 1927–8, p. 1.

autumn rice. It has already been said that the most important factor in the growth and maturity of the winter rice crop is rainfall in October. In 1927–8 there was a general failure of rainfall in October. But it appears that the effects of the failure of rainfall in October were more disastrous in the moribund than in the active delta.

CHAPTER IV

CROPS AND DENSITY

In this chapter we shall study the relation of crops to rural density from the point of view of both agricultural productivity and agricultural security. The choice and the combination of crops in a tropical region are determined not only by the range of environment of particular crops, but also by the pressure of the population upon the soil. In previous chapters we have indicated the ranges of environment of different crops grown in the Ganges Valley. The broad distinction between crops that we observe throughout the Ganges Valley is that between dry and wet crops. Dry crops such as wheat, barley, millet, maize, and gram predominate in regions in which rainfall is not heavy, artificial irrigation is indispensable, the mean summer temperature is high, and the water-table is so low that wet crops with their surface root-system cannot grow. On the other hand, wet crops, such as rice and sugar-cane, are adapted to heavier rainfall, lower temperature, and a higher water-table. But it must be noted that although this broad distinction between dry and wet crops is a fundamental one, yet the distribution of harvests in any region of the Ganges Valley exhibits a combination of both dry and wet crops within the limits of a particular natural environment. Only the predominance of either dry or wet crops varies from one region to another according to differences in the conditions of rainfall and temperature. But there is another factor which determines the choice and the combination of crops, viz. the pressure of the population on the soil. In every country the increasing pressure of the population upon the soil has led to the substitution of heavy-yielding for light-yielding crops. In western countries, for example, there has been a decrease generally in the area devoted to small grains, because the production of small grains is unsuitable to intensive farming which is always the consequence of a high density of population. Moreover, as the pressure of the population upon land has increased, there has been a shifting of the wheat belt, as in America, owing to the substitution of forage crops, heavy-yielding root-crops, such as potatoes, sugar-beets, turnips and stock-beets, and different kinds of truck-farm produce, for wheat, because it has been found that although wheat is an important commercial crop yet it is a light-yielding crop suitable to the methods of extensive farming. In this way the transition from the stage of extensive farming to that of intensive farming has always been marked by a change in the choice and combination of crops. In the Ganges Valley we find a similar change in the choice of crops which has been brought about by the increasing pressure of the population upon land. The prevailing type of farming that has evolved there may rightly be characterized as intensive subsistence farming based on the production of heavy-yielding crops as far as possible within the limits of the natural environment and the economic resources of the agriculturists. In fact, when the cultivators grow valuable commercial crops from which they raise money for cash payments they have naturally to depend for their subsistence on the cultivation of heavy-yielding food crops. Thus we find in the Upper Ganges Valley an enormous increase in the area under rice, and in the area under gram and peas which are commonly raised as second crops on rice lands in winter. The second remarkable feature has been the development of the cultivation of maize. Maize is a valuable crop itself and, by reason of its early maturity, tends to increase agricultural security. Moreover, it provides the cultivator with sufficient food till December, so that he is able to sell most of the *rabi* crops. Thirdly, we find a tendency to grow more and more of barley, the most heavy-yielding crop in the *rabi* harvest. In the eastern portion of the Upper Ganges Valley in which natural conditions are not so favourable to the cultivation of wheat, the yield of wheat has been estimated to be one-fifth less than the yield of barley on average land. Now since barley has been adopted as an article of food, and to the cultivator, who tries to keep as much of food crops for his personal consumption while he relies on commercial crops for the necessary cash, a higher outturn is an important consideration, barley has taken the place of wheat, juar and other light-yielding crops. Even a valuable commercial crop has sometimes to yield place to a heavy-yielding food crop. For example, the cultivator has sometimes preferred to grow maize or rice instead of sugar-cane and then to sow a *rabi* crop on the same field, thus obviating the necessity of long fallowing which is incidental to the cultivation of sugar-cane. Lastly, the change in the direction of more intensive subsistence farming is further indicated by the increase in the area under *kodon* and *mandua*, two other cheaper food grains, and by the substitution of pure wheat for mixed wheat which has always a lighter yield.

Lower down the valley of the Ganges and particularly in the Ganges Delta, the natural environment is particularly favourable to the cultivation of wet crops. Rainfall is heavy and evenly distributed, summer temperature is not as high as in the upper portion of the Gangetic Plain, river floods supply silt and moisture to the soil, and the water-table is high enough to favour the growth of aquatic plants having surface root system. The most important crop in this wet zone is rice, a particularly heavy-yielding crop, the high productivity of which is supplemented in the Ganges Delta by the high return of a valuable commercial crop like jute.[1] Rice requires a mean summer temperature of 75 to 77 degrees. The largest rice regions have an annual rainfall of 50 inches, and a rainfall of 5 inches a month during the growing season. The ideal conditions for the cultivation of rice are fulfilled to a pre-eminent degree in the Ganges Delta. On the other hand, the climate of the deltaic region is so moist that the wheat crop is liable to suffer from rust, the stem of the wheat plant becomes coarse, and the grains come out soft and mealy and poor in nitrogen. Hence wheat is an unimportant crop in this region. Now the predominance of rice cultivation in this region, as contrasted with the predominance of wheat culti-vation in the comparatively arid regions of the Gangetic

---

[1] The variety of paddy which gives the highest yield is transplanted aman paddy, which requires a clay soil and about 1¼ feet of water almost from the time of planting to harvest time.

Plain, implies an agricultural economy which favours a particularly high density of population. A full justification for this important generalization of agricultural economics has already been given in a previous chapter. Another wet crop which has been until recently a valuable commercial crop in the Ganges Delta is jute, which is excellently adapted to the moist climate of the delta. In the active delta jute is grown on the water-logged land in an excessively damp atmosphere. As it is a crop which exhausts the soil to a great extent it is grown to best advantage in the active delta in which river floods leave deposits of fertile silt on land and the cultivators have not to use manures. But jute may be grown equally well on high lands beyond the reach of river floods. Indeed, jute grown on such lands has a better fibre than jute grown in the lowlands of the delta. But jute cultivation on high lands is impossible without manures. Hence the cultivation of jute in the highland tracts of the delta, particularly in West and Central Bengal, is confined to the highly manured lands near the village sites, while the lowlands are devoted exclusively to the cultivation of winter rice. Thus obviously the importance of the jute crop is greater in the active than in the moribund delta and makes for higher agricultural productivity and higher density of population.

From the point of view of agricultural productivity the contrast between the Ganges Delta and the drier regions of the Gangetic Plain on the one hand, and the contrast between the active and the moribund delta on the other, become quite obvious when we observe the distribution of rainfall over the entire agricultural season and the timing of agricultural operations in relation to the sucession of crops. In the dry regions of the Ganges Valley the *kharif* and the *rabi* constitute the two harvests. The distribution of these two harvests no doubt depends upon soil and configuration of land. In the waterlogged region the principal staple is rice and the main *rabi* crops are usually gram, peas, and barley. On the dry lands between the rivers and the depressions the usual crops such as cereals, pulses, millets, cotton, sugar-cane, and oil-seeds are grown. The river valleys have their distinctive series of crops characteristic of lighter soils, such as bajra, cotton, and hemp. But the importance of either the *kharif* or the *rabi* crops depends essentially on agricultural water-supply. For example, important *kharif* crops like rice and sugar-cane predominate in the eastern portion of the Upper Ganges Valley, because this tract enjoys greater advantages in respect of both natural and artificial irrigation. On the other hand, important *rabi* crops like wheat and cotton predominate in the comparatively arid tracts of the western portion of the Upper Ganges Valley in which the natural environment is favourable to the growth of dry crops. But both the harvests are mostly dependent on sufficient and well-distributed rainfall. A poor monsoon or its early cessation becomes disastrous in its effect upon the *kharif* crops, and a failure of the *rabi* crops can be averted only if there is favourable winter rainfall. On the other hand, particularly in the eastern and the central portions of the Upper Ganges Valley, excessive rainfall is disastrous to the *kharif* crops. Only when excessive rainfall is sufficiently general and well distributed has it the compensatory effect of increasing the area and the yield of the *rabi* crops. Winter rains also should not be excessive, otherwise excessive dampness will injure the *rabi* crops. In the Middle Ganges Valley, the early rainfall, the monsoon rainfall, and the winter rainfall are distributed in such a way that three cycles of plant life can be completed in the course of the entire season. Thus the *bhadoi* harvest, which is reaped in autumn, is followed by the *aghani* harvest, which is reaped in winter, and is followed again by the *rabi* harvest reaped in spring. For the success of the *bhadoi* crops showers in March and ante-monsoon showers in April are indispensable, because otherwise preparatory tillage is impossible. In the Upper Ganges Valley early rainfall is so scanty that the season cannot begin as early as in the Middle Ganges Valley and the Ganges Delta. Moreover, rainfall during the monsoon season is not so heavy as to facilitate quick germination and rapid growth of early sown crops so as to enable the cultivators to raise another crop in the winter harvest. Again, so far as the contribution of double-cropping to agricultural productivity is concerned there is also a contrast between the dry regions of the Upper

Ganges Valley and the Middle Ganges Valley. As we have shown above, in the Upper Ganges Valley the increasing pressure of the population upon land has been relieved to some extent by extensive double-cropping, which means mostly the cultivation of inferior food-grains like gram and peas as catch crops. But the double-cropped area has been limited by scanty rainfall and the absence of the facilities of artificial irrigation. In the Middle Ganges Valley, on the other hand, the contribution of double-cropping to agricultural productivity is greater whenever the *rabi* crops are raised as second crops, not after the *aghani* but after the *bhadoi* harvest. But, as already discussed above, the main economic problem in this region is the problem of agricultural insecurity caused by too much dependence on *aghani* rice, the success of which is bound up with favourable rainfall during the Hathiya asterism. Extensive cultivation of winter rice no doubt co-exists with high density, but it is sad to reflect that the predominance of winter rice co-exists with great agricultural insecurity in regions where the entire agricultural economy depends precariously on sufficient and well-distributed rainfall. In the Ganges Delta the early rainfall, the monsoon rainfall and the winter rainfall are normally so heavy and so well-distributed that three cycles of plant life are possible, as in the Middle Valley. But in the Ganges Delta rainfall, both early and late, is so heavy and so well-distributed that meteorological conditions are far more favourable to high agricultural productivity. Early rainfall in March, April, and May is often heavy enough to permit of preparatory tillage and early sowings. And if the *bhadoi* crop thus gets a good start it can be harvested early with the help of sufficient monsoon rainfall, so that the same land is fit to receive the transplanted seedlings of *aman* paddy. This is never possible in the Middle Ganges Valley, which receives less than 4 inches of rainfall between March 1 and May 1931, and the *bhadoi* crop cannot get as early a start as in Bengal. Thus in the Ganges Delta it is possible for cultivators to get a heavy-yielding crop of *aman* paddy from the same land which has already borne a valuable crop like jute or a crop of *aus* paddy. This kind of double-cropping is the secret of the economic prosperity of the active delta which supports such a phenomenally high density of population. Another point of contrast between the Ganges Delta and the dry regions of the Gangetic Plain is the comparative insignificance of the *rabi* harvest in the former region. In the Ganges Delta the *rabi* crops predominate only in the dry tracts of the moribund delta, in which natural conditions are unfavourable to the cultivation of the heavy-yielding crops of the *bhadoi* and the *aghani* harvests. In fact, the *rabi* crops are generally half as valuable as summer and winter crops. Hence usually they are raised after either the *bhadoi* or the *aghani* crops as cheap catch crops on which little labour or attention is given. In the active delta such crops can indeed be grown more extensively. But their value is not tempting enough to a cultivator who can get good crops of rice and jute with so little labour. He does not feel inclined to plough his land twice or thrice, when it is caked to its hardest, for the sake of the few rupees which the *rabi* crop will bring in. Hence the cultivator concentrates either on the *aman* or the *aus* harvest and tries to get an *aman* crop after the *aus* harvest if he can. In fact, he thinks of raising spring cereals or pulses only when he finds that the land is not low enough for two crops of rice.

Let us next consider the contrast between the active and the moribund delta as regards the choice of crops. In the active delta weather conditions are so favourable that the agricultural season starts earlier than in the moribund delta; preparatory tillage is finished earlier, and the *bhadoi* crops can also be sown earlier. Moreover, rainfall is sufficiently heavy to enable the cultivators to harvest the *bhadoi* crop and transplant the *aghani* rice crop earlier. In the moribund delta, on the other hand, early rainfall is not heavy enough.[1] The season begins later and the *bhadoi* and the *aghani* crops cannot be harvested earlier. Hence the cultivators have to choose between the *bhadoi* and the *aghani* crops. Where early rainfall is sufficiently heavy and well-distributed the cultivators grow *bhadoi* crops to a large extent, and where they have to depend mostly on the monsoon rainfall winter

---

[1] The rainfall in March, April and May is 9·63 inches in the moribund delta, while it is 17·92 inches in the active delta.

rice becomes necessarily the staple crop. We shall see later
how this exclusive dependence on the winter rice crop in
certain tracts of the Ganges Delta has caused great economic
insecurity, and how some of the blackest spots on the famine
map are those where the cultivators have to rely too much on
the *aghani* rice crop as in certain districts of North Bihar.

The following table illustrates the distribution of harvests in
the different districts of Bengal included in the Ganges Delta:

PERCENTAGE OF NET CROPPED AREA
(Excluding orchards)

	Bhadoi	Jute	Aghani	Rabi	Double-cropped
Burdwan . .	17	1·5	83	14	14
Birbhum . .	19	—	78	3	3
Bankura . .	7	—	87	10	5
Midnapur . .	14	1	71	18	4
Hughly . .	23	12	64	11	9
Howrah . .	32	23	53	14	12
Average for West Bengal . .	18·6	—	72·6	16·6	8
24 Parganas .	18	6·3	77	4	10
Nadia . . .	83	14	25	56	64
Murshidabad .	43	2·9	50	40	33
Jessore . .	30	9	42	21	17
Khulna . .	12	2·6	92	7	11
Average for Central Bengal .	37·2	—	57·2	25·6	27
Dacca . . .	27	22·4[1]	41	23	35
Faridpur . .	35	23·8[1]	72	24	33
Bakarganj . .	11	2·7[1]	95	7	13
Tipperah . .	44	20·9[1]	74	18	38
Noakhali . .	45	5·3[1]	90	14	50
Average for the Active Delta .	32·6	—	74·4	17·4	33·8

[1] Percentage of cultivable area.

The table shows clearly the importance of the *bhadoi* and the *aghani* harvests and the comparative insignificance of the *rabi* harvest throughout the Ganges Delta. Of the *bhadoi* and the *aghani* harvests the *aghani* is distinctly a more important harvest. The crops of the *bhadoi* harvest are *aus* rice, and jute. *Aus* rice is a coarse grain consumed by the poorer classes alone. In the moribund delta it is grown on high lands and requires much less water than winter rice. It yields a smaller return than *aman* or *boro*. The yield of *aus* rice (husked) is estimated to be 906 lbs. per acre as against 1,000 lbs. per acre in the case of *aman* rice.[1] The price fetched by *aus* rice is also lower. But this crop supplies the cultivator with food and his cattle with fodder at a time of the year when both are scarce. It is also reaped early enough to permit of the preparation of land for spring cereals, pulses, vegetables, potatoes, and sugar-cane. In the active delta *aus* rice is also grown together with *aman* on low lands where the depth of water does not exceed two feet at the beginning of the rainy season. The plant grows to a height of a little over three feet, and the stalk does not grow sufficiently fast to keep pace with the rice of the flood level, so that *aus* rice cannot grow at all in the marshy areas. Jute, the other more important crop of the *bhadoi* harvest, can be grown on high as well as low lands. But, as already said, in the moribund delta its cultivation is confined mostly to the highly manured lands near the village sites, while in the active delta it is grown also on low lands and thus competes not only with *aus* rice but also with *aman* rice sometimes. In the *aghani* or the winter harvest the only crop is *aman* rice. It is cultivated in low lands with a clay soil and requires much more water than *aus* rice. In the moribund delta *aman* rice is sometimes grown on high lands, but only when they are close to canals, tanks or any other reservoirs of water. But mostly this crop occupies the extensive lowlands separating the village sites throughout the alluvial tracts of Western and Central Bengal. In the active delta *aman* rice is grown usually on low lands which are inundated during the rainy season.

---

[1] *Quinquennial Report on the Average Yield per Acre of Principal Crops in India for* 1926–7, p. 12.

It can be grown on lands which do not go more than six feet under water in August and September. The cultivators grow numerous varieties of *aman* paddy, being guided in their choice of seeds by the height of the land. For land on which a crop of *aus* or jute has already been raised one of the *bhadra-mashi* or long-stalked, quick-growing varieties has to be used. On the other hand the varieties grown on low lands which produce *aman* only are classified as *asharhi*. Now it is obvious that a heavy-yielding crop like *aman* rice, which finds the best environment in a monsoon region like the Ganges Delta, should naturally be the most important crop on the success of which the stability of the rural economy so largely depends.

An examination of the above table shows that, in the following districts included in the Ganges Delta, the *aghani* rice crop occupies more than 70 per cent of the net cropped area:

Districts	Percentage of net cropped area under Aghani rice
Burdwan	83
Birbhum	78
Bankura	87
Midnapur	71
24 Parganas . . .	77
Khulna	92
Faridpur	72
Bakarganj	95
Noakhali	90
Tipperah	74

When interpreting these crop statistics from the point of view of rural density we must not lay undue emphasis on the high productivity of the *aman* rice crop, and ignore the agricultural insecurity caused by too much dependence on a single crop, however heavy-yielding it may be, which depends for its success too precariously on the monsoon rainfall and particularly on rainfall in September and October. Indeed, from the point of view of agricultural security, so far as it depends on favourable natural conditions under which winter rice is grown, we find an interesting contrast between the moribund and the active delta. In the old delta the cultivation of *bhadoi* crops such as jute and *aus* rice is confined to the high lands near the village sites, which are highly manured and grow a variety of crops in the autumn and the spring harvests. Hence, as the statistics show, only a small area is under the *bhadoi* crops. The area under the *rabi* crops, some of which are raised as second crops and some independently, is also small.[1] We have seen that in this region the extent of double-cropping (which means usually the cultvation of spring crops after either the *bhadoi* or the *aghani* harvest) is small, because there are extensive areas of single-cropped rice land, and consequently double-cropping is confined mostly to highly manured lands near the village sites. In fact, the laterite clay soil of the old alluvium in West Bengal is very difficult to work, as it turns into a mass of most tenacious mud in the rainy season and becomes as hard as stone in summer. On account of this difficulty in many places nothing but winter rice to which this soil is well suited, can be grown.[2] But, as explained in the last chapter, the balance of the entire agricultural economy in the moribund delta rests on sufficient and well-distributed rainfall. For the success of the *bhadoi* crops rainfall is required at frequent intervals from April onwards, but it must not be heavy or continuous. For the success of the *aghani* harvest, on the other hand, the most favourable rainfall is the premonitory shower in May or early June. 'The rainfall in the latter half of June and July should be heavy, otherwise transplantation will be hampered, and there should be an interval of comparatively fine weather so as to permit of weeding operations being successfully carried on. Rainfall in September should also be heavy, and it must shade off into fine

---

[1] The difference between the percentage of the rabi area and the percentage of the double-cropped area indicates the extent to which rabi crops are raised independently and not as second crops.

[2] The rice seedlings are planted when the rains have set in and the clay soil has been softened by deep ploughing.

weather with showers in October. The most important factor
in the growth of transplanted paddy is rainfall in October,
on which the outturn of this crop entirely depends.[1] Thus
if there is failure of rainfall in the beginning of the monsoon
season the prospects of the *bhadoi* harvest become very
gloomy, and if there is a premature break of the monsoon,
with failure of rainfall in September and October, there is
always a danger of the total failure of the *aghani* rice crop.
The reason is that in the old delta the scope and facilities of
artificial irrigation are very much limited, and in years of
drought the irrigated area forms only a small percentage of
the net cropped area. In fact, the cultivator in this region
seems to be so completely at the mercy of the weather that
it is very often impossible for him to save his *aghani* rice crop
when there is failure of rainfall or when it is badly distributed,
and consequently he has to subsist on maize or inferior millets
until the harvesting of *rabi* crops in the latter part of March.
But the helpless position of the agriculturist is easily realized
when it is remembered that the *rabi* crops occupy only a small
percentage of the total cultivated area, and that, when there
is a premature termination of the monsoon, there is bound to
be a shrinkage in the area and yield of the *rabi* crops too
owing to want of moisture at the time of sowing. Thus in
most of the districts included in the old delta in which *aman*
rice occupies more than 70 per cent of the net cropped area,
we invariably find acute economic distress amounting to
famine whenever the monsoon rainfall is short or badly
distributed. In this respect some of the tracts in the old
delta resemble too closely the Middle Ganges Valley, where
also there is the same predominance of winter rice and a
similar delicate adjustment of the timing of agricultural
operations to meteorological conditions. It would be interesting in this connexion to mark out some of the blackest
spots in the famine map of Bengal. Take, for example, the
district of Bankura. Here as much as 87 per cent of the net
cropped area is devoted to the cultivation of winter rice.
There is no complete system of irrigation works to counteract
the effects of a failure of rainfall. Moreover, in this district,

[1] Pp. 261-2, Ch. IV.

'an ample and well-distributed rainfall is especially necessary, because the country is undulating and the soil porous, thus helping rapid drainage and percolation.'[1] Hence, whenever the rainfall is short or ill-distributed in this district there is great economic distress, and there are some tracts, for example, the northern part of Sonamukhi thana, which are especially liable to drought and consequent famine. Again, in Midnapur as much as 71 per cent of the net cropped area is devoted to winter rice. In the absence of a complete system of irrigation works the fortunes of the agriculturist in this district depend largely on ample and well-distributed rainfall. Such agricultural insecurity is further enhanced by the configuration of land. 'A part of the district being high and undulating and a part flat and low-lying, most estates are liable to suffer to some extent from the vicissitudes of the seasons. If the monsoon sets in early with very heavy rain the crops on the lower lands cannot be grown at all or are damaged by submersion, while if it sets in late or ceases prematurely the crops on the high sites suffer from drought.'[2] Another district in which the cultivators have to depend precariously on ample and well-distributed rainfall is Khulna. In this district as much as 92 per cent of the net cropped area is normally under *aman* rice. A sufficient and seasonable rainfall is essential for the growth of this crop for special reasons. 'The soil in many parts is more or less impregnated with salt; and before seedlings can be grown and transplantation effected the salt must be washed out. Consequently, any deficiency of rainfall at these critical periods reduces the area under cultivation. At the same time ample rain is required to keep the water of the rivers and *khals* sweet, especially as the silting up of the rivers at their heads has caused them to remain salt for a much longer period than formerly.'[3] Thus a failure of rainfall or its bad distribution seems to be all the more disastrous to agriculture in Khulna and readily creates famine conditions.

[1] *Gazetteer*, Bankura.
[2] *Gazetteer*, Midnapur. As already explained, human interference with drainage levels has also increased the difficulties of agriculture in Midnapur by causing over-flooding of land. It must be remembered that some tracts in West Bengal are liable to famine due to this cause, viz. Arambagh and Khanakul thanas of the Hughly district.
[3] *Gazetteer*, Khulna.

19

In the active delta winter rice is cultivated as extensively as in the old delta, but the natural conditions in the active delta are such that it is not exposed to agricultural insecurity due to the vicissitudes of the seasons. Take, for example, the district of Bakarganj. Being a recent alluvial formation the land in this district is so low that it goes under water during the period of annual inundation, and it is only in small areas that the soil is suitable for crops other than winter rice. Hence 95 per cent of the net cropped area in Bakarganj is under winter rice, so that cultivators have to depend upon the success of this crop to a much greater extent in this district than in Khulna, Bankura, or Midnapur. But the danger of drought here is not so great as in the moribund delta and the dry regions of the Ganges Valley. The rice crop here no doubt needs rain at the right time, but rainfall is certain, and delay, although damaging, is not ruinous to the whole crop, as agriculture depends to a greater extent on river economy. In fact, what ensures the safety of the winter rice crop in the active delta is heavy rainfall in September and October, combined with regular river floods. Thus the natural conditions in Bakarganj are so favourable for the cultivation of winter rice that the cultivator pins his faith on this crop rather than allow experiments with summer crops.[1] Take again a district like Noakhali, in which as much as 90 per cent of the net cropped area is under winter rice. Here the cultivator has, no doubt, to trust to the certainty of sufficient rainfall in the end of September and in October to make a good crop of winter rice. But it never fails him, and he gets a good crop even when winter rice has been transplanted late. Hence it is easy for him to depend safely on extensive cultivation of winter rice for which the soil also is especially suited. In Tipperah also there are tracts which are so low that summer crops cannot grow there at all, and the land is devoted entirely to winter rice. The particularly high proportion of the cultivated area under winter rice in the centre and the south-east of the district is explained by the fact that in those parts late rain is more

[1] In the southern portion of Bakarganj, which is a typical recent alluvial formation, a very small area is under crops other than *aman* rice, and *aus* rice is cultivated less than in the north of the district.

plentiful than elsewhere, thus enabling *aman* rice to be transplanted later.

Let us now consider the significance of the varying percentage of the *bhadoi* area in the Ganges Delta. As already said, the crops of the *bhadoi* harvest are *aus* rice and jute. Both of them can be grown on high as well as low lands. In the moribund delta the cultivation of *aus* rice is commonly confined to high lands beyond the reach of river floods. The cultivation of jute is also confined to highly manured highlands near the village sites. But in the active delta jute can be grown on *chars*, where the land always retains sufficient moisture, and in the low-lying country where it stands in three or four feet of water. In fact, the rich alluvial soil of the *chars* gives the highest outturn and also produces the finest fibre. *Aus* rice can also be grown on lands which are not too low, although the characteristic crop of the low lands is the heavy-yielding *aman* rice crop. Thus it follows that the predominance of the *bhadoi* harvest in the absence of jute, or in other words, the predominance of *aus* rice, is most often an indication of the extent of high land which is beyond the reach of river floods, and in which river economy has almost ceased to play its part in agriculture. It is clear from the statistics given above that, except in Hughly, Howrah and Nadia, the area under jute in the moribund delta is insignificant and *aus* rice is the only crop in the *bhadoi* harvest. Now, this overwhelming importance of *aus* rice in the *bhadoi* harvest throughout the moribund delta is clearly a sign of the inactivity of the delta-building rivers and the deterioration of soil fertility. In fact, wherever the delta has ceased to be active there has been an increase in the area under *aus* rice at the expense of the area under *aman* rice. For example, in Jessore, in which the process of land formation has been completed in comparatively recent times, the area under *aman* rice has contracted due to deficient floods, but on the other hand the area under *aus* rice has increased.[1] In the northern portion of Faridpur which has also become a part of the moribund delta in recent times we find a remarkable predominance of *aus* rice, the area under which occupies

[1] We find this tendency particularly in the Magura sub-division of Jessore.

two-fifths of the net cropped area in the Goalundo sub-division and nearly one-third in the Sadar sub-division, while very little of it is grown in the other two sub-divisions.[1] Take again the contiguous district of Khulna. Here also the chief *aus* growing areas are the high lands in the north-western part of the district where the process of land formation has been completed. In Kalaroa, Satkhira, and Tala, situated in the inland tract, the *aus* area is 55, 21, and 31 per cent respectively, while it does not exceed 7 per cent in the rest of the district. There is another important fact which must be taken into account when we consider the significance of a high percentage of cultivated area under *aus* rice. Not only is *aus* rice inferior to either jute or *aman* rice from the point of view of agricultural productivity, but its cultivation also precariously depends on sufficient and well-distributed rainfall, particularly in the months of March, April, and May. Hence this crop is more likely to fail in the moribund delta, where early rainfall is smaller in amount and more liable to be deficient in abnormal years.

In the active delta *aus* rice is usually sown broadcast like *aman*, and except in marshy areas which go under water to a great depth during the rainy season it is commonly grown together with *aman*.[2] For example, in Faridpur *aus* is commonly grown with *aman* in localities where the depth of water does not exceed two feet at the beginning of the rains. The *aus* crop is harvested in July and August, and the *aman* crop is left to mature and be reaped in winter. The object of growing *aus* and *aman* together is to ensure greater agricultural security. If the level of water on land is high enough, a good crop of *aman* rice is obtained although the yield of *aus* crop is low. On the other hand, if the level of water during the flood season is low, the *aman* crop has a lower yield, but the loss is compensated by a good crop of *aus* rice.

[1] *Aus* is as important as aman in the north of the district, half as important in the centre of the district and but one-tenth as important in the rest of the district.

[2] In fact much of the *aman* rice might be classed as aus 'as the dates for sowing and reaping are dependent upon the level of water which is convenient at very different periods of the year at different points in the fringe.' Radhakamal Mukherjee, 'Agricultural Contrasts in the Bengal Delta', *Indian Journal of Economics*, July 1928.

Sometimes under favourable conditions half a crop of *aus* and a three-quarter crop of *aman* are obtained by sowing *aman* and *aus* together. In Tipperah also the early *aus* that is grown in the new alluvial accretions is transplanted like *aman* and gives a very heavy crop, although, if the flood rises too fast, a part of it is destroyed. Thus it appears that the conditions under which *aus* rice is cultivated in the active delta are far more favourable. But the most distinctive feature of the *bhadoi* harvest in the active delta is the predominance of the jute crop. As already said, jute can be grown to best advantage in this region. As a crop which is adapted to the moist climate of the Delta and exhausts the fertility of the soil, it finds the best natural conditions of growth in the alluvial accretions and lowlands of the active delta, which receive fertilizing deposits of river-borne silt during the rainy season. It appears from the statistical table given above that, with the exception of Bakarganj and Noakhali, in all other districts of the active delta jute occupies a conspicuous place in the *bhadoi* harvest. Bakarganj and Noakhali are the typical rice districts of the Ganges Delta. There *aman* rice is the most important crop, and the cultivator relies on summer crops to a very small extent. In explaining the remarkably small extent of jute area in Bakarganj, the late Mr. J. C. Jack, I.C.S., observed that 'in the south of the district this is probably due to the difficulty of getting it to market when the great rivers are turbulent and in flood, but apart from this in the lower grounds salt water stands when the jute plants are young and kills them'.[1] But everywhere else in the active delta the importance of the jute crop cannot be exaggerated. Owing to the increasing pressure of the population on land and the high value of jute as a commercial crop until recent times, jute has displaced *aus* rice and other *rabi* crops to a very large extent. We find this typical change in the character of crops in the district of Faridpur. As Mr. J. C. Jack observed in the case of Faridpur, 'At the present day the cultivators may be said in three-fourths of the district to depend on jute for a comfortable livelihood. Spring crops are only grown as catch crops where formerly much dependence

[1] *Survey and Settlement Report*, Bakarganj, 1900 to 1908, J. C. Jack, I.C.S.

was placed upon them, rice is grown for consumption where formerly it was grown for sale, and jute is increasingly grown every year with far greater profit than was ever won from the crops which it has displaced.' Indeed, the nature of jute production is such that the cultivation of even *aman* rice sometimes suffers considerably for the sake of the jute crop. 'Even when it might possibly be better to leave it a little longer on the ground a cultivator will take up his *aus* crop to make room for winter rice, but he would not treat jute in the same manner. As soon as the *aus* crop is cut he will set to work at once to prepare the land and transplant winter rice, but when jute is cut his labours with it have been by no means finished. What he cut first has steeped long enough before the cutting is finished and it cannot be left while he prepares the land for the winter crops. A few days too long in the water will ruin it, and the process of stripping and drying it keeps him and all his family busy for some time longer, before the transplantation of *aman* crop can be thought of.'[1]

In conclusion, let us consider the contribution of double cropping to agricultural productivity in the moribund and the active delta. It has already been discussed in a previous chapter why the twice-cropped area is much greater in the latter than in the former region. The main conclusions may conveniently be summarized here. In the moribund delta the total amount of rainfall during the critical months is much smaller than in the active delta. Moreover, the soil does not get sufficient moisture and silt from the seasonal floods. Hence the cultivators have to choose between summer and winter crops, and a summer crop cannot be followed by a second winter crop. Where the *bhadoi* is the main harvest it cannot be followed by a winter crop, not only because the rainfall in September and October is insufficient, but also because there are no river floods which leave the soil moist after the rainy season. Where the *aghani* is the main harvest the cultivator cannot possibly allow experiments with summer crops to interfere with its chances. Consequently the second

[1] *Survey and Settlement Report*, Tipperah, 1915–18, W. H. Thompson, I.C.S. It may be noted in this connection that the production of jute, like that of rice, requires a large labour force and thus necessitates a high density of population.

crops are usually *rabi* crops grown after either the *bhadoi* or the *aghani* harvest. But the cultivation of the *rabi* crops is hampered by uncertain winter rains and lack of the facilities of artificial irrigation. Thus it appears that unfavourable natural conditions have been responsible for the small extent of the double-cropped area in the moribund delta. In the active delta, on the other hand, rainfall in March, April and May, and again in September and October, is so ample and certain, and the floods of the rivers in June, July and August rise and fall with such unfailing regularity, that both summer and winter crops can be grown on the same land and in the same season. Indeed, if the cultivator likes he can also grow a *rabi* crop on land sown with winter rice provided that the winter rice crop has not been harvested late, because if it is harvested late there is not sufficient time for wheat or barley to ripen before the rain in March and April, which would spoil it. Secondly, it must be noted that not only is the double-cropped area more extensive in the active than in the moribund delta, but its economic importance is also greater in the former than in the latter region. The *rabi* crops, as already explained, do not possess the same import-ance in the Ganges Delta as in the comparatively arid regions of the Upper and Middle Ganges Valley. Hence it is obvious that the contribution of double-cropping to agricultural productivity varies directly as the extent to which the *bhadoi* crops are succeeded by *aghani* rice on the same land and in the same season. From this point of view double-cropping makes a greater contribution to agricultural productivity in the active than in the moribund delta.

APPENDIX

A NOTE ON THE DENSITY OF POPULATION
IN RELATION TO AGRICULTURAL WATER-SUPPLY

THE correspondence between the density of population and the facilities of agricultural water-supply can be demonstrated by another method of approach. It is obvious that the density of population per square mile depends on (a) the number of villages per square mile, and (b) the average size of each village. Density per square mile will be high if the average size of each village is large and, at the same time, the number of villages per square mile is large. Density per square mile will be low if the average size of each village is small, and, at the same time, the number of villages per square mile is small. It is also clear that density will be high if the number of villages per square mile is very large, even if the average size of each is small, and that density will be low if the number of villages per square mile is very small, even if the average size of each is large. As a matter of fact, however, a study of the nature and geographical distribution of human establishments indicates that the density of population per square mile is high or low, usually under the second set of conditions assumed above. As we shall see presently, the causes which make the average size of each village small but the number of villages per square mile so large that the density of population per square mile becomes high, and the causes which make the average size of each village large but the total number of villages per square mile so small that the density of population per square mile remains low, are essentially the climatic and hydrographic factors which determine the facilities of agricultural water-supply in a certain region.

It is apparent that the average size of each village becomes necessarily small when the prevailing type of human settlement is the hamlet type, which presupposes a scattering of human habitations. In this case the causes which prevent human establishments from being collected in groups so that the land becomes dotted with innumerable isolated hamlets are the climatic and hydrographic factors of human environment. As Vidal De La Blache says: 'Where a diffusion of waters, variety of exposure and fine dissection of the landscape occur together there are all the necessities for a permanent abode. So the groups consist of the members of a single family with possibly a few neighbours in addition. There is nothing to require the varied services which life in a village community implies. Habitations scatter.'[1] Thus the hamlet type of human settlement is found in the rugged and mountainous sections of Serbia and Bulgaria where there is a supply of water everywhere, and the forest is 'close enough to supply the timber necessary for building purposes and for winter fires.'[2] It is true that this type of scattered establishments may be accompanied by a type of life which is semi-agricultural and semi-pastoral and does not permit of a high density of population. But this is not always so. In fact, the most striking example of the hamlet type of settlement co-existing with intensive agriculture and high density of population is found in the case of Lower Bengal and the narrow coastal strip of Malabar and Travancore. Here, as La Blache says, 'Heavy rainfall and abundant water-supply encourage scattered settlement'.[3] Thus in Lower Bengal large compact villages, where periodical markets are held, are usually found only on the banks of the rivers. Otherwise the country between the ridges is dotted with hamlets consisting of small groups of houses scattered through the rice and jute fields, and tiny hamlets rear up their heads wherever there is high ground raised above the flood level. The low lands, which receive an abundant supply of natural irrigation bear rich heavy-yielding crops like jute and rice, and the dense population, which is necessary for the cultivation of these crops, and which can only be supported by such heavy-yielding crops, is distributed in innumerable small hamlets. Hence in this region the density of population per square mile is very high, because the density of hamlets per square mile is high although the average size of each hamlet is small, and this is due to favourable climatic and hydrographic conditions which have ensured an abundant agricultural water-supply.

As contrasted with the hamlet type of human settlement, there is the compact village which is characteristic of broad plains having a relatively uniform soil and relief. Under such natural conditions need is felt for centralizing agriculture in some place. 'A co-operative agreement as to dates in the agricultural calendar and the time for certain tasks is adopted for the advantage of all concerned. Necessity for co-operation in the regulation and

---

[1] Vidal De La Blache, *Principles of Human Geography*, p. 300.
[2] Ibid., p. 304.   [3] Ibid., p. 312.

control of water, driving of wells, upkeep of certain public works and preparation of the environment to make it favourable to crops—such things mean consolidation.'[1] In certain parts of Europe the broad level plains can be ploughed in long unbroken furrows, and crops can be raised on a large scale by the same methods, with the same machinery and at the same seasons—sowing, weeding, harvesting being carried on everywhere simultaneously. Such an agricultural economy is 'consistent only with a type of occupation in which the entire space for living purposes is centralized.'[2] The result is the formation of large clustered villages. In oriental countries the necessity of co-operation for the regulation and control of water has very often led to the formation of compact villages and the growth of strong village communities. In Tonkin, for example, 'between the dykes built for the control of floods there are little compartments in which water accumulates during the summer rains in *arroyos*, pools and ponds, artificial in part. And here the Annamese of the Delta has built his village. . . . The cisterns where rain-water collects as in the *johls* of Bengal, are filled from the small pools lingering after summer rains and floods. By strengthening their borders and controlling the flow a precise and minute regulation is accomplished entirely in keeping with the labour-supply.'[3] This type of rural economy which is based on the community organization of compact villages, is similar to what we find in India, where also the necessity of guarding against irregular and insufficient rainfall has been responsible for the growth of village groups. Before the construction of canals in Northern India and the dykes of the Cauvery and the rivers of the Carnatic in Southern India modest primitive methods for the control and regulation of water had been in existence for long ages, thus fostering the growth of compact village groups. Again, the necessity of artificial storage of water by means of dams in the Middle Ganges Valley and Madras has also impelled men to pool their resources, so that population there has naturally tended to concentrate in big villages. Similarly, artificial irrigation by means of wells and tanks, as in the Upper Ganges Valley, has also required a co-operative organization and favoured the formation of compact villages. But it must be borne in mind that the same causes which have led to the evolution of compact villages have prevented a high density of population per square mile. The number of such villages per square mile always depends upon the facilities of artificial irrigation which each village can command, and the

[1] Ibid., p. 300.   [2] Ibid., p. 293.   [3] Ibid., p. 311.

number has been small owing to the inadequacy of agricultural water-supply. Hence the density of population per square mile has remained low, because although the average size of a village has been large, the total number of villages per square mile has been small. The situation can be contrasted with what we find in regions in which the hamlet type of settlement prevails. There, as we have seen, an abundant supply of natural moisture has favoured such a large increase in the number of isolated hamlets per square mile that the density of population per square mile has become necessarily high.

It is very interesting to observe that in the whole of Northern India the geographical distribution of the hamlet type and the village type of human establishments corresponds very closely with varying climatic and hydrographic conditions which determine the facilities of agricultural water-supply. The compact type of village may be regarded as the characteristic type throughout Northern India except the Gangetic Delta. In the Punjab a village 'has so many inhabitants, is so complete in itself with its organization and with its various trades, so well enclosed within its mud walls that it resembles a tribal camp. Between grassy slopes busy with stock-raising, markets and fairs, the regulation of valley floods by means of primitive sluices and the driving of wells near elevations, necessitate co-operation.'[1] In the Upper Ganges Valley the same type of compact village meets our eyes everywhere. As Mr. E. H. H. Edye observes, 'The isolated country house or farm so familiar in Europe has no counterpart here'. The high density of population has thus resulted in great overcrowding, and 'if village densities were calculated on the area of the inhabited site, and not on that of the site and the village lands, they would generally be greater than that of any town.'[2] It is interesting to note that the average size of a village is much larger in the western portion of the Upper Ganges Valley than in the eastern portion where the scattering of human habitations is due to the fact that the water-table is accessible, and the ease with which wells can be constructed has enabled the population to cover uniformly the entire area of loose mellow soil. The Middle Ganges Valley is also generally a land of large villages, although in the hilly regions of South Bihar the lack of uniformity of soil and relief and the barrenness of the country have led to a diffusion of habitations which co-exists there with a very low density of population. Here, as already said, the evolution of the compact

[1] Vidal De La Blache, *Principles of Human Geography*, p. 312.
[2] *Census of India*, 1921, Vol. XVI, Pt. I, p. 33.

village is due to the necessity of co-operation for the regulation and supply of water. A water-supply cannot be obtained by sinking a well or digging a tank equally well everywhere. Consequently 'the growing population has to find accommodation by overcrowding the existing houses or adding yet another house to the congested village site.'[1] In rural Bengal, on the other hand, the tendency for people to swarm in compact villages is discouraged because 'The cultivator uses very little indeed which his own land cannot supply. A water-supply can be obtained by sinking a well or digging a tank equally well in almost any spot. The property of a landlord or middleman is usually far stretched and interspersed with the properties of others, and labourers who have not land of their own are very few indeed. In these circumstances it is not surprising to find the homesteads scattered over the whole face of the countryside. Each cultivator has selected a suitable spot for a homestead on his own land, dug a tank or made untidy irregular excavations to obtain earth to raise a site and build houses on. The process is still going on.'[2] In this way the increase in the density of population has been accompanied by a multiplication of scattered homesteads which has been facilitated by an abundant agricultural water-supply.

[1] Ibid., 1911, Vol. V, Pt. I, p. 44.
[2] Ibid., 1921, Vol. V, Pt. I, p. 124.

INDEX

ACTIVE DELTA

Agricultural productivity in, 273–4, 279–80, 282–6

Agricultural security in, 273–6

Agricultural water-supply and double-cropping in, 245–6, 247–8

Aman rice and economic prosperity in, 290–1

Boundary of, 233 f.n.

Choice of crops in, 279–80, 282–6

Cultivable area in, 212, 233

Cultivated area in, 212, 233

Density in, 207, 209, 212, 233

Distribution of rainfall and double-cropping in, 246–7

Distribution of silt in, 270

Double-cropping and density in, 245–6, 247–8

Effect of the distribution of rainfall on the harvests in, 261–2

Floods and double-cropping in, 245–6

High productivity of *Aman* rice in, 285

Importance of early rainfall and rainfall in October in, 261, 262

Importance of flood irrigation in, 267, 268–73

Migration from north to south in, 207, 234, 238, 239

Percentage of cultivated to cultivable area in, 212, 233

Pressure of population on the purely alluvial tracts of, 233, 234, 238

Rainfall in critical months and distribution of harvests in, 247–8

Rainfall and density in, 260

Sanitation in, 208, 209

Scattering of habitations in, 298, 301

Soil in, 269, 270

Zones of, 233, 234, 238

ADEQUACY OF CULTIVATION

Introduction, vi

AGRICULTURAL CONTRASTS

In the Ganges Valley, 213 f.n., 277–84

AGRICULTURAL DEVELOPMENT

And colonization, 213, 220, 223, 232, 234, 235, 236, 237, 238, 240, 241, 242

And reclamation, 6, 7, 16, 17, 21, 22, 23, 27, 213, 217, 220, 222, 223, 225, 231, 234, 241, 242 f.n.

And the sugar tariff, 13

Nature of, in India, Introduction, vii, viii

Two-fold tendency of, in the Upper Ganges Valley, 58

AGRICULTURAL PRODUCTIVITY

Introduction, xii, xiii

And combination of crops in the Ganges Valley, 93–6, 194–7, 277–83

In the regions of the Ganges Valley, 280–3

AGRICULTURAL-ECONOMIC ENVIRONMENT

And density of population, Introduction, vii–xiv

As an ensemble, Introduction, vii

Interference with, Introduction, vi

Vital factors of, Introduction, vii

AGRICULTURAL SECURITY

And cultivation of *Aus* rice, 292, 293

And double-cropping, Introduction, x

And wells, 69–76, 119

And winter rice, Introduction, xiii, 100 f.n., 121 f.n., 127, 130, 133, 193, 194, 287–91

In the Ganges Delta, 262, 266, 267, 272, 273–6, 287–91

In India, Introduction, xi, xii, 100 f.n.

In Middle Ganges Valley, 173–4, 176, 177, 178, 183, 184, 185, 193–7

In regions depending on rice and millets, 100 f.n.

Relative, in well-irrigated and canal-irrigated districts, 69–76, 80–5

303

BENARES

Density of population in, 5, 6
Double-cropping in, 45, 46, 55
Extension of cultivation in, 6

BHAGALPUR

Cultivable area in, 131–3
Density in, 131, 132, 133, 134
Distribution of double-cropping in,
  157–8
Emigration from, 131, 133, 134
Extension of cultivation in, 131–3
Floods in, 132, 132 f.n.
Immigration into, 131, 133
Insignificance of irrigation in north,
  178
Internal migration in, 132, 133
Nature and value of second crops in,
  157–8

BIRBHUM

Deforestation and soil erosion in
  west, 227–8
Double-cropping on *Do* and *Sali*
  lands in, 249
Flood prevention in, 228
Internal migration from West to
  East in, 228
Lack of irrigation and small extent
  of double-cropping in, 249
Pressure of population in east, 228
Second crops in, 249

BOWLEY

Introduction, v

BULANDSHAHR

Density of population in, 29
Double-cropping in, 53, 56
Extension of cultivation in, 29, 53

BURDWAN

Cultivable area in, 226
Derangement of drainage levels and
  agricultural decline in, 226–7, 264
Intensive double-cropping on the
  highlands of, 248
Low density in the laterite portion
  of, 227
Second crops in, 248
Small extent of double-cropping in
  the laterite portion of, 248

CANALS (*see* IRRIGATION)
20

CARBON-DIOXIDE

And plant life, 60–1

CARVER, 96 f.n.

CATTLE

Function of, in a rice region, 98

CAWNPORE

Density of population in, 17, 18
Double-cropping in, 47, 54, 55, 56
Extension of cultivation in, 17, 18

CENTRAL BENGAL

Double-cropping in, 250–2
Drainage in, 264–6
Forest clearance in *Sunderbans* of,
  213
Increase in density in, due to
  deforestation, 213
Low density in, 213, 213 f.n.
Nature and sources of irrigation in,
  266–7
Water-logging and defective drain-
  age in, 264–6

CHAMPARAN

Canal irrigation in, 178
Cultivable land in, 120–3
Density in, 119–23
Distribution of harvests in, 200
Double-cropping and economic pros-
  perity in, 165–6
Double-cropping in, 154–5
Extension of cultivation in, 119–23
Fever and density in, 121
Immigration into, 122, 123
Index of prosperity for, 200
Second crops in, 154
Spill irrigation in, 177

CLIMATE (*see* RAINFALL)

And the limits of cultivation of crops,
  87–92, 188–90
In Central Gangetic Plain, 64, 65
In Eastern Gangetic Plain, 63, 64
In Ganges Delta, 260, 279
In Middle Ganges Valley, 114, 169–70
In Western Gangetic Plain, 65

COLONIZATION

And density, 213, 220, 223, 232, 234,
  235, 236, 237, 238, 240, 241, 242

Printed in the United States
by Baker & Taylor Publisher Services